Wish and Fulfilment

A HISTORY OF SHIPLAKE COLLEGE

Shiplake College and environs in 1958 and 2000

Wish and Fulfilment

A HISTORY OF SHIPLAKE COLLEGE

H.E. Wells-Furby

GRESHAM BOOKS LIMITED
in partnership with
SHIPLAKE COLLEGE

The title of this book is taken from Peter Abelard's Hymn

O quanta qualia

as translated by J M Neale seven centuries later.

Ubi non praevenit rem desiderium
Nec desiderio minus est praemium

freely translated as:

Wish and fulfilment can severed be ne'er
Nor the thing prayed for come short of the prayer

Abelard, as an eminent early twelfth-century teacher, contemplating the future of the Spirit, declared with confidence:

Nostrum est interim mentem èrigere
Et totis patriam votis appetere . . . Et ad Jerusalem

In Neale's words:

Now in the meanwhile, with hearts raised on high
We for that country must yearn . . . seeking Jerusalem

Published by
Gresham Books Limited
The Gresham Press
46 Victoria Road
Summertown
Oxford OX2 7QD

in partnership with
Shiplake College
Henley-on-Thames
Oxfordshire RG9 4BW

ISBN 0 946095 41 8

Design & typesetting by John Saunders Design and Production
Printed and bound by MPG Books Ltd., Bodmin, Cornwall

Contents

Foreword

WHEN PART ONE of *Wish and Fulfilment* was conceived, Shiplake College meant little to me. I was aware of an increasingly successful rowing club and once or twice I had caught a glimpse of a fine new Sports Hall beyond the cricket field beside the main road along which I occasionally travelled between Henley and Reading. I had never ventured down the drives and knew nothing of the remarkable early history of the College or of the fascinating background to its development into a nationally recognised school of substance and worth.

There is within our community enormous pride at what has been achieved, not only in those first twenty-five years, but in the fifteen since then. Our fortieth anniversary week of celebrations, the sponsored walk, the Commemoration Service led by the Bishop of Dorchester, the memorable assembly addressed by the founder himself and the concluding open-air fireworks concert will always remain for me a highlight of my time at Shiplake.

To mark that important milestone in the life of the school the Governors agreed that, although now retired, the original author should be asked to attempt the challenging task of bringing *Wish and Fulfilment* up to date. Challenging because, in December 1993 after a lifetime of commitment to Shiplake, Hans Wells-Furby retired. But although the reader will appreciate that Hans's knowledge of the last five or so years was limited, he has still managed to keep closely in touch and the story in Part Two is as diverse, fresh and fascinating as was Part One.

A remarkable history has thus been continued, not this time from the lawns of Tudor Cottage, but from Hans's home in Somerset, and I wish to record the huge debt owed to him by the College and to extend our thanks for the hours of painstaking reading and research.

Edward Hatchett's splendid foreword to the original book has admirably stood the test of time, is as relevant today as it was in 1983 and serves as a fine introduction to this combined volume.

N. V. Bevan
Spring Term 2001

Foreword

to the 1984 edition of *Wish and Fulfilment*

TWENTY-FIVE YEARS in the life of a long-established school, although spanning perhaps five generations of boys and two or even three headmasterships, is a relatively short time. For a new school the first twenty-five years can seem to be a very long time indeed.

Shiplake has been most fortunate in that the faith of the founders has been so ably supported by the courage and dedication of those who followed, that we have what we see today. It is a story of such achievement that it had to be told, and who better than Hans Wells-Furby who has been, not on the side-line, but in the thick of it for most of the time.

The amount of research that has gone into this book has been prodigious and Hans has dealt most ably with the personalities involved. With one exception, himself, and it falls to me in expressing the appreciation and gratitude of the Board of Governors to Headmasters, Staff and all who have made Shiplake College such an agreeable community, not to forget the Author's very special contribution over the years.

It is not too invidious of me to record that we have been very well served by our Governors, men distinguished in many walks of life, who have given unstintingly of their time and the benefit of their wide experience and have always been ready to assist and advise the Headmaster whenever necessary.

Lastly perhaps, but not least, a word on finance. Always a new venture is difficult and a school is no different. At an early stage a close link was established with Barclays Bank, and they have never hesitated to give us their full support. At times they must have been uneasy but have continued to see us through to a situation that today must be regarded as not unsatisfactory.

Long may it all continue.

'Historians tell the reader more about their own times than about the period they are describing' is an old adage which all students of history are taught to absorb. In *Wish and Fulfilment* Hans Wells-Furby has had to combine the two influences. It is very difficult to remain objective when one is living through a story but the typewriter, pattering away on the lawn of Tudor Cottage, while most of us were enjoying our holidays, has managed to achieve just this.

The story is a venture of faith, a nineteenth-century event in a post World War II setting – it will be enjoyed by all who are connected with Shiplake.

E. P. Hatchett
Governor 1976 to 1991

College has been about young people and their development. For this reason I have tried to avoid the method used in many school histories; that is, to allocate a section to each headmaster. This is easy enough when you have former pupils spread over most of the present century who say 'I was here in so-and-so's time' or 'I came just before this war or that war'. I have tried to avoid being sentimental. Equally, I have tried to avoid the approach of the school prospectus (to include everything) or the style of the school magazine (everybody must be mentioned).

I have been helped immensely by reading a wide range of school histories, mostly written during the last fifty years. The closer one gets to modern times, the more a history tends to concentrate on the basics. The historian of the Eighth Army operations in Italy told me, 'Don't read it, it's all about supplies'! The history covering the first fifty years of one of Oxford's newest colleges, St Peter's, deals mainly in terms of board meetings, balance sheets and fund raising. Finding the wherewithal to continue and to expand is a vital ingredient of the story of Shiplake College. The way in which more up-to-date school histories have dealt with this aspect of school management has been a great help to me. Dealing honestly with disputes, difficulties with governing bodies, resignations and personality clashes is a feature of recent school histories, and again these books have shown me how to attempt it.

Many of the people involved with the launching of Shiplake College are still alive. Indeed Peter Carter-Ruck was the guest of honour at a recent Speech Day and Alexander Everett addressed the whole school on May 1st, 1999, the fortieth anniversary of our foundation.

Curiously, most school histories (often books marking 150 or perhaps 400 years of a school's existence) become strangely reticent when they deal with recent times. More than one school history names only recent headmasters. Such an approach would be impossible with a history of Shiplake College's first forty years. There simply would not be any history if we did not mention people alive and flourishing at the moment.

Boarding schools founded since the 1840s had substantial problems in their early days; they were often similar to our own. I think it is immodest to compare our early beginnings with those of schools now great and famous, but it is encouraging that they generally began without endowments and without vast pre-launch capital. They were often handicapped by serious personality clashes. It would be possible to expose and over-exaggerate the human failings uncovered in the first two or three years of this school's existence by writing along the lines of a Sunday newspaper. However, to do so would be as big a distortion of what happened as to go to the other extreme and pretend nothing ever went wrong. One can only hope to deal firmly, factually and fairly, but not, I hope, prematurely with these difficulties.

Chapter 1 on the history of Shiplake Court from medieval times to the early nineteenth century is based on the substantial history of Shiplake written by Mrs Climenson some ninety years ago and also on some researches carried out by sixth formers in the early days of Shiplake College. Our knowledge of the building of the present mansion by Robert Harrison was increased by meetings I had with Robert Harrison's granddaughter and various of his nieces and nephews almost thirty years ago. Time has not permitted a thorough revision and updating of this material. It is, in fact, a summary of articles published in the College magazine before 1965.

Much of the Shiplake story up to 1982 was drafted while John Eggar was still alive. I looked forward to hearing his comments on the finished work. He would have said there was 'too much about him'. He would also have said, with a twinkle in his eye, 'I don't remember it happening quite like that', and I would then have directed him to the document upon which my conclusions were based. While we would from time to time have disagreed, his undoubted objectivity would have meant that my difficult task of being both friend and historian would have been combined successfully.

When headmasters make the right plans, when governors and administrators get new buildings open on time, when schoolmasters reorganise and adapt, when new boys improve, each is only doing his own job. The real volunteers in the educational process in the world of independent schools are the parents. They choose the schools, they pay the fees. There is a lot about governors, headmasters, staff and boys in this history. The prep school headmasters who recommend us and the parents who give us their confidence over a period of three or five years are amongst the most important contributors to our success. Unfortunately it is too difficult to be positive about the size of their contribution, but, of course, no parents really means no Shiplake. It is to them more than to any other group that our initial success is due.

Taking up the joint invitation from the Governors and Old Boys to continue the story has proved even more interesting than I expected and I am as grateful for the opportunity as I begin the second half in 1993, as I was in 1982.

While Part Two began as a continuation of *Wish and Fulfilment*, I hope it will stand as its own account of two decades of a story worth telling – for its increasing pace, achievement, partnerships and confidence building. Reviews in the months after publication of Part One emphasised some approaches worth retaining beyond 1982. *The Prep School Review* stressed the value of commenting on post-war education. Many policies would not make sense without looking at the broader picture, in education, politics and economics. Even in the best-managed schools, tense situations arise and young people are quick to sense an 'atmosphere' among staff. Shiplake's early days were eventful and uncertain, but 'Conference and Common Room' approved the 'courage' shown in relating our early problems to those who had never heard of them. As far as I remember from writing in 1982, I had no desire to indulge in calumny, nor did I want to be over-charitable. I just followed the best examples I had found in biographies and in recent school histories. It was therefore welcome to be praised for being 'Not evasive, but tactful, judicious and direct'.

Being at Shiplake is important to those who have come here. Understanding where we have come from gives a meaning to life. Shiplake has come rapidly to a position of some strength and I hope this book makes clear how this happened.

I must admit to some inconsistency in the use of surnames, Christian names and initials; to maintain variety and informality I have decided not to standardise this. Ladies have a Miss or Mrs and I have generally given a Mr to members of the governing body.

I must thank Mrs Jackie Leigh for many hours of typing the first draft - always cheerfully done. She has had the help of Miss Monica Tomalin in making sense of my handwriting! My thanks are also due to the many people who have answered questions, often when they have been very busy themselves and particularly to Barry Edwards for rounding things off and Alexander Everett for his personal view of our humble beginnings.

H.E. W.-F.

Part One

WISH AND FULFILMENT
Shiplake College's First Twenty-five years

CHAPTER 1

The History of Shiplake Court

IT IS 90 YEARS since the publication of Mrs Emily Climenson's substantial history of Shiplake. While this work can be faulted, it does represent a lasting contribution to local history and the ground covered is not likely to be worked over again. We have ample evidence that the first Shiplake Court was a home from 1265, or earlier, and the present school perpetuates an occupation of the site which has lasted over 700 years. During the fourteenth and fifteenth centuries, Shiplake Court was part of the property of the Englefield family. The Englefields provided an early Tudor Speaker of the House of Commons and at much the same time built a mansion which survived on the site until 1804.

We know rather more about the Englefield family than we do about the house they built. The family can best be described as significant rather than important. They had been landowners in Berkshire and Oxfordshire for centuries in contrast to many of the new gentry who rose under the Tudors. Sir Thomas Englefield was Master of the Court of Wards during the long-drawn-out period of Henry VIII's divorce from Catherine of Aragon. Francis Englefield inherited from his father in 1537 and was knighted at the coronation of Edward VI. He was imprisoned in the Tower in 1551 for supporting Mary Tudor in her refusal to accept the Protestant prayer book. The rest of Englefield's life was dedicated to the support of the old Catholic ways. When Mary became Queen, Englefield was made Master of the Court of Wards and became a Privy Councillor at the age of 31. In 1559 the new Queen Elizabeth I dismissed him from all his appointments. Englefield took up residence in the Spanish Netherlands and was still there in 1563 when the Queen ordered his return to England. His disobedience led to the immediate confiscation of his goods and estates in England. In 1573 Shiplake Court and its estate was leased by the Crown to Sir Edmund Plowden. The Plowdens were, and still are, a Roman Catholic family in Shropshire. Their connection with Shiplake was to last slightly over a century.

During the time of the Englefields and Plowdens one can say that, while nothing of national importance took place here, Shiplake Court did have its connections with events of national significance. Edmund Plowden was a

The original Shiplake Court at the time of the Plowdens in 1765

Member of Parliament until severe persecution of the Roman Catholics after 1580 forced him into seclusion. Meanwhile, Francis Englefield had settled in Spain where he worked as an agent trying to obtain aid for the English Roman Catholic refugees in the domain of Phillip II. There Sir Francis died in 1596, aged 74.

The loyalty of the Plowden family to the old faith was undoubted. During the seventeenth century four sons of the family went abroad to be educated as Jesuit missionaries. The house itself was plundered in 1643 by parliamentary troops at the time of the battle of Caversham Bridge. The downfall of James II in 1688 brought the Plowden connection with Shiplake to an end. William Plowden followed that Roman Catholic monarch into exile and commanded a regiment at the Battle of the Boyne in 1690. In the same year, William's mother Penelope sold Shiplake Court and 1500 acres of land in order to finance her son in exile. William was eventually allowed to return to England and settled at Plowden where he lived until 1740.

In Mrs Climenson's history there are copies of two drawings illustrating Shiplake Court, one of which is reproduced above. They suggest that the old Shiplake Court was slightly further to the east, a few yards further away from the church than the present mansion. The house was 'H shaped', facing towards Reading and the road ran past it to the north on the line indicated by the milestone standing in front of Everett House.

Shiplake College owns two buildings of historic interest. They are Tudor Cottage and the Tithe Barn. These buildings were probably standing in the last days of the Englefields and they certainly saw the Plowdens come and go. Mr Whittington found considerable remains of very old woodwork during his restoration work in the barn's more remote parts. The name 'tithe barn' is probably a misnomer. Before 1539 the Abbot of Great Missenden took the Great Tithe from Shiplake and the vicar received the Small Tithe. I have seen no documentary evidence that suggests that the barn was ever church property as it would have to be in order to be a tithe barn.

Appropriately, this history has been written at Tudor Cottage and the story of the new school has been recorded in one of the oldest homes in this area. For most of its history Tudor Cottage was church property and could be more appropriately called The Clerk's Cottage. There is a tradition without documentary evidence that Tudor Cottage was two cells for the use of monks coming from Great Missenden Abbey to conduct the church services here. A document dated 8 October 1685 lists amongst the Shiplake Parish property, 'North thereof is bounded from the roadway with a growing hedge a church house conteyning two bayes of building with a little garden plott bounded with the church yard'.

On 25 September 1759 Tudor Cottage is again listed as 'house containing of two tenements one of which the Parish Clerk lives in rent free according to an ancient custom of the parish and the other is occupied by Sarah Bushnell widow who pays one pound per annum rent for the same'.

To continue the story of Tudor Cottage up to the building of the present Shiplake Court, nobody knows for certain whether the church sold it to Robert Harrison or whether it was purchased earlier by Mr George Cherry who thus added it to the Shiplake Court estate. The first Lord Phillimore, writing of staying with his grandparents at Shiplake House before 1855, describes it as 'lived in by Dame Sylvester, an old woman never seen without her old poke bonnet: the cast off one standing up by the fireside and used to hold coals'.

The only thing that survives from the medieval Shiplake Court is between the tennis courts and the towing path. There is a largely silted up 'fish stew' – an artificial enclosure for keeping fish.

During the eighteenth century Shiplake Court belonged to the Jennings family. They had originated in Reading as merchants and Robert Jennings, the owner from 1689, appears to have been Headmaster first of Reading and then Abingdon School before he took over his father's business interests. There is a monument to him and his son above the main door of the Parish church. The old Shiplake Court fell into decay during the ownership of Henry Constantine Jennings (1731–1819). He travelled extensively and spent extravagantly. Shiplake

Connections through marriage of Robert Harrison of Shiplake Court

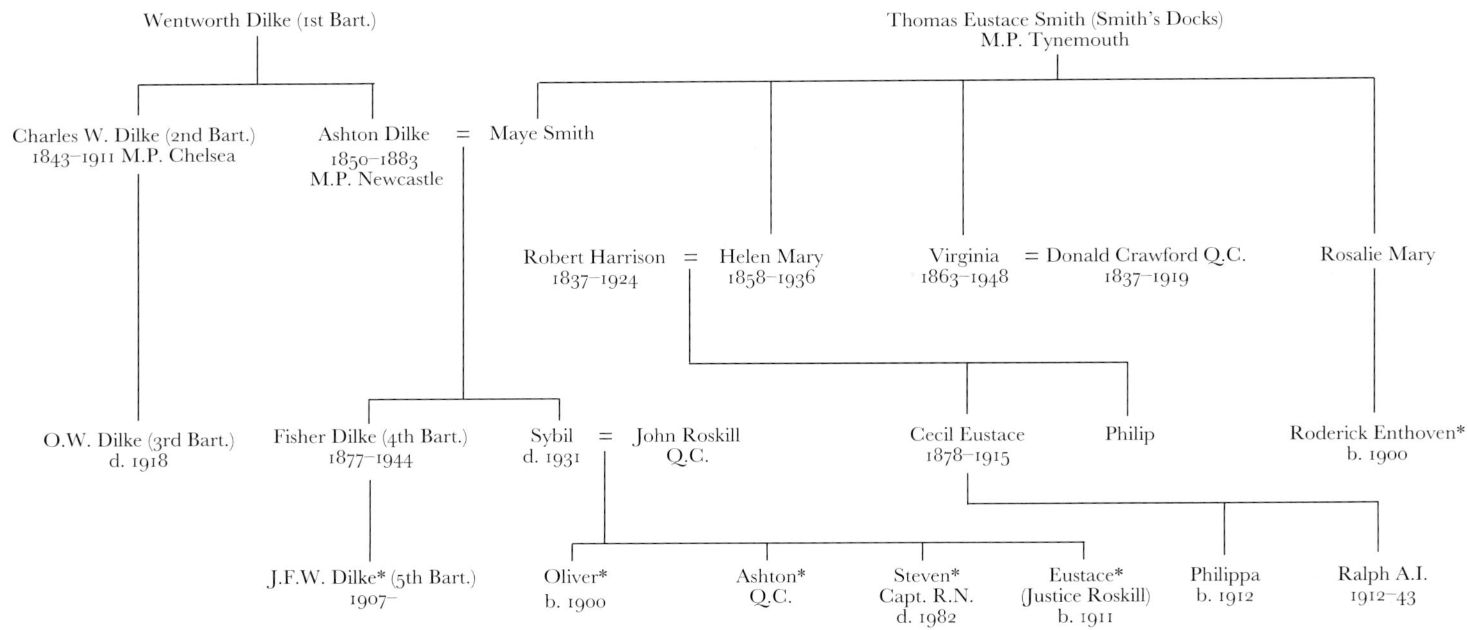

* Alive 1970

Helen and Robert Harrison in May 1915 with their grandchildren, the twins Ralph and Philippa

Court was neglected, then leased and finally sold in 1802. There is a persistent tradition that the old Shiplake Court was burnt down and this was mentioned again recently by a member of the Plowden family who happened to look in on his travels between London and the Welsh borders. There is, however, ample documentary evidence that in 1804 the old Shiplake Court was demolished for the value of the building materials. One has to remember that the house was getting on for 300 years old and was structurally probably past saving. Mid-

Crawford, a Liberal MP, that she had committed adultery with Sir Charles Dilke, who had been a Cabinet Minister until the previous month. On the basis of Mrs Crawford's confession her husband obtained his divorce in February 1886. Mrs Crawford's confession was evidence against herself, but not evidence against Sir Charles Dilke. Neither Sir Charles nor Mrs Crawford gave evidence at the original divorce hearing. One has to remember two things; firstly, a century ago involvement in a divorce was tantamount to social ruin, and secondly, until 1924 all detailed evidence given in divorce cases could be published in the press. Dilke vehemently denied involvement with Mrs Crawford, but as he had not appeared in court he had great difficulty in reopening the case. This was achieved by persuading the Queen's Proctor to intervene and claim that the divorce had been unfairly granted. Technically, Dilke was just a witness for the Queen's Proctor. His evidence was evasive and in the course of 500 questions put to Mrs Crawford she made the most astonishing admissions about her own conduct. She was ruined anyway, but she also ruined Sir Charles Dilke. The rightness of Sir Donald Crawford's divorce was confirmed by the Courts, but even so Dilke did not rest. He set up a committee to try to clear his name.

What is certain about all this? First of all, Mrs Crawford became a reformed character; she adopted the Roman Catholic faith; she was an early left wing member of the London County Council, but she never made any attempt to clear Sir Charles Dilke. The second thing is quite sure: Mrs Crawford was never properly cross-examined about the evidence she gave. Not so certain is the evidence collected by Dilke's committee. Mrs Crawford had had several affairs, particularly with a Captain Foster whom it was claimed she was protecting when she named Dilke. Even less certain is the committee evidence that Mrs Crawford had been led into a career of adultery by her older sister Mrs Harrison who was supposed to have passed Captain Foster on to her sister! None of the allegations against Mrs Harrison was widely known until Roy Jenkins published a life of Sir Charles Dilke in 1958. Then Mrs Harrison's granddaughters were totally surprised that she had 'a past'.

The Dilke Case has received considerable publicity over the past forty years. A full length play was staged in the West End in 1964. It was advertised as 'Not suitable for children'! There has been more than one television programme on the subject and in 1979 Mrs Harrison was again the victim of careless publicity at the time of the Sargent Exhibition at the National Portrait Gallery. The page of catalogue notes accompanying Mrs Harrison's portrait, painted in 1886, is highly inaccurate. It speculates on the impact of the Dilke scandal and Mrs Crawford's conduct on the marriage of Robert and Helen Mary. However, as the article has Robert Harrison entertaining leading musicians at Shiplake Court the year before he bought the land and two years before building began, all the information is highly suspect.

Robert Harrison's nephews suggested to me a number of years ago that he probably never knew about his wife's private life. It would certainly have been very unimaginative to build a country mansion in an area where the other main landowner was Sir Walter Phillimore, who had appeared for the Queen's Proctor when Dilke attempted to have the case reopened in 1886. Like Virginia Crawford, Mrs Harrison became a convert to the Roman Catholic Church. Her nephews remembered her this century as a person with great sympathy for the problems of the young. They remembered also a lively person and a compulsive chatterer. 'Uncle Robert, when he wanted to say something, used to tap on his cigarette box in order to get silence.' The nephews of Mr and Mrs Harrison felt that Shiplake Court, when it was built, was Robert's taste entirely. He admired Tudor styles and collected the sixteenth and seventeenth century furniture that filled it. 'It was not to her taste at all, and she had no regrets about selling the house and its contents soon after Uncle Robert died.'

The present Shiplake Court as it stands comes towards the end of the Victorian period of building great country houses in Tudor style. Ernest George and his partner at that period, Harold Peto, were the architects. Their practice in building large country houses declined in the 1890s and they switched to Queen Anne style buildings in London at the beginning of this century. Later in life Ernest George was knighted and elected a member of the Royal Academy.

The estate that Robert Harrison bought at auction in September 1888 comprised 362 acres of farm land with a river frontage from above Phillimore's Island and near Wargrave Ferry. There was a farm house – the present home of Burr – there were well-timbered grounds with old elm and walnut trees. Incidentally, the walnut trees were much missed in the 1960s by visitors who had not seen the grounds since 1920. Harrison must have swept away most of the farm buildings he bought when the farm was transferred to its present site on the Reading road. The auction particulars referred to three barns and yards, three stables, a cart shed, a granary and five labourers' cottages. In front of a walled kitchen garden was the site of 'an old manor house'. The whole estate was described as adjoining the estates of Sir Walter Phillimore and Colonel Baskerville. A modern note was struck in the sentence which referred to the property being 'of interest to land speculators and building companies to acquire the riverside building site of great prospective value'.

There are no surviving Harrison family papers. We have no idea what Mrs Harrison destroyed when she left Shiplake early in 1925. Mrs Harrison herself died in 1935 and her possessions were stored with Druces. Their depository was destroyed during the Blitz and Mrs Harrison's granddaughter, Philippa, had no idea of what might have gone into the store. Robert Harrison himself was a keen photographer. Someone remembered the Tithe Barn being full of old glass plates. These relics of Victorian photography were all thrown away over 70 years ago. A few of the photographs taken by Robert Harrison appear in Mrs office until 1990 was Mr Harrison's business room, but the billiard room has totally disappeared having been converted partly into the servery and partly into the marking room and the masters' cloakroom. The masters' common room, entirely panelled in oak, with oak floors and ceiling, was the original dining room of the house and, as recently as 1959 in the school's first term, everyone sat down to meals there.

Originally the spiral staircase in the great hall was at the library end but was moved by Lord Wargrave in the mid 1920s. The bay window, now, sad to say, converted to a fire escape, was full of hothouse flowers throughout the year. They were Mrs Harrison's particular interest.

The room numbering of the main building on the first and second floors is a relic of the BBC's use of Shiplake Court. Numbers 101 and 103 were the main bedrooms of the house; the main guest bedrooms were the present Skipwith House sewing room, the room next door to it and the resident tutor's room over the common room. What is now the sick wing was partly occupied by senior resident staff and the rest of it by nursemaids. The Headmaster's sitting room was the day nursery and the two large rooms next to it the night nurseries. On the top floor, room 216 was the original sewing room. Some of the servants' rooms still survive; some have been divided and the rest of the partitioning was done to increase the accommodation during the years when the BBC owned the property and is therefore about 60 years old.

The staff that Robert Harrison employed is a reminder of the world of 'upstairs, downstairs'. On a salary of £70 per year Robert Harrison's butler eventually retired and opened a shoe shop! The rest of the inside staff consisted of two footmen, a housekeeper, a cook, three parlour maids, two nursemaids and an uncertain number of teenage maids learning their job. The latter were paid £5 a year and keep. Outside, the gardener had six assistants and his responsibilities extended to the kitchen garden across the road, now occupied by the Orchard Close estate. Two full-time mechanics were required for the water plant and electricity. A coachman and two grooms were also employed; they lived in the 'careers room' and the two rooms above it.

The grounds were laid out by Alfred Parsons, RA, and by the time of the *Country Life* article in 1906 the gardens were well established. A rose garden, from the dining-room side of the house across the entire lawn where the present swimming pool stands, was a main feature. In the winter, evergreen shrubs stood in tubs on the main terrace; in the summer months, they were replaced by exotic tropical plants from the greenhouses. The view from the terrace included Lynch Island, which in 1906 was virtually without trees: it was just a flat grassed-over island. The mass of spring flowers on the river bank and in the orchard are a survival from the Harrison period.

Life at Shiplake Court between 1891 and the outbreak of the First World War is a matter for detective work. The reputed price of the mansion and the other buildings was £30,000. That is an understandable figure if one remembers that the labourers working on the construction site would have earned a pound a week or less and the really skilled masons, carpenters, joiners and wood carvers would at the most have been paid two pounds a week.

The Harrisons certainly furnished Shiplake Court magnificently. When the contents were dispersed by auction in March 1925, the sale lasted four days. An advertisement in *The Connoisseur* lists a wide range of Elizabethan, Jacobean and Flemish furniture. In addition there were William and Mary, Queen Anne, Chippendale, Hepplewhite and Sheraton chairs and a wide range of tapestries, carpets and antique ornaments. Ernest George and his partner Harold Peto were keen that their clients should furnish their homes properly. There is a tradition that Harold Peto used to come down to Shiplake and rearrange furniture to his way of thinking. As soon as he had gone, Mrs Harrison put things back where she wanted them!

The banking firm of Barings failed in 1890 and Harrison is supposed to have lost money as a result. Certainly, he never seems to have used Shiplake Court to the extent that the lavish building suggested. The Henley show was held at Shiplake from time to time, then the village flower show was held annually in the grounds and the hunt met there once a year. Harrison was High Sheriff of Oxfordshire in 1900 and President of the Liberal Association. He was for many years a JP, a member of the Parish Council and manager of the village school. He seems to have been a reasonably generous patron of local causes, but he does not appear to have entertained in a particularly lavish way. We have a picture of the home just before 1906 from the pen of Lady Ottoline Morrell. She was half-sister of the Duke of Portland and was married to Philip Morrell, an Oxford solicitor who won South Oxfordshire for the Liberals in the sensational 1906 general election. Lady Ottoline felt that as president of the local Liberal Association Robert Harrison rather patronised them, but she liked Mrs Harrison – an intelligent woman caring for books and art – and was impressed by the house; it was full of beautiful things, Sargents, Whistlers and many other treasures.

Harrison's sons both took up careers in the army. The elder son Cecil served in the Boer War, and the Rifle Brigade museum at Winchester has a small circular table in which the officers of the 2nd Battalion carved their names while on active service. 'C. E. Harrison' is written boldly across the table in a large round hand. His portrait had been painted by Sargent when he was ten. It was exhibited at the Academy in 1888 and was again on view to the public in the posthumous Sargent Exhibition in 1926.

The history of Shiplake Court is inextricably bound up with that of the twentieth century. It has been affected by wars, rising prices, shortage of labour and social change. Neuve Chappelle, in March 1915, was the first of many British offensives to go wrong. Cecil Harrison, by then a major, was killed in action leading an attack by the 2nd Rifle Brigade. He left a widow and two children – the twins Ralph and Philippa. His widow spent the rest of her short life nursing the wounded and died in the influenza epidemic of 1919; there is a memorial tablet to her in the parish church. The twins were left in the care of their elderly grandparents. During the war Robert Harrison devoted his energy to producing as much food as possible from Shiplake Court farm. This was stressed in his obituary in the local press in 1924.

In 1921, Harrison was unsuccessful in selling the estate. It was a period when a vast amount of English property changed hands at low prices. Robert Harrison died in November 1924 and is buried in Shiplake churchyard within sight of the mansion he built. He left a rather curious will. He gave £10,000 to his son Philip – a major in the Artillery – and he left everything else to Mrs Harrison to dispose of as she wished. Mrs Harrison had very little business experience, but she seemed determined to get rid of Shiplake Court and its estate as quickly as possible. She sold the whole property to Mr Reginald Mardon of Haileywood, who presented the farm and land to Reading University and sold the house to Lord Wargrave.

Mrs Harrison moved first to Wargrave House and then to a flat in Regent's Park. She died there in November 1935 and was buried in the Great North London Cemetery, a Harrison family enterprise. In 1948 her sister Virginia Crawford was buried next to her. Robert Harrison's grandson Ralph was commissioned into the Royal Air Force in 1931; by 1943 he had reached the rank of Wing Commander. He was killed in a raid over the Ruhr in June that year.

Lord Wargrave, previously Basil Golding, had been a figure of some significance in the Conservative Party before the First World War. Subsequently he concentrated on his business interests and was, amongst other things, Chairman of Rolls Royce. He was a bachelor and used Shiplake Court really as a week-end cottage to entertain his friends! At his death in 1936 the property passed to a nephew who had little use for it. The British Broadcasting Corporation bought Shiplake Court in 1941 for £15,000 which is considerably less than Harrison had spent on the place 50 years earlier. The purchase price included furniture, carpets and rather more land than we have now. A small school – Ladbroke Grove – had occupied the house for a while before the BBC. The Corporation's original intention had been to use Shiplake for expanding the overseas service, but it seems to have been used at first for storage purposes. In 1943 the Monitoring Service moved from Evesham to Caversham Park and Shiplake Court became a hostel for members of staff; the hostel closed in 1953. The BBC cast around for some other use for the estate, including the idea of making Shiplake Court the BBC Library. Nothing came of any of these schemes and the property was put on the market in 1958. By this time, the contents that had come with the house in 1941 had been disposed of by the BBC and most of the ornaments and statues in the grounds had been transferred to Caversham.

The late Sid Smith had come to Shiplake Court in 1941 as the third gardener to take charge of the grounds. In the last few years of the BBC he had been caretaker and he remembered the wide interests of the numerous would-be purchasers. The plans to turn Shiplake Court into a school were a relief to a rather harassed local community who feared other and possibly more detrimental forms of development.

CHAPTER 2

The First Two Terms

NINETEEN FIFTY-NINE is one of those years that are easily remembered. The summer was long and fine and in the brilliant autumn that followed Macmillan won the general election associated with the slogan 'you never had it so good'. Shiplake Court had been bought for educational purposes the previous December and opened as a boarding school on 1 May 1959.

In March the *Daily Mail* published a centre page article under the heading 'If your son fails his Public School'. The article was based on interviews with Alexander Everett, the headmaster-to-be, and George Spencer-Brown, who was to be senior tutor. There was a significant trend – independent schools were flourishing, then they were also under attack for being outmoded. The public schools were not increasing the number of places available as fast as the demand grew. Alexander Everett was prepared to take boys who could not get in elsewhere. He aimed at a school of 120 and believed that coming to Shiplake might prove better than getting into a long-standing public school. This was a reasonable view as Everett had some experience of prep school teaching and had been involved in starting one.

The records of the school's first year are sparse. A company was formed with Mr and Mrs Everett as directors, together with Peter Carter-Ruck and Aubrey Goodwin. Tradition has it that the purchase price of the property was £16,500; the records show it was £17,500. Of course the property boom had not begun and large houses were viewed with suspicion as potential millstones for any owner. Even so a 40-room mansion with a stable and garage block, three cottages, an island, a boat house and reasonably sized grounds constituted a first-rate bargain.

The rest of the year's records show that a chance was missed in February 1959 to purchase the Red House – now the home of Burr – and that other improvements cost little by comparison with the inflationary standards of the 1980s. The basement was converted to showers and changing rooms for £1,000. The previous owners, the BBC, had already divided the top floor into numerous single rooms with plenty of wash basins, baths and lavatories. It cost £417 to tar a quarter of a mile of front drive – the back one cost £6,000 in 1977! A dust tennis court was tarred and rewired for £400 – retarring in 1982 cost over £4,000. Two laboratories were created in the stable yard for £1,000 and the field sown for £750. In February, when these figures were noted, plans were going well.

Within two weeks of the school opening problems appeared. The Red House had been bought by the Waller family and there were going to be right-of-way problems. The fees at 100 guineas a term were too low and would have to be raised to 130 guineas. A guinea was one pound one shilling – a pound and five pence to those who have grown up with decimal currency. Some of the first parents were to find £136 a term a real strain. Finally the senior tutor's relations with boys and staff were unsatisfactory and he would be asked to leave. More optimistically, plans were being made to increase the 30 boys of the first term to 120 as soon as possible. For the first time, building a dormitory block was mentioned. The existing buildings would be sufficient to teach 120 boys but not to sleep that number.

The fourth Board Meeting in September recorded 'a high demand for places' and hoped to build a dormitory block starting early in the spring term. A Development and Endowment Fund was mentioned for the first time. Five of the original entry had been asked to leave.

On 14 January 1960 David Skipwith and his solicitor Fraser Bird joined the Board. The resignation of Mr Everett as headmaster was reported. David Skipwith was now headmaster and E. M. Burr was to be the bursar. Two weeks later another Board Meeting decided to spend £600 on emergency accommodation by May when the school would total 95 boys. The target for September 1960 was 120. A loss of £323 was reported for the second term, but the January-March period was expected to produce a surplus of £1,312. Three Houses were named, Common Entrance was to be adopted and Mrs Everett was to be resident Governor on a three-year lease.

Behind these few facts officially recorded lay considerable problems and strains. Probably the first year of the school's history was the most difficult, but strains and successes, doubts and optimism abounded for another ten terms.

Some of the famous boarding schools founded in the nineteenth century had substantial problems; early headmasters were found wanting, backers and patrons proved wayward, there was unrest amongst boys, capital was hard to find and debts were incurred. Other schools ran smoothly from the onset. History was repeating itself. In the early days of the school, there were almost two worlds – the boys' world of classes, games, bedtime and breakfast which functioned quite normally, and the adult world of serious rifts that were developing between Mr and Mrs Everett, together with Mr Everett's uncertain grasp of the management of the school. These were a potential threat both to the day-to-day running of the school and to confidence in it.

Mrs Eunice Richardson was a widow when she met Alexander de Morley

Everett at Ashfold School. Her first husband had died suddenly in 1954, leaving an estate of some £31,000. A significant factor was the educational problems of her own son, who later became Shiplake's first sixth former. It is easy to identify the problem in two ways: personal and nationwide. There were boys who needed a 'different' type of school and there were many who needed a school if they were unable to get into their father's or brother's school. Alexander had ideas and some vision. Eunice had some capital. They married in February 1958 and set about finding a home for the school they envisaged.

Shiplake was one of a number of schools then starting in country houses; they were a feature of the 1950s. Most were short of capital and remained small till they closed. The larger the mansion and the estate, the more the scope for expansion. Shiplake Court benefited from its nearness to London and its rural situation. However, parental support is the key factor in building expansion. If the Everetts had turned out to be a happily married couple running a small business efficiently, Shiplake Court would probably have remained the small and unusual institution they envisaged. What went wrong and led to a rescue operation headed by the original Chairman and Deputy-Chairman?

Central to the problems were the personalities of the founders. Alexander Everett was an ineffective schoolmaster and by no means a leader of men. His personality did not match his vision. Mrs Everett was kind but excitable, her moods were unpredictable; she wanted to be needed, but she was difficult to work with. Basically she was lonely and the failure of her marriage to Everett made her bitter. In the years before 1963 when she left Shiplake, her personal problems were obvious because she lived in a school. None the less it was her money and her generosity that made the school possible.

In retrospect, starting the school in September 1959 with 60 boys might have been wiser. To run a school with 30 boys, many of whom did not settle, provided some income, but rather a false start, especially as the initial fee was too low and produced only £3,000 income for the period May–July.

The teaching staff was of uncertain quality for the first two terms. The first biology teaching was distinctly eccentric, the first modern linguist drifted away, a successor was suspected of false pretences, a failed medical student and a would-be poet completed the list of the ineffectual. Things were very much held together by David Skipwith, who arrived as senior tutor during the first term. It was not till September 1960 that all boys in the school were following structured courses leading to 'O' Level GCE. Before that, only 12 fifteen-year-olds seemed to be working with a purpose.

Alexander Everett had a vision of a small, friendly and 'different' school. Choice was to replace compulsion, there were to be no bells, few rules, staff and boys would mix freely and share common rooms and Christian names would set the tone of the tutorial system. A friendly atmosphere is the only relic of the earliest days. Considerable talent as a headmaster might have made these ideas

The Stable Block in May 1960 – no upstairs classrooms

work, but having a senior tutor from the outset (and starting with the wrong one) underlined how little experience Alexander Everett had of the older boy. In a nutshell Shiplake's first head was not headmastering material.

However, our first Head set important standards in some respects. He insisted on good quality furniture and equipment. Ex-War Department furniture was not bought. The result was that Shiplake began with a high quality appearance. He was concerned to protect the wooden floors by requiring micro-cellular soles for all shoes, but the cheerful and easygoing atmosphere did not prevent vandalism.

Adults overestimate the amount of attention the young pay to the grown-up world, but the emotional public conflicts between Mr and Mrs Everett could not be missed. They would have been far less obvious in the privacy of a home. Whatever their personal problems they had invited parental support and taken young people into their care. However, Mrs Everett owned the school and had put almost all her liquid capital into it.

Mr Carter-Ruck and Mr Goodwin were well aware of the Board's responsibility to the parents and boys, well aware, too, of the deteriorating situation and they could see clearly the school's potential. Restructuring the school and redefining its aims would be for the benefit of the boys and would, incidentally, protect Mrs Everett's investment. On academic and personal grounds Mr Everett had to go and Shiplake began its third term with David Skipwith in charge.

What had the boys made of these troubled first two terms? From the frequent comings and goings of the staff they drew the obvious conclusion that all was not well. However, they liked Alexander Everett and while they spoke kindly of him, they quickly forgot him. They had responded well to his efforts to tidy the estate, got involved in camping on the island and shared his enthusiasm for cars, but they felt the atmosphere was too prep school-ish, too slack and they often felt 'talked down to'. Most preferred certainty and wanted to get on with a job of work. Their day-to-day problems were overcrowding and boredom. Non-study holders had only a bed, a chair and a tuck box. On winter evenings there was often little to do except hang around resident staff. The compulsory Sunday afternoon walk was a most unpopular event.

Pressure to get things right gradually came from the increasing number of professional people involved with the school. The school doctor, A. J. Salmon, Mr C.R.E. Gillett, formerly a university lecturer and Harry Sykes, a veteran ex-member of the Pangbourne staff, were three men who could see the obvious deficiencies. In mid November 1959 two key appointments were made. W.R. Hartley had taught at St Edward's in the 1930s. He joined the school after his post with the consular section of the Foreign Office ended. J.F. Foster came to Shiplake after three years at Oxford and three in the educational branch of the RAF. Their experience and influence were invaluable from the outset.

The first two terms were not without achievements. The Oxford and Cambridge Board agreed that the school could be a GCE Centre; in 1961 the Oxford Appointments Board handled vacancies for staff. Their Educational Secretary, A.R. Woolley, after his visit pronounced Shiplake to be 'one of the future great schools of England'. Certainly in rowing we now come near that. Alexander Everett was quoted in the *Daily Mail* as saying 'I hope we shall have an eight at Henley one day'. From the start no boy was admitted without interview; this became less of a burden when more boys came from prep schools. Boys from agencies had to be interviewed at length, but prep school boys were known through headmasters' reports before they arrived. The policy to recruit after Common Entrance became established during 1960.

In spite of difficulties the rate of material progress was considerable. During the first term all teaching took place in the main building. The great hall was a sitting-room area and the 30 boys took meals in the present common room. The ground floor rooms of the stable block were the chemistry and biology labs and the present Head of English's room was a physics lab. Rooms 10, 11 and 12 only came into use in May 1960. A boxing ring occupied Room 3 for a while. The car club and boat building shared the barn – then partly open to the weather. In

January 1960 every available space was being used. What is now Skipwith day room was a dormitory. The Sister had a bed-sit in the tower, the tower room was the sick bay and a room on the top floor was the surgery. The present sick bay was part of the Everetts' flat. Alexander Everett used the bursar's study as his office but David Skipwith ran the school from the rooms now used by the Skipwith resident tutor. Since January 1960 bursars have used the same office in the front hall.

Shiplake village was much smaller in 1959. Many of the larger private houses had belonged to the same people since the 1920s. It is hard now to understand the opportunities that we missed in the early days. A school at Shiplake Court was a more welcome form of development than an hotel or a country club or a 40-unit housing estate on the grounds, but the school was a newcomer and had to merit a welcome. The Everetts were not good mixers. David Skipwith was charming, but shy. The Vicar was new. The Doble family at Shiplake Farm, the other farmers and the local residents were bound to wonder about numbers of boys wandering the countryside.

The Red House had been part of the Shiplake Court Estate, but it became a separate property in Lord Wargrave's time. When it was offered to the Everetts, they attempted to drive a hard bargain thinking that no one would want to buy a house in the middle of a school. In fact Mr and Mrs Waller, the purchasers, and their family spent ten happy years there. The Wallers had many local friends and the school's attempt to stop them using the main drive lasted till 1963. Whatever the legal position it was a silly policy. The decision to build the dormitory block (now Everett) in front of the Red House deprived the Wallers of their view. This created another awkward situation. Until 1963 the boys were the school's best local ambassadors. Soon after he arrived John Eggar joined the Parish Council, but he and Pam had to give a great deal of thought to improving our relations with the village. He was head of an increasingly conventional school, but the feeling that this was an odd kind of school lasted a long time.

Alexander Everett left Shiplake with a large Land Rover equipped for an overland journey from Alaska to Tierra del Fuego! Somewhere in the American wild west he encountered a circus with a sick elephant. His Land Rover replaced elephant power in erecting the 'big top'. Alexander remained as Ringmaster for some months and the overland journey was forgotten.

On 2 January 1961 all was normal at Shiplake. I departed for Switzerland with a school ski-party. The staff were in a state of near panic when the ski-party returned. Alexander Everett was back! He was living in the flat. Mrs Everett was pleased to see him. Was he back to take over again? Was David Skipwith in a hopeless position? Was everything gained in 1960 to be lost? To those who met him for the first time, Everett seemed mild and rather ordinary. The basis on which he finally severed his connections with the school belongs to the story of David Skipwith's headship. The summer after he left, Mrs Everett obtained an

The Great Hall – a multi-purpose room

1960 – ready for lunch

– music rehearsals in the Great Hall

The lawn above the tennis court

An early science lesson

annulment of the marriage and in due course she asked to be called Mrs Richardson.

Alexander Everett visited Shiplake in one of John Eggar's early summers. He expressed great pleasure at what he saw. The school was obviously developing as he had hoped. At least he had the satisfaction of knowing that some of his intentions had been fulfilled in ways he liked.

The impressions of Stewart Cowley (below, set down in 1982) and those of the late Sidney Smith are valuable postscripts to a chapter written mainly from official records:

'My first headmaster at Shiplake was also the school's first headmaster and I suspect that we were each as confused as the other. Even at twelve years old I seemed to sense that we were all part of some obscure experiment; there were few rules and fewer disciplines and most of those that existed grew out of the boys' own need to establish some sort of operational framework.

'A pecking order was arrived at quite quickly, largely through brute strength. I recall one older boy who established a fairly senior position by the simple expedient of calling every boy into an upstairs room one by one, kitting them out with boxing gloves and plastering them all over the walls.

'The headmaster himself also appeared to favour unconventional methods of establishing authority, but the rich and original atmosphere he helped to generate during those first days remains a clear and valued memory.

'The laws of England clearly extended to school life, but beyond that it was hard to know whether one was likely to fall foul of the rules. The boys themselves were an extraordinary mixture of the gifted and the idiotic with a clear bias towards the latter. Although we were so diverse in background and character there were so few of us that we were bound together very closely. Staff and pupils were all new boys trying to cope with an unfamiliar situation.

'The strange and unorthodox beginnings of the school attracted many members of staff who were equally strange and unorthodox. I suppose such a situation would tend to appeal to (a) younger, able men who saw the chance to make a mark and grow with an emerging public school and (b) older or less able men who had nowhere else to go. Initially the school seemed, on reflection, to attract an inordinate number of the latter. Certainly we had more than our fair share of extraordinary characters.

'In the early days, the school and its surroundings was a paradise. There were a mere thirty of us rattling around a network of buildings that was like a deserted warren. Hardly a quarter of the place was actively used, the rest was an uncharted labyrinth that belonged solely to the boys. Small wonder that so many infringements went unpunished when a culprit could go to ground and remain undiscovered for days at a time. Almost every boy in the school had a room or refuge that was exclusively his by the unwritten code of that era. The basement, unlit and empty, could only be explored by torchlight and the stable block was a dusty, rubbish-filled no man's land, unpoliced by the staff and the scene of all sorts of misdemeanours and sinister enterprises.

'Clubs and societies abounded with staff only too pleased to be offered some justification for using another space. As time passed, however, more and more of these areas were conquered, mapped and absorbed into the administrative fabric of the school. By the time I was near to leaving about the only refuge remaining was within the walls themselves. On the upper floor of the main building a narrow space ran behind the walls carrying the water pipes, with access doors to most of the single studies. A few of the old timers had keys made and furnished the tunnels with old car seats, wine racks and even electric light.'

Mr and Mrs Sidney Smith are well remembered by early Old Boys. Sadly, 'Sid', as he was affectionately known to early generations, died during 1983. He remembered with considerable affection some of the early 'rogues'. He encountered an American in the potting shed at 7.30 one morning. The lad was smoking a cigar, and proudly declared 'I am off for good as soon as the bus comes'. Sid persuaded him to go back and have some breakfast and think again. Incidentally, our early Americans were not a success. Their inevitable reaction was 'you're not going to push us around like these Limeys'. Mr and Mrs Smith had long-standing local connections, and they came to live in the Lodge in 1941.

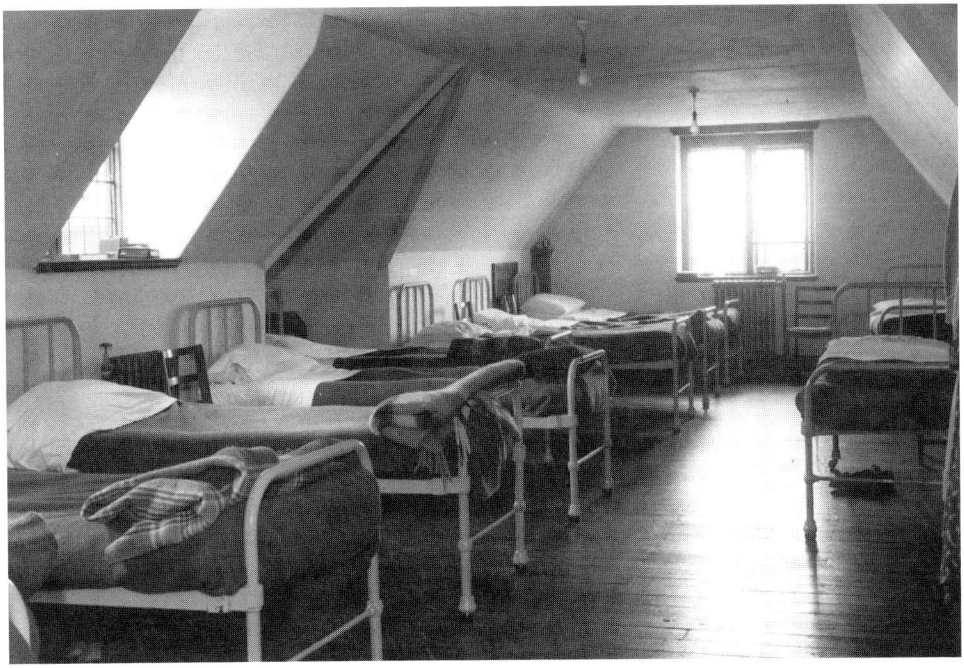

A dormitory in the 1960s
(the Social Services inspectors in 2000 might have something to say about this)

1 May 1960 with a few hours to spare. The glass went into the frames literally hours before the new boys arrived. It was a mainly fine summer – otherwise the draughts through empty knot holes might have caused problems. To complete the story of the huts, during the summer term the Board decided to build a second hut which would contain more sleeping space, together with adequate washing and lavatory facilities. Both huts were to be properly lined and would have night storage heaters. The final cost of all this was £4,088! The huts were probably a good investment as they sheltered one-third of the school until December 1961 and a smaller proportion after that.

Two young men between sixth form and Oxbridge took charge of the hut in the summer of 1960. One now has his own house at Marlborough, so the experience cannot have been too terrible! From 1960 to 1962 R.S.C. Wood, a bachelor, in charge of English, lived in a bed-sit at the end of the huts, not surprisingly called 'the wood shed'. There were still some boys in the huts when John Eggar arrived and using the huts in daytime only became one of his urgent priorities.

'All headmasters are busy in their first year.' This is a theme that we shall return to when we discuss the first years of John Eggar and Peter Lapping. It was David Skipwith's style to let his colleagues be busy and he provided a polish or a 'civilised' style to their enterprises. Progress was greatly helped by the boys. The arrival of school ties and house ties, the first cricket fixtures, the starting of rugby football, all were greeted with the greatest enthusiasm. More important milestones were the first Confirmations (30 June 1960) followed by the first Prize Day on 9 July. By the time DJS reached the end of his first twelve months in office the Duke of Edinburgh Awards had begun; the first school play and the first carol service had also taken place.

David Skipwith suggested *The Court* as the name of the official school magazine. The first edition recorded these numerous firsts plus many more, including the first six inter-house competitions. The first squash rackets report was provided by David Welsh who remained in charge until July 1982, thus setting a record unlikely to be beaten.

Organised sport got going in the second year. At the end of April 1960, the seeded cricket field was ready for use. It had been planted in the very dry summer of 1959, and made slow progress in the early months. In that very first term, David Skipwith organised some cricket nets on the front lawn. There was one tennis court in use, a fair amount of swimming in the river and a good deal of hanging about. In the winter of 1959/60 soccer was played, and Peter Clements – the school carpenter – refereed the first inter-house games!

The early rowing was supervised by Mr R.E. Burgess – an Old Etonian – who had rowed for Oxford in 1911. Beginners first tugged at an oar while sitting in a 'bank-tub' watching themselves in a mirror. Coaches still believed you should start to row on a fixed seat. The only serviceable boat throughout the summer of 1960 was one fixed-seat four.

David Skipwith had a good deal of experience as a games organiser from his Bloxham days. He gave every encouragement to those who got things moving. Several cricket fixtures were played in the summer term of 1960. A Headmaster's XI, raised for Prize Day, just got away with a draw. Bloxham sent us a team of mixed ability which we beat, and we just scraped home against a useful Radley Under Fifteen side. Two or three prep. school games were also played by our junior cricketers. There was every temptation to get going as, even in its first season, the square was magnificent. To give it a chance, we only played on half of it for the first two summers.

John Foster ran the rugby in the early days, and in our first full rugby term, Pangbourne, Radley and Bloxham gave us fixtures at the right level. From the outset, our First XV was able to hold its own against Third XVs or Under Sixteen sides from neighbouring schools. It took much longer for junior rugger sides to establish themselves, and the Rugby Club must have been in existence here for almost a decade before our Under Fourteen and Under Fifteen fixtures ceased to be rather one-sided. We just did not have enough strength at those levels.

Inter-house rowing in the early days took the form of timed races. One after the other the three main houses rowed as fast as they could from the lock to the boat houses, and the fastest crew was judged the winner.

Boxing was another sport which started early in the school's life. David Skipwith had run boxing at Bloxham, and simply got into contact with his friends at various schools in the neighbourhood. This is perhaps the point at which one should stress how much the start of inter-school fixtures owed to the helpful co-operation of independent schools in the area, all being willing to respond to a personal request for a fixture at our levels.

As soon as we started playing rugby, the size – or rather lack of it – of our playing fields became a problem. During the early years we had the temporary use of fields by the lock, and others half-way to Henley. One rugby pitch was sited where Konrad Engber's market garden is now, and First XV Rugby was played by courtesy of Mrs Green on the other side of the road beyond the waterworks.

The official policy was to undertake one new sport per year until we had a complete coverage. The cricket and rowing clubs can date their existence here from 1959. September 1960 saw the start of rugby football, followed in the spring of 1961 by athletics. Hockey followed in the spring term of 1962.

Golf, squash and tennis were successful minor sports from the very early days. The early generation of Old Boys must have everlasting memories of the time spent going to and from the squash courts in Henley. Golf was at its strongest up to about 1966. Until the membership of the Henley Golf Club grew too large, our boys were able to go round at weekends with Ronnie Hartley, as well as in mid week. A number of 'fathers and sons' matches were played until 1965, when full members at the Henley Golf Club had to take priority, especially at the

The First XV in 1961

weekends. There is no doubt that the business success of two of our early sixth formers owes a great deal to their acquiring a low handicap during their time here, and they seem to have spent most of their holidays on their local links.

For the first three years, our inter-school fixtures were, not surprisingly, few in number. House matches counted largely in the season of each major sport. Boys seemed to play with a determination and confidence in house matches, yet failed to show anything like the same spirit in inter-school matches. Some coaches felt this approach was still a problem here until the early 1970s, but since then it is quite clear that playing for the school has become more important than house matches. However, the spirit in which house matches are played here owes a great deal to the tradition built up in the early days. In retrospect, the remarkable thing was the rate at which junior house competitions developed.

Between 1960 and his departure at the end of 1965, John Foster watched exactly 50 First XV matches, and he put in an appearance at a good many junior fixtures as well. John Eggar lent his full support to the Rugby Club. His years at Repton had convinced him that a skilful game, such as soccer, was unsuitable for many a clumsy adolescent. However, this type of big strong boy always had a place in a rugger team. From 1964 the Rugby Club used visiting referees. They, too, made a helpful contribution to improving our standard.

Certainly in John Foster's last two seasons, the rugger did justify bringing in Society referees.

There was little disagreement in the summer term between the rowing and cricket authorities. Only one boy with a good prep school cricket reputation insisted on becoming an oarsman. Most of the time those who rowed did so because they had enjoyed little cricket success at prep school. Very many turned out to be useful oarsmen, and the Cricket Club never had any desire to impose their game on those who had come to dislike it. In the early days there were just not enough boys to enable the cricket and tennis clubs to have a separate identity. Members of the First XI generally turned out as the school's First VI, and tennis fixtures were deliberately arranged on days when there were no cricket fixtures. The early sporting days at Shiplake were marked by a great deal of enjoyment, a fair amount of uncertain weather, much enterprise, even more improvisation – and a good deal of confidence that we were getting somewhere in the long run.

In his work for music between 1959 and 1963, Derek Healey showed it was possible to do a first-rate job under difficult circumstances. Eventually we lost him to a composition studentship in Italy. He is now a Professor of Music at the University of Oregon.

During the spring term of 1960, D.F.K. Welsh and I were interviewed and appointed to the staff. DFKW remembers David Skipwith's shyness at interview, and a boy who wandered in and 'asked for sixpence'! My own recollections are of Daniel Maynard-Taylor, Charles Pepper and Nicholas Findlay who were to show me round. They did this in great detail and convinced me of the merits of Shiplake Court. Another recollection is of the frankness with which DJS explained the departure of Alexander Everett and the role of Mrs Everett. Also appointed on a part-time basis to help with French was Mrs Edna de la Praudiére, who stayed till July 1972 and became our first lady member of the Old Boys Club. She attended the 1999 celebrations in her 89th year. There also arrived, on a week-to-week basis, the former head of mathematics at Pangbourne, P.T. Robinson. In fact he stayed till December 1962 and played a key role in the establishment of 'O' and 'A' Level Maths. 'Robbie' enjoyed bad health; he had a fund of cynical stories about schoolmastering, the 1914–18 war and Rhodesia in the 1920s. He probably had more impact on the staff than on the boys and was the first president of the common room. He was a type of schoolmaster now extinct; loved by some, feared by many junior colleagues and yet with an influence for good hard to define – without him, Shiplake would have been different.

The most significant appointment DJS made in the summer of 1960 was that of Col. W.H.C. Travers. 'Jim' was a Sapper – Woolwich and Cambridge educated. He offered to teach physics, promised to speak his mind and help with any practical tasks. He did all this and much more from September 1960 until July 1974.

The School, 1962

Michael Burr was the original Tutor of 'Burr'. He was part-time bursar and taught geography. He had a wide range of local contacts and in his time here supervised the completion of several tasks, in particular the stable block conversions and the green hut project. Soon after he left he became Head of Falcon Manor, Towcester. W. R. Hartley took over as Tutor of Burr, Col. H. W. Newell became full time bursar and a full-time geographer was appointed.

From 1960 young staff were paid somewhat more than they could expect elsewhere, but older men with varied experience in the armed forces or the colonial service were recruited for as little as possible. This may have been a contributory factor during 1961–2 when DJS came under fire from this group. The staff in residence put up with cramped conditions and, from the headmaster downwards, getting a bath involved an early hike in a dressing gown.

Who were the boys who saw Shiplake through the first four years? They had a lot to put up with – it was school policy to prevent them watching television, having private radios or record players. It was also policy to insist on compulsory Sunday afternoon walks. They were caned for quite moderate offences. They were made to do sides 'on special paper drawn from housemasters' – that must be one of our oldest rules. Then there were 'circuits' for trivial offences; a circuit consisted of putting on running kit at an official time and running from the check point – the Bursar's window – down to the river and round the quarry back to the starting point. It was soon scrapped because it made exercise a punishment. Some things did not happen – DJS always said there would be compulsory pre-breakfast PT as soon as we had an instructor, but by the time Ken Dalgetty was appointed in 1961 the whole thing was forgotten.

The autumn term in 1960 began with a staff meeting – this was a milestone of a sort – for the first time the school had a qualified professional staff. Twelve out of fourteen had been at Oxford or Cambridge. Regular staff meetings did not come till 1961–2.

As bursar, Colonel Newell quickly showed his ability to get on with people, he was good with strangers and took some of the strain of dealing with Mrs Everett. He had previous experience as an aide de camp – this proved most useful. He also developed a considerable loyalty to David Skipwith.

Running the school was greatly helped by the Governors forming a General Purposes Committee (later Finance and General Purposes Committee). Even so, the full board continued to meet with great frequency. The main subject was the new dormitory block. The plans provided a basic building of seven rooms capable of sleeping eight plus a small senior study and a day room. Changing rooms, lavatories, washrooms, Matron's department and a study would be at one end. This building would cost £20,000; a housemaster's residence could be added for a further £5,000.

By October 1960 £12,300 was available for the project. This money had been offered by 40 parents at an Endowment Fund meeting on 27 July. The guardian of one of the boys, Col. F.N. Richardson, was the moving force behind proposals that parents should subscribe to debentures repayable after seven years. Thus future income would pay for a building now. Some delay was caused by an alternative scheme to buy house property and convert it. However, parents had subscribed to provide a new extension and a decision to build was taken in February 1961; the site was cleared during the Easter holidays.

This decision led to a revision of the overall plan for the school. One new boarding house automatically created a house of fifty boys. Therefore the school should aim to be three houses of fifty each. The other two houses would share Shiplake Court and the huts. If the number of boys rose above 120, more classrooms would be needed. The most rapid solution was a 'terrapin' building to be fitted up as a biology laboratory. This was the first building on what was then the kitchen garden and the sections were lifted over the wall by a large crane during the summer holidays in 1961.

During the early months of 1961 the House system took shape. As Alexander Everett left things, a boy at Shiplake banked pocket money with his tutor. You could see your tutor after lunch about pocket money, leaves and sides; he was available for any problem. He saw you about half-term reports and wrote an end-of-term report about you. All those in your tutor group formed a house for sports purposes.

In March 1961, boys were told that from the next term, dormitories and studies would be arranged by houses and the dining hall would be divided into house areas. These arrangements made supervision of tidiness a house matter – it coincided with there being enough senior boys to take on house responsibilities. This was all in preparation for Everett (John Foster's house) going into the new block when it was finished. The hoped-for date, September 1961, turned into January 1962. At the same time DJS was gradually handing over his house to me.

Three years after opening, Shiplake had a proper house system. In some schools this took considerably longer – at St Edward's, Oxford, 60 years. By January 1962 each house had its own accommodation to match the organisation that has really taken shape since January 1960.

From the time of Colonel Newell's arrival school records are more detailed. For instance, on 11 October 1960 the Governors dealt with twenty-one items. This is typical of the care and attention given to the school's problems and needs during the first five years. In the early years the utmost vigilance was needed and the accounts were audited once a term.

As many know, the present masters' common room is the original dining-room of the mansion. From January to July 1960 one of Alexander Everett's experiments survived. At break and tea the common room was confined to staff use – at other times boys could come in to meet staff. The staff dined in a pleasant room – formerly the housekeeper's – next to the kitchen. By

September 1960 this had become a matron's bed-sit and the staff had departed to the servants' hall – opposite the kitchen. The boys had full use of the present masters' common room until summer 1961 when it became a dormitory for one term – while we waited for the new building to be finished. The staff moved back in January 1962 – for good!

A very important meeting of the Governors took place on 6 February 1961. They appointed a special committee to look at all aspects of school accommodation and asked it to meet in two weeks' time. They then moved on to the key issue of Alexander Everett's return to Shiplake. The staff offered their full support to David Skipwith in writing, making it clear that if Everett remained, they could not. Everett in fact agreed to leave in return for (1) a final financial settlement and (2) an agreement to mention his part as a founder of the school in the prospectus.

The day-to-day difficulties caused by Mrs Everett were explained to the Governors by three senior members of the staff; they emphasised the desirability of her moving out of her flat in the school. The agreement made thirteen months earlier that Mrs Everett would be resident governor for three years from January 1960 seems not to have been mentioned. This would have helped the staff to understand that no immediate solution was possible, but would also have shown that the situation would not last for ever. Perhaps it was forgotten or perhaps it was part of the general secretiveness that was quickly abolished by John Eggar on his arrival.

All that could be arranged in the afternoon of this hectic day was a redefining of the relations between the school and the resident governor. The aim was to stop her wandering round the school at all hours, interfering in the school office and giving orders contrary to those of the headmaster and bursar. Looking back, this was the high-water mark of good relations between DJS and staff he gathered. While two essential decisions were made, it was not a day Shiplake could be proud of: There was some loss of temper and dignity, some evasion, some bluster, but a lot of progress.

Victorian headmasters were convinced that schools always knew better than the parents. Even they were aware of some parental pressure, and school numbers could fluctuate alarmingly depending on the reputation of individual heads. Parents began to worry seriously about accommodation standards a hundred years ago. Many a twentieth-century autobiography begins with a blistering attack on the boarding-school system. Parental indifference to tales of suffering at school forms another part of the literary attack on boarding school life. I remember being horrified at a pony club camp just after the war when I heard a mother loudly declare 'We shall have much more time to ourselves when we can pack Andrew, our youngest, off to boarding school'. Some of our early parents at Shiplake took the line 'Here he is, he's all yours for the next twelve weeks, I don't really want to see him until Christmas'.

Shiplake has been very fortunate in the parents it has had as partners. We know the children have to be at school until they are at least sixteen, and parental support for our fund-raising, and for the Duke of Edinburgh Award expeditions, their attendance at musical and dramatic performances and their encouragement of our early sixth formers are evidence of true partnership.

In the early 1960s, at least half the school still came and went by train. Widespread car driving has made Shiplake an easily accessible school for parents in the south-east. While we have to a considerable extent become a regional school, in 1983 60 boys were here because their parents were involved in business overseas and received fees support from those businesses. In addition there were 32 sons of serving officers.

Shiplake has never made the mistake of regarding parents as a nuisance. There is now a conference for parents of each age group during the course of a school year. This system evolved during the 1970s as academic and career pressures mounted. Most parents are realistic about their children; few expect too much, though some ignore considerable achievements.

During Shiplake's first twenty-five years, the parents consistently fell into three groups. Ten per cent were not UK citizens, 45 per cent were themselves pupils at boarding schools, and the remaining 45 per cent were new to boarding education, their sons being the first generation to be educated away from home.

A large number of those here in the early sixties had fathers who had been at public school and brothers who had gone to public schools. The bulge in the post-war birth-rate led to higher standards for the Common Entrance examination pass. Under DJS Shiplake was aiming to provide on a smaller, less intensive scale, everything they would have found at father's or brother's school. These included courses to 'O' and 'A' level, a wide range of sports together with a Cadet Force, boarding-house life and, most important to DJS, Church of England centred religion.

The overseas residents early on were a small percentage – 1960 saw the beginning of long distance flights by jet liner and those whose fathers worked in what was left of the British Empire got home far less frequently than today's expatriates! In a sense inter-continental air travel did for Shiplake's expansion what the railways did for the mid-Victorian boarding scholars.

In the spring of 1960, the Governors had decided that Shiplake should recruit as far as possible from the preparatory schools. No boy has ever come to Shiplake without an interview, but prep school reports quickly improved the interviewing process and Common Entrance scores (however modest) helped 'setting'. The number of boys who failed to fit in fell rapidly.

There were some boys who were disappointed at having to come to Shiplake and remained so to their last day here, but the great majority responded well to the pioneering atmosphere, and to being involved in so many 'first ventures'. They certainly knew that impressions on and off the field in our early fixtures would count more than anything in keeping the first ones and getting more. Also, so much had to be done from the outset with boys' help that estate work has never been a punishment.

There were some bonuses – boys at Shiplake never had to agitate for the abolition of school caps – we never had them. 'Fagging' and personal service to seniors was never allowed; school traditions, like the uniform, were simple and practical. Ideas and criticism from boys were always acceptable provided they were phrased with 'please' and 'sir' somewhere in the suggestion. Old boys will remember that DJS frequently spoke of the 'tone and repute of the school' – he left them in no doubt about their part in improving both.

We had our first athletics season in February/March 1961. The weather was very mild, but in 1964 Shiplake was to follow most schools in shifting the whole athletics effort into the early weeks of the summer term.

It was now school policy to introduce one new activity a year. 1961 saw the start of the Army Cadet Force which we hoped would become the Combined Cadet Force in due course.

For part of 1961 we had a Head Boy – the first. Then there was a twelve-month gap. The only candidate suitable for the job in the autumn of 1961 declined to serve! That year also saw the rifle range in use and a literary magazine *The Phoenix* raised a useful sum for charity. One of our longest surviving societies – the Young Farmers' Club – was founded most enthusiastically by Simon Stracey.

During the summer of 1961 Everett House – as it is now known – took definite shape. Placing it next to the main building of 1889–91 had considerable architectural implications. Windows had to be of similar size to those in the Court itself; timber had to be a feature of the façade, but we saved over £1000 by not using an exactly matching brick. The large grey tiles of the roof of Everett were selected to match the large slabs of Forest of Dean stone on the main building. We did not realise that, in five years' time, the weight of this stone roof would compel total removal – with the capstones, there were four hundred tons of material on the move! Re-tiling in 1968 was, fortunately, done at reasonable cost – we were lucky to have to pay only £5,000 for the job. Replacing heavy stone roofs also had to be done on other mansions designed by Ernest George and Peto.

From the outset, the school medical officer was Dr Tony Salmon, helped by partners in the 'Hart' practice. Dr and Mrs Salmon took more than a passing interest in College music over the years and were the link between the college and the Henley Symphony Orchestra.

The surgery and sick wing were fairly primitive in the early days. The sister had a bed-sit in the tower and two small rooms were the surgery and sick bay. In 1964 a substantial part of what had been the Everetts' flat was assigned for health needs. There were now two sizeable wards and a surgery as well as a bathroom. Sister had to wait until 1974/5 to have a substantial flat of her own.

the housemasters needed guidance in general and some specific definition of responsibilities, but DJS failed to produce this. This was another case of Shiplake taking a big step forward without DJS as headmaster making sure that things worked out properly.

John Foster was officially appointed Second Master in February 1962. This promotion was a well deserved reward and vital in view of DJS's increasingly uncertain health. Curiously, the appointment was made for one year and according to school records was never officially renewed. In spite of this, John Foster remained second master till he left in December 1965.

In the spring term of 1962 we played our first hockey. M. Le Mesurier was in charge, assisted by Colonel Travers. The first-ever fixture was against Henley Town Second XI.

M.W. Mash arranged the first cross-country fixtures during this term and also provided the first worthwhile organisation for the Duke of Edinburgh Award. We had joined the scheme in the autumn of 1960 – rather too soon – and a year passed before the early members made much progress. Michael Devas was presented with his Gold Award at a Cadet Force parade on Speech Day in June 1962.

Some difficulties were purely material. Before Stowe became a school the ability of local water supplies and sewerage system to cope with a school of several hundred were studied. No such feasibility studies appear to have been made at Shiplake Court before it became a school. Water pressure problems occurred in several of our new buildings. At one time watering the cricket square left the labs high and dry. There was no main drainage in Shiplake parish when the school opened. An expensive sewerage system was dug into the orchard area – it lasted eight years before we were able to connect with a newly finished main drainage system.

For many years limited resources meant that the Boat Club did its own maintenance – visiting craftsmen did overhauls from time to time, on the spot. Early in 1962 we obtained the services of a full-time groundsman and he was bought a second-hand tractor, a smooth roller and a set of gang mowers. Before this, the playing field was cut by contractors, rarely at the right moment! For the first two seasons the cricket master prepared the pitches himself. 1964 was the last year he put up the nets – John Eggar said this was 'infra dig' and instructed the bursar's department to do it in future!

Thirty-five years ago, the word 'environment' did not have its current meaning. In its first twenty years Shiplake's environment has been threatened three times. In 1964 plans for the M4 motorway still envisaged a route north of Reading: the result would have been a motorway on stilts crossing the water meadows opposite the College and crossing the Thames at Lynch Island! The road danger moved in 1971 to the other side of the estate, when a road widening scheme threatened the lodge and part of the playing field. In 1981 the Thames frontage was again under threat – this time from plans for gravel extraction. In 1971 and 1981 the College was actively involved, with other local organisations, in protecting a uniquely unspoiled area less than 40 miles from central London.

It is curious that while many important decisions were made in Shiplake's first few years, something quite minor should be left unresolved for far too long. In May 1961 a generous parent offered £100 towards the cost of the school obtaining a Coat of Arms from the College of Heralds. This donation amounted to nearly two-thirds of the cost. Blazer badges and 'colours' ties were amongst the things the early Shiplake boys would miss. It was not until February 1963 that the Governors and the Heralds finally agreed on the exact details. Ties, badges, prizes, library book plates, school printing, all benefited from this Grant of Arms. Luckily the son of the benefactor remained till 1964!

The school motto was taken from the stained glass in the great hall screen. Bursar Newell thought that the words in each panel were from Fuller's Worthies, but we have been unable to prove this. The original Latin master reduced 'Discreet example is the best sermon' to three words and David Skipwith got DFKW to reduce it to 'Exemplum docet'.

As far as one can see, Shiplake has no connection with the Viking invasions. There is a tradition that a Saxon war party raiding up the Thames burnt their ships here and retreated overland to Southampton Water. This event has nothing to do with the name Shiplake which refers to sheep washing and not to ships. A Viking army camped at Reading during the winter of 870/1, but they came overland on horseback from East Anglia. Once the Viking ship became part of the coat-of-arms it was clear we should never get rid of it. This unaccountable mistake was later perpetuated by the Viking ship scene in the 1979 pageant.

M.M. Gilliat began his twenty years of service at Shiplake in May 1962. He had met David Skipwith at St Andrew's, Grahamstown and he had been a member of the party on the overland drive back to Europe in the autumn of 1958. Mike Gilliat had been teaching at Rossall and took over the English department soon after he arrived at Shiplake.

Thanks to a generous offer from three parents it was financially possible to begin work on the accommodation for the Everett housemaster. As usual with any building, the job took about a month longer than expected and John Foster and his family hurriedly moved into Everett just before the autumn term began in 1962. I then moved into Shiplake Court and began a tradition of managing Skipwith from there.

An important meeting of the governing body took place on 24 May 1962. The Governors decided to begin negotiation with Mrs Everett's accountants. They also set aside the money to build a boat house in the quarry to accommodate fours, and Viking I was ordered. This was the first and decisive step towards our present position as a rowing school. During this meeting, David

Skipwith became ill and was rushed to hospital. As he himself said, his 'heart monitor did some alarming things'.

Because DJS was quite ill, John Foster ran the school during June and July 1962. He read David's report at Prize Day and it gradually became clear that Shiplake could run without David Skipwith. He himself began to ask if he 'could do without Shiplake?'

The resignation of David Skipwith was one of Shiplake's better-kept secrets. On the last full day of the autumn term in 1962 DJS told John Foster that he would be in charge next term and immediately afterwards told the other housemasters. He then told the staff in the presence of the chairman of the Governors that he was leaving because of a disagreement with the chairman. David spoke as if he then expected the chairman to say a number of things that might annoy the staff. The chairman preferred to look ahead at 1963 . . . The headmastership would be widely advertised and existing members of staff were welcome to apply. He regretted that the school would lose the services of Mr Skipwith as headmaster and as a Governor. DJS rather dramatically replied that he had only resigned as headmaster and hoped to contribute more to the school's progress as a Governor.

When left alone, the staff decided to meet early in the afternoon. During the next few hours the immediate sympathy for DJS evaporated and the meeting quickly drew a distinction between DJS as a person and as a headmaster. Some people actually changed their views during the meeting. The final decision was that the teaching staff would do nothing. A few were disappointed by this decision – DJS's task had always been very difficult and Mrs Everett's presence was an additional strain. On the other hand the feeling had grown considerably during 1961–2 that Shiplake needed a different headmaster.

Having looked at records for the second half of 1962 I have come to the conclusion that it was fortunate that the staff decided not to protest or offer resignations. As DJS said, 'I offered my head on a platter and the Chairman took it'. Resignation is always a bad tactic. 'I told him not to do it', said James Newell. If David Skipwith had published his letter of resignation (dated September 14 1962) we would all have seen how flimsy his grounds for resignation were. He complained of the Board's slowness in taking the steps necessary to

(i) pay off Mrs Everett, and
(ii) obtain Charitable Trust status.

The Board Meeting of 8th October considered this letter and reminded DJS that steps were being taken according to a timetable to which he had agreed.

The normal mid term meeting took place on 22nd October. The Board agreed to bid for Shiplake Vicarage and discussed terms to pay off Mrs Everett. As far as the Headmaster's resignation was concerned, the Board resolved that

DJS's views were ill founded. More problems had been caused by the school expanding too fast than by going too slowly.

On 26 November (25th meeting of the Board since December 1958) the Board considered an offer from DJS to withdraw his resignation. They quickly decided that further discussion was not necessary and the stage was set for the dramatic announcement at the end of term. Letters to parents were sent out shortly before DJS told the school 'I am going to become one of this term's leavers'. I don't think the boys were terribly surprised. Why should the turnover rate of headmasters be any less than that of staff and matrons? There was a curious tendency for boys to ask, not 'Are you leaving?' but 'Are you staying?'.

I only had two visits from amongst my 43 parents. They were more concerned about the impact on boys' progress than critical of the school's development. Only one father said, 'I sent Roger here as a personal vote of confidence in David Skipwith', but he was prepared to wait to see what the next headmaster would be like.

Friends and admirers of DJS may feel I have been too harsh to him. I always enjoyed working with him – you never felt you were working for him – there was so much scope to take charge of things and do things as you liked. DJS was delighted that something was being done properly and left you alone. Seeing the documents covering the period of his resignation caused me to change my views. Exasperation seems to be the explanation of his resignation letter. His tactics were very poor. The more observant boys saw that David Skipwith was 'straight out of a *Boys' Own* adventure story'. Square shouldered, firm of jaw and resonant of voice, he presented an imposing figure but the warmth that lay too close to the surface was an obvious hindrance. Young boys are not noted for their scruples and tend to regard compassion as an opportunity to escape the true effect of retribution.

We saw David Skipwith at regular intervals between 1963 and 1966. He arranged and managed cricket fixtures between Shiplake and the South Oxfordshire Amateurs. He did GCE examining and gave lectures to prep schools. 'An African Overland Drive' was his first. He returned to Yugoslavia to take colour slides for 'With Tito and the Partisans'. His last trip was to a cousin in Peru where he hoped to gather material for lectures on 'Peru and the Incas'. He died at Panama on the return voyage. The oak lectern and reading desk in the Chapel were presented by Old Vikings and Staff in his memory. We probably never saw David Skipwith at his most effective. With the permission of Bloxham School we print their tribute to a versatile schoolmaster:

DAVID SKIPWITH

The news of David Skipwith's death came to all of us as an unhappy surprise in June. He had made a brave recovery from the thrombosis trouble which necessitated his return from South Africa, where he had gone to teach after leaving Bloxham. And we had had welcome visits from him up until quite recently both as a lecturer and cricketer. His end came suddenly from a heart attack whilst on a cruise at Panama. His splendid work at Bloxham and for Bloxham will long be remembered by a wide range of Old Bloxhamists and colleagues. His contributions to the academic side in French, English and history: and also in the cricket, boxing, rugger and hockey were invaluable. His jovial efficiency as Housemaster (shades of the Camel-Corps and odours of herbal-tobacco!) will remain in the minds of many former Wilberforce boys who were under the old 'Skip'. And his wide network of friends far beyond the reaches of Bloxham brought in many refreshing contacts to the school.

In grateful memory of him a special Requiem Service was held in the School Chapel, the celebrant being Rev. Michael Covington, who in 1956 became school Captain and Captain of DJS's House. The School, the Staff and the O.B.s were all represented for this family farewell.

CHAPTER 4

A Fresh Start

THE CHRISTMAS 1962 holiday muted discussion of the sudden departure of David Skipwith. The start of the next term brought an unexpected problem which absorbed all our energies – the big freeze of 1963. Severe frosts began before Christmas and heavy snow at the new year settled and remained for two months. The last snow on the playing field melted on 10th March. In the first week of January, Bursar Newell declined the chance to share in the use of a bulldozer – 'This will all be gone by the start of term'. What we did have for the start of term were almost unusable drives! There was no second hockey season at all. Ken Dalgetty kept the school fit and active almost single handed. Curiously, we had few of the 'nothing to do' problems that seemed to arise during periods of snow at the end of the 1970s and early 1980s. There were three possible explanations for this: the school was only 135 strong, much of the pioneering attitude remained and TV had just been recognised and the houses now had their own sets.

The first decision John Foster made was to introduce the three-weekly order card. He wanted the boys to know more often how well they were doing. Housemasters needed more information about boys' progress and it would be easier to answer parents' questions or chase the idle. Only later was the card re-shaped so that a boy could compare his second order with his first.

John Foster was a man of great energy and enthusiasm. In his second term he took control of Everett House and drew up the timetables. Early in 1962 the Governors appointed him Second Master. He was acting headmaster from January to August 1963 and continued as second master until December 1965. Sarah Foster was the first child of many born to serving members of staff.

From his own school days at Kings, Canterbury, he knew about ambitions and expansion. His Headmaster there was the egregious, yet highly successful Canon Fred Shirley. Apart from running a house, devising the first timetables, teaching a full load of science and generally co-ordinating things, John Foster ran the rugby and swimming, produced a play every year, began the Careers Department and 'did', for want of a better word, the school calendar. As acting headmaster he found time to interview and select the September 1963 entry unaided and dealt with the usual school problems. His report at the 1963 Speech Day was a vigorous outline of a fine, if temporary, stewardship. He did much to make Skipwith's three years as Headmaster a success. DJS always called him a tower of strength. This book should remind people of how much he did contribute.

David Skipwith had started an Old Boys Club in 1962 but fell ill before its first gathering. This was something John Foster had to keep going. The period from February to August 1963 was almost a refounding of the school. With the departure of Mrs Everett now a virtual certainty, it was possible (without embarrassment) to

(i) appoint a leading schoolmaster to the vacant headship and provide him with a modern flat in the school,
(ii) invite a number of distinguished people to join the Board of Governors,
(iii) prepare a programme of improvements leading to a full-scale recognition inspection.

The immediate results of this programme were 85 applications for the Headship, a plan to increase the governing body to twelve and the purchase of the Vicarage in March 1963. A short list of candidates for the headmastership was drawn up with the help of A. Chenevix Trench, Headmaster of Bradfield and F. F. Fisher, Warden of St Edward's. From these John Eggar was appointed on 18th March.

In May, four new Governors joined the Board: Warden Fisher, Roger Goodenough (Regional Director of Barclays Bank), Sir Colville Deverell and Hubert Beales.

As a result of the Board's satisfactory negotiations with Mrs Everett, she moved to Rustington in Sussex early in August 1963 and the school recognised her as Founder-Patron. She attached great importance to this and the school happily agreed to recognise it prominently in the prospectus. Her investment in the school was repaid over a five-year period.

The summer term of 1963 was a happy one, with problems being resolved at some speed. The Cadet Force reached 100 and visited Berlin in July. Blazers and colours ties were on sale at last. The Boat Club IVs entered nine regattas and a second appeal to help pay for the Vicarage was launched with the active help of Colonel F. N. Richardson. In addition, a second terrapin building for chemistry was agreed. The one sad note was the death on a world tour of Revd Henry Kendall, the first man of wide educational experience to serve on the governing body. He was one of many St Edward's School influences upon Shiplake's development.

The governing body had a knack of being flexible. A number of new boys were sleeping in what had been David Skipwith's study, but there was an urgent need for more dormitory accommodation in the main building. In June 1963 the

Governors decided to lease Rodborough House* in Mill Road for two years so that the incoming headmaster could live there. Mrs Everett's large flat could then produce two perfect dormitories, a sick bay, surgery and bed-sit for Sister, plus a reception room for the headmaster. The existing sick bay and surgery would also become dormitories. This had all been worked out between the Governors and John Eggar and John Foster by early July, when the Governors took the vital decision that a house for the headmaster would have to be built within two years.

The summer of 1963 ended with the Boat Club overshadowing the cricketers for the first time. Three different crews had taken part in a total of 34 races against 27 different crews and won 19 of them. Not surprisingly the Governors agreed to an independent rowing budget from 1964 onwards.

The term had begun with 144 boys in the school; 23 left at the end of the term – many of these had been here since September 1959 or January 1960. Thirty-one new boys were expected in September so John Eggar took over a school of 152 boys, three housemasters, one bursar, one school secretary – the ever present Miss Monica Tomalin – a sister, two matrons, fifteen full-time teaching staff and two part-timers.

What had been achieved after four years and one term? We had done better in some respects than some nineteenth century foundations – these are the nearest historical comparisons we have. Nineteenth-century schools attracted numbers, but found finance for expansion hard to obtain. It was characteristic of the twentieth century to move faster than the nineteenth.

This history must model itself on the frank and factual information provided by many school centenary histories. I hope comparison with famous schools is not immodest. At Shiplake within four years two headmasters left after disagreements. At Radley the first six departed after similar disagreements. In contrast, however, Bloxham was 37 years old before a third headmaster was needed.

At Shiplake, the house system was well established after three years. It took fifteen years at nineteenth century Radley. At St Edward's, tutor groups emerged after 30 years, and a full house system began after 60 years. Shiplake reached its planned 120 after two years. It took Bloxham 78 years to reach 110. Malvern was below its planned target of boys in the school for 40 years. In the slightly longer term, it took Radley from 1847 to 1925 to reach the number Shiplake attained between 1959 and 1982. Shiplake's resident Founder was here four years – Bradfield's resident Founder was there for 30 years!

Was the school fortunate to survive its early troubles? While things seemed alarming to those with inside knowledge the school was never in serious danger of 'folding' during the period 1959–63. The biggest threat was financial. A company may not trade when its liabilities exceed the value of its assets. Mrs

* Years later the owner of Rodbrough House, Mr Tom Rosser, became a governor!

Everett's total capital had gone into purchasing and improving the property. There was little margin for error. Overdrafts were hard to obtain in the days when the pound was a reserve currency. In the second term £323 was lost but the third term was budgeted to produce a surplus of £1,300 and the actual total surplus for 1961 was £8,900. Every penny of this was needed to finance accommodation for those who wanted to come here. The determination of Peter Carter-Ruck and his Board of Governors to ensure success showed itself in careful financial control. One could quite see why Shiplake Court and 40-room mansions like it barely survived as private houses. In 1960 it cost £10,000 to keep the grounds tidy and to heat and clean the buildings.

The other possible threats were failure of leadership and failure to educate the boys in a responsible manner. One boy left as a result of Alexander Everett resigning: parents were not put off by changes in staff; they were remarkably understanding and were quick to notice improvement and slow to criticise. When David Skipwith left at the end of 1962 some parents did point out that their sons being here was a personal vote of confidence in DJS. Forty of the first 120 parents subscribed £12,300 to the Development Fund between 27 July and 21 October 1960.

Rapidly changing staff is supposed to be a bad sign. When John Eggar came to meet the staff of 15 (in March 1963) he was told that he was the fiftieth appointment. We have no official record of those who worked at Shiplake during our very early days because the first salary and wages books were destroyed – to save space! First of all I can only identify 43 appointments and this total breaks down as follows: five part timers; five pre-Oxbridge 18-year-olds helping in various capacities; five employed when the school could only offer meagre salaries in the early months; seven who stayed for between five and twelve years and five who were still here when John Eggar left.

The balance of sixteen who taught at Shiplake and moved on did include quite a number of good schoolmasters who came as a result of the policy, begun in January 1960, of strengthening the staff. David Skipwith was disappointed that many of these did not stay longer. They left for one of three reasons: they were disappointed with the ability range to be taught; they were too high powered for the opportunities here; they had reservations about the leadership provided by Skipwith himself.

In 1959 the staff was not good enough – by 1962 they were possibly too good!

None of these difficulties constituted a threat to the school's survival. The continuing danger was Mrs Everett's caprice and the possible walk-out of all the staff. The answer to this was the patience and skill with which the Board persuaded Mrs Everett to limit her interference.

While one has considerable reservations about what was achieved in the first years, the start was at least adequate. Since then we have, like most independent schools, survived political pressure, criticism, and the stresses of rapid inflation.

Long ago, rising costs were supposed to put schools of our type out of existence: there would be a point at which parents would cease to make the sacrifices necessary to have their children at boarding school. In addition we have, like all other schools, stood up to the pressures of the modern examination system which have distorted the summer term in a way we did not dream of in the 1940s and 1950s.

A more technical threat to the school's survival was a provision in the 1944 Education Act concerning the registration of Independent Schools. From 1957 proprietors of independent Schools had to register with the Ministry of Education. Under this regulation a Head/Owner could be banned from (i) running a school and (ii) teaching. Those associated with the owner could be banned from running a school. There were only two cases up to 1982 brought under this provision – they concerned ill-treatment of children and unsuitability of secular education.

In the summer of 1960 we had our first visit from an HMI, Mr Arnold, and it was our policy to welcome his regular visits as a way of knowing when we would be ready for a full-scale inspection. The Oxford and Cambridge Examinations Board had already taken a good look at us and were prepared to make us a GCE centre.

The danger that one of these threats or a combination of them would force a closure was never great. David Skipwith was very vigilant to make sure that boys' contacts with possible sources of scandal were watched carefully. Friendships with girls and with bachelor staff, and men offering lifts were subjects on which DJS coached the early housemasters with considerable success. David knew he would not be very good at dealing with a scandal if it arose and therefore followed a policy of prevention. It was fortunate that drugs became a problem for schools at the end of the 1960s and not at the start.

The boys made a huge contribution to Shiplake's survival. They showed visitors around in a gentlemanly way; when visitors returned to the Head's study they said at once how charming every boy had been. The 'chemistry' of the place was, in John Foster's view, very important. Something was happening to build up boys' self-esteem. David Skipwith's influence got some work going; the staff liked the boys and believed they could succeed. The too easy-going atmosphere of the first two terms at least persuaded the boys to like the place. They liked it enough not to alarm their parents by reporting the more bizarre events. Many, seeing grown-ups close at hand for the first time, thought that was really how they behaved! This has been said to me by a surprising number of the 1959–60 intake.

In the days when Common Entrance standards were shooting up, it was very easy for children to be branded as failures. The eleven-plus was having much the same effect in the maintained sector. With all its early blemishes, Shiplake attracted a good number of professional staff interested by this new venture in private education. The people who really mattered, the governors and the key members of the teaching staff, were committed to the welfare of the boys. It was, of course, a fight to get the school going but the educational goals were quite quickly defined. All Shiplake's Heads shared the wish to help the late developer and believed it could be done.

CHAPTER 5

John Eggar Settles In

BEFORE ARRIVING, John Eggar said more than once that he looked forward to the challenge of being Shiplake's Head. In fact, many of the worst difficulties had been overcome before he came, but his main problems during the first three years were not only the unfinished business, but also wholly unexpected challenges. Under the first heading there was 'what to do with the Vicarage?' John felt that the appeal launched early in 1963 was ill-conceived. Additionally, he felt some staff changes were needed; Charitable Trust status was not finalised until March 1964, and, most important of all, the time for a full-scale visit by Her Majesty's Inspectors had to be arranged. The unexpected challenges varied from the discovery, in 1966, that the whole main building had to be re-roofed, to the economic consequences of thirteen years of 'Tory rule' coming to an end. Selective Employment Tax and a ban on increased prices were two other unexpected problems which come to mind.

If John Eggar ever really thought, as he said, that 'coming to Shiplake was a nice little job to use the rest of my time', events did not let him think so for long. In his view, every boy deserved more than one chance: success depended on getting the balance right in both large and small matters. Big improvements at Shiplake would come from increased income. Much of the early expansion was encouraged by small improvements; rooms were re-decorated, the external painting was standardised, classroom lighting was improved. The groundsman was given a chance by being given £300 worth of new equipment. The loan book scheme replaced the sale of books to individual boys. The expansion of the Tuck Shop created a Headmaster's Fund for non-academic amenities. The houses were provided with a small termly allowance to improve day rooms and stimulate community life. Most important of all, the ending of the system of charging parents for coach trips to 'away' games and expeditions lessened the burden on parents of the most vigorous boys.

Twenty years later, the Crowder twins (our original day boys) and Victor Durman spoke for those who came in 1960: 'We had much more inducement to work after JDE came. In John Eggar's first three years at Shiplake, the facilities

The original cricket pavilion – opening ceremony

of the school improved considerably: two new classrooms were provided by using the space in the stable block roof. They were reached by the outside stairs and walkways. The Ministry of Defence provided us with a third green, but very much at the same time as the Army Cadet Force changed into the CCF. By arrangement with Colonel R.G.H. Phillimore, the Phillimore Estates, and Mr F.E. Doble, the school obtained the long-term use of the field between Shiplake House and the main road. The boys have always known this as the 'new field'. The empty space beyond Tudor Cottage and in front of Robert Harrison's gazebo was filled in by Court Mead. As a result, in the summer of 1965, Mr and Mrs Eggar became resident. The building of the first cricket pavilion is best described in the chapter of humorous events! It came into use in May 1965.

Not until January 1965 did we obtain full use of the Vicarage, built in 1907 to replace the large white house still known locally as The Old Vicarage. As soon as he arrived at Shiplake, John Eggar decided that a fourth boarding house was needed to get the right balance in the school. David Welsh was appointed Housemaster, duly supported by his wife Jenny, and the tradition of naming a house after its first housemaster was maintained: Welsh House came into active being in January 1965. There was no way of avoiding what had already been done in the case of Everett three years earlier – to put a whole generation of new boys into a new House. In Everett this had the effect of making the house too strong, first at junior and then at senior house level. This became true of Welsh House to some extent in 1968 and 1969. To give Welsh House adequate leaders from the outset, a number of senior boys were given the chance to transfer to the new house. Those who moved to improve their chance of promotion were all volunteers. One of the results of this is that the Old Viking list has some boys from the mid-1960s who are listed as belonging to two different houses, the second being Welsh.

In the spring of 1965, the School numbered 182 – an increase of 30 over the 152 grand total when John Eggar had arrived. The numbers game was one which governing bodies and headmasters tended to play in different ways. To governors, more boys means the problem of finding increased facilities. To heads, increased numbers means pleasing the prep school heads and parents, and represents a way of paying for future improvements and new buildings, whereas the governors tend to regard increased income as a way of reducing the size of borrowings. After 1990, this expansion applied much more to day pupils and far less to boarders. The total of 120 envisaged in 1960 soon became a target of 150. Now, three years after John Eggar arrived, the immediate target had become 200.

In Shiplake's early days we had the greatest help from schools in the Oxfordshire and Berkshire area. They tended to be boarding schools of 300 in number. They gave us fixtures and advice. 'Two hundred is an economic number' we were often told. 'The next economic number is 400'. At 300 it was suggested we would have the worst of both worlds. You stick to 200, was the warning! It sounded like sage advice. There is, however, documentary evidence that already in February 1965 John Eggar was thinking of 250 as a maximum. As things turned out, the school remained around the 200 mark from 1966 to 1972, and it took until 1975 to bring the numbers up to 250. The thinking behind advising us to remain around 200 was to keep down overheads. It was suggested that once you went much above 200 you would need an assistant bursar, a second sister resident in the sanatorium area, and altogether the ancillary staff would increase costs rather faster than the increased number of boys justified.

In the autumn term of 1963 the First XV played ten fixtures for the first time. In 1964 the Boat Club gained in strength yet again – the First IV won four events out of seven and was runner up in three more. In those far-off days, the summer term lasted until late in July, and August Bank Holiday was on the first Monday in the month. In 1964 and 1965, First and Second IVs joined together, rowing as an VIII in the Bank Holiday weekend regattas. There was one at Maidenhead on the Saturday, and Henley Town and Visitors Regatta was on the Monday.

By the end of 1964, those taking part in the Duke of Edinburgh Award Scheme had gained three Gold Medals, twenty-one Silver and sixteen Bronze.

It was steady progress of this type which enabled the school to survive a totally unexpected shock.

At the end of May 1964, everyone connected with Shiplake was upset by the death of the Bursar in tragic personal circumstances. Lt. Col. H.W. Newell had previously been bursar of the Islamic College in Mombasa and became our first full time bursar in 1960. Known for some reason as 'James Newell' his career as a soldier had included some service as an ADC. At Shiplake he was very good with visitors, putting strangers at their ease. He was very much a hero of our early difficult period and saw the humorous side of most situations. Those who were here in 1964 will remember something of the circumstances surrounding his death, but they are not part of the College history.

Colonel Newell had been Shrewsbury's fast bowler in 1923. He was always a good shot and he first saw the possibility of the quarry face as a safe back to the rifle range. It is a pity we did not think of calling it the Newell range when the school was still full of people who knew him.

H.M. INSPECTORS ASSESS FIVE YEARS OF PROGRESS

Lenin was the son of a Government School Inspector. Some GCE history candidates know about Victorian school inspectors, and the system of payment by results, but otherwise public knowledge of the work and responsibilities of Her Majesty's Inspectors for Schools was an area of uncertainty. Shiplake's experience of Her Majesty's Inspectors was neither Tsarist nor Scrooge-like. In fact, our experience was entirely helpful in the best traditions of the Inspectorate. Mr Arnold – a name of good omen – was the first HMI to take Shiplake under his wing. He did everything to advise and encourage. Mr Wingate Saul was the Chief Inspector during the full-scale inspection we had during the autumn of 1964. 'Recognised as efficient by the Ministry of Education' was the status sought by us and enjoyed by the bigger independent schools. Recognition would be followed by periodic full-scale inspections. Recognition said something to parents about standards of teaching and of accommodation. It acknowledged the aims and ethos of the school. Until Shirley Williams removed recognition from independent schools in 1978, only teachers in Recognised Schools were able to join the Ministry's Superannuation Scheme. Thus, for two reasons – evidence of reaching some standards and as a means of attracting and keeping staff – Recognition was important after only five years' existence.

The report of a team of inspectors was a booklet running to several pages. Quite reasonably, the Ministry required the school either to publish the entire report or none of it. A school should not just print 'convenient extracts'; this is a very reasonable approach – because schools would quote the best bits and omit the parts which recommended improvements. In keeping with this policy, this history therefore does not quote from the 1964 Inspection Report.

When the Inspectors were here, each sat at lunch at the end of a table. The boys were not shy about asking questions: 'Why are you here?'; 'What exactly is your job?'. The inspectors formed a good impression of the boys' poise and sociability, but they told us by word of mouth that they were not so impressed with the GCE results obtained between 1961 and 1964. In 1983/4 the gap between personality and exam grades was still there. Ten years later Headmaster Nicholas Bevan believed that improved teaching had closed the gap . . . indeed he said so in a letter to *The Times.*

In March 1965 the Ministry granted 'provisional Recognition'. John Eggar was slightly disappointed, but one feels that full Recognition at once would have meant that a five-year-old school would be allowed to go un-inspected for up to ten years.

In March 1967, Mr Arrowsmith, the new District inspector, brought a team to Shiplake for the second time. Soon after this, the school was told that 'Recognition need no longer be regarded as "provisional" '. After this we continued to enjoy visits from our local inspector. Help was particularly valued on the subject of new laboratories and new methods of maths teaching. This happy relationship continued until Mrs Williams's manpower-saving decision during the time of the Callaghan administration.

While the Recognition Inspection and plans to open Welsh House were the most significant developments in the autumn of 1964, a variety of other things were happening. The school was improving, changing, becoming more busy.

The Duke of Edinburgh Award began to make a useful contribution in the years after 1963. There was a real need to channel the energies of the adventurous. Gold Awards were won by several boys who had been involved in an unpleasant episode in John Eggar's first year. A camp was set up on the Berkshire side of the lock; the capture and cooking of a local prize cockerel led to their detection and correction. The leader was heard of commanding a tank at Bovington and another emigrated to the United States, served in Vietnam and is now a police officer in Texas.

Driving away a car without leave, various roof-top parties, and many minor infractions of school and State rules were discovered and dealt with sympathetically by John Eggar in his early days. He believed that no boy should have his school career ruined by his first and major mistake. A knifing, love affairs between boys, and bounds breaking were examples of this reckless tendency. What lay behind these undesirable activities? Was Shiplake growing into a larger school with rather more misfits or adventurously minded than we needed? The solution to these problems lay in several directions. An increased number of senior boys in the Sixth Form resulted in better prefect material. John Eggar provided the prefect training. He had more experience and was less likely to take boys' protestations at face value than some members of the staff.

The fact is that in the very early days too many misdemeanours went undetected, and JDE's experience increased the detection rate. Fewer trouble-makers amongst the entry was part of the answer, but unfortunately Welsh House suffered during its first two years from two persistent 'criminals' who had to leave us in the end. An educated public opinion was the boys' main contribution, and the arrival of a chaplain with a great deal of schoolmastering experience was a further help. The Duke of Edinburgh Award was undoubtedly a helpful bridge between the individualistic boy and the school authorities, and got both working energetically together.

The memorial to John Eggar's service here is the sports hall. It was being built during his last two terms, and curiously 'a gym' was almost first on the list of high priorities he drew up on arrival in 1963! The £7,000 possibly needed in 1963 for a small purpose-built gymnasium was well beyond Shiplake's resources in his early terms, but it is a measure of John Eggar's persistence that the project was nearly complete by the time he left.

CHAPTER 6

A Church of England School

SHIPLAKE COLLEGE was a Church of England school from the outset; for its first five years every boy was required to go to one of the regular services in the village church. The vicar of Shiplake, then the Reverend John Overton, had arrived at much the same time as the school. He prepared the first Confirmation candidates, took some divinity lessons and welcomed the school at Sunday services.

The early policy was to leave the 60, then 90, then 120 boys to choose one of the four Sunday services. These were early Communion, Sung Eucharist, Matins and Evensong. The policy of trust worked quite well; very few failed to go on Sunday and housemasters were quick to spot the absentees and have a quiet word! There were two 8.45 a.m. services on weekdays in the church with the senior boys reading lessons and there were prayers in the Great Hall on the other mornings. Two of these sessions in the Great Hall were dropped in favour of voluntary private prayers in the church itself.

Looking back, we ought to have had our own chapel before we appointed our own chaplain. A 'school' chaplain licensed by the Bishop meant that we could have our own Sunday service of the communion type. It would mean an end to every Shiplake parish service being almost dominated by a block of schoolboys. When, as an alternative, we took the whole school to Sung Eucharist on Sundays our numbers absolutely swamped the parish service.

When the first chaplain, the Reverend Peter Tidmarsh, conducted our own Sunday service in the parish church, other problems emerged. Most were a matter of timing. The bells would have to start ringing before we had finished and one choir was assembling whilst another was going. The vicar was making preparations whilst the chaplain was disrobing. In fact, the situation was not unlike the townspeople versus the monks in places where both shared the same Abbey Church in the Middle Ages.

Relations between a head and a chaplain and between a chaplain and a housemaster can never be defined. In a school the chaplain has to provide what the head wants; there can always be full and frank discussions but a chaplain has to defer to policies defined by a head. Playing off a chaplain against a housemaster is always a temptation for some boys. A wise housemaster will always be glad that there is someone in the community that a boy can see when he is reluctant to tell parents, housemaster or head what he has done or to pass on what his worries are. A wise chaplain listens first without making promises and then suggests the next course of action.

I have already suggested elsewhere that one of David Skipwith's failures was not to have a policy about the role of a first chaplain at Shiplake. A chaplain always had to be a partner in the care of young men. He cannot rigidly insist on his priestly functions to the exclusion of head and housemaster. John Eggar had these needs clearly in mind when he appointed Basil Wilks as our second chaplain. Thanks to many years of teaching experience before ordination, BWW got the balance right. He did take his anxieties to the head, he did make boys go from him to their housemaster when he felt that it was the right course, he explained other problems to housemasters advising them of the line he was taking, but he did offer a secure, confident refuge to any who felt utterly alone.

The need to fit into the pattern of Shiplake parish church services on Sunday removed the element of choice of which service to go to from the boys themselves. It seemed silly to bring boys back from Sunday leave as early as 5.30 for a compulsory evensong because it was the only time when we could have a service. Somehow school worship had to be put on a different basis from compulsory walks, compulsory letter writing and compulsory club activities.

The key lay in the urging of the then Bishop of Oxford: 'It is time that the College had its own chapel'. The only solution, John Eggar felt, was to use the Tithe Barn on Sundays and to make much the same use as we were already doing of the parish church on weekdays. With our own chapel we could have morning services at the same time as the village and we could invite a wide range of preachers. Naturally, as long as we used the parish church we had to consult the vicar about the choice of preachers, especially of laymen. A generous loan made it possible to make the barn weatherproof and to provide stacking chairs in large numbers. I do not think the 'loan' has ever been repaid as the benefactor allowed it to become a gift. The official records are not quite clear about this.

J.W. Whittington had come to Shiplake via Bristol University and Kodak Limited to strengthen the modern languages department. Over the years he gave much of his spare time to strengthening the barn. He advised on the felting and tiling of the roof and did much of the cladding of the exterior with elm in 1966. The Head and BWW bought some second-hand church furniture to give Chapel services in the barn a start. Mr Whittington played a vital part in the conversion of the barn into a multi-purpose hall, but in 1966 the ideas of the 1980s were undreamed of. Mr Whittington's early contributions included protecting the organ (bought in 1967) from accidents when the barn was used as a gym. Permanent storage was constructed for an altar given by the Knoll School of Woburn Sands. The lectern and chaplain's desk were the Old Vikings' memorial to David Skipwith. During 1967 our Sunday chapel services took a shape that served us well into the early 1980s. The central event of the week was a slightly shortened Sung Eucharist led by a hardworking choir. An early Communion, with a later Matins, generally enlivened by a sermon from a visiting headmaster, represented an alternative. The choir normally had a day's outing at least once a year. Year after year, Miss Tomalin took care of the altar linen and kept the surplices white.

It was just as well that Shiplake got its chapel organisation right at this stage in the school's development. The years 1968–1972 were the years of hostility to organised religion at most boarding schools. 'Why should we?' was the frequent cry. It is no use pretending that many saw the early service as anything else but a chance to make an early start to Sunday leave. On the other hand, a chapel committee with representatives from each house also played a part. Sunday chapel collections, notorious for the usual halfpennies, buttons and housemaster-issued sixpences were abolished. The committee adopted a charity for one or two terms and organised a termly collection for the good cause chosen. These were well supported and led in the 1970s to two major efforts for Dr Barnardo's and then for a Guide Dog for the Blind. Apart from the Poppy Day collection every November, boys have not in recent years been asked to support local flag days. The boys are thus left in no doubt about the extent of the calls upon their pockets for charitable causes each term.

To those of Shiplake's early generation, the present Shiplake Sunday may be something of a shock. Do you remember the rule that no casual clothing might be worn except between the main building and the river on summer Sundays? Winter Sundays seemed at times like an organised campaign to prevent boys from watching television.

In 1964 the Inspectors had felt there should be a day in every week when a boy should be free to choose what he did instead of another day of compulsory sport; thus began a minor sports and a minor activity day. One result of this was that club meetings moved from Sunday evenings to a mid-week afternoon, thus clearing the way for Sunday leave to end late. The doubts about the success of chapel services in the barn, which were strong when we first started, proved to be unnecessary. There is a benefit in a multi-purpose hall. Plays, films and exams shared fairly regularly in the use of our place of worship. Sunday chapel was thus part of routine life, not a special occasion in an otherwise remote and little-used chapel.

The opening of the sports hall in 1980, followed soon after by the well-deserved retirement of Basil Wilks, led to reconsideration of the place of the Tithe Barn in the school's life. JWW had completed his second reconstruction of the barn in 1977: there was now an altar end concealed behind folding doors and a film projector box was at the other; this was the most acceptable way of adapting the barn. As the gym equipment moved out of the barn, the arts committee moved in. Profits from summer balls financed further improvements; we were now in the age of video. The actors wanted to get away from the Great Hall. Plans soon became realities: the organ found a permanent home at the other end of the barn, and the altar was moved at the same time. A stage would give those at the back a better view, impressive stage lights were installed and new doors connected the barn to adjacent rooms. Smaller holes then led central heating pipes into the barn so that it became, amongst other things, a warm lecture room and video centre. Old Boys will remember, with mixed feelings, acts of fortitude in a freezing barn. However, the warm winter temperature from September 1982 was probably the biggest physical shock the ancient structure has experienced!

Tithe Barn Chapel services ended with the 1980s and only a few members of staff can now recall the services there. As the organ wore out there was less reason for crowding the school into the barn. There was also increasing opportunity to conduct some services in the Parish Church of St Peter and St Paul and an electronic organ was installed in the Great Hall Gallery. Experimental services in the Great Hall itself attracted considerable support from parents, confirming plans to end twenty-five years of Tithe Barn services. Unfortunately, storage problems prevented the regular use of chapel furniture given for the barn, and after several changes of chaplain, its very existence has been forgotten.

CHAPTER 7

Four Years of Consolidation

THE SIXTH OF JUNE 1964, twenty years after D-Day, was John Eggar's first Speech Day. A fine morning was followed by an exceptionally wet afternoon. Amongst the visitors were Miss Philippa Harrison, granddaughter of Robert Harrison, and his nephew Roderick Enthoven. They were both delighted to see the house they remembered being enjoyed by so many people.

In 1964, the Governors – very much with John Eggar's prompting – decided to drop the name 'Court'. The managers of Shiplake Church of England Primary School felt, quite rightly, that they were well and truly Shiplake School, so we became Shiplake College. At much the same time, Mr and Mrs F.E. Doble renamed Shiplake Court Farm simply by leaving out the name Court; thus the name of Shiplake Court went out of regular use in this area after some 700 years.

One of the school's early personalities finally gave up in 1964. This was Geoffrey Gaskell. He had been a regular soldier from 1914 to 1945 and had reached the rank of Brigadier. After Hitler's war, he had worked for the Blood Transfusion Service before joining the youthful students at the Slade School of Art. He was perhaps not a very good artist, nor much of a teacher, but he was a kindly man, a generous host, and the most genial of bachelors. Due to economic factors and lack of space, art teaching remained on a part-time basis until the 1970s – the David John era.

In July 1965 we said goodbye to the handful of boys in the Upper Sixth who had joined in 1960 and had completed five years in the school. Those who came in September 1961 could also fairly claim to belong to the pioneer generation. They left the Upper Sixth in July 1966. The new boys coming into the school now found Shiplake very much like any other school – a bit short of changing rooms perhaps, a bit crowded, but the incomers had little idea of how much they owed to the leavers, boys who had put a great deal into making a small school a success. Staff and boys were rather less of a team in the years after 1966. While much good was achieved, the boys developed more of a 'them versus us' attitude. The school lost something special when the last of the origi-

Shakespeare on the Terrace

Henry IV's seizure of the throne from Richard II has not been easy. As the play opens news is brought of a victory over the Scots at Holmedon for him, which seems at last to have brought some measure of peace to the kingdom. But it is a peace which is soon to be shattered . . .

King Henry IV	**C. Mantel**
Prince of Wales	**M. A. Rawlings**
John of Lancaster	**G. R. Bell**
Earl of Westmoreland	**D. J. McNeill**
Sir Walter Blunt	**J. R. A. Nayler**
Earl of Worcester	**M. A. Law**
Earl of Northumberland	**A. B. Docker**
Hotspur, his son	**P. J. Shakespeare**
Edmund Mortimer	**H. Wyndham-Smith**
Earl of Douglas	**S. R. Moller**
Owen Glendower	**J. W. Turner Lashmar**
Sir Richard Vernon	**J. S. Cullis**
Sir John Falstaff	**N. M. Lyttelton**
Poins	**K. de C. Hepburn**
Gadshill	**P. J. H. Judges**
Peto	**J. M. Smith**
Bardolph	**D. Guillaume**
First Carrier	**P. de Meo**
Second Carrier	**R. M. Green**
Sheriff	**P. J. H. Judges**
Vintner	**A. J. S. B. Batten**
Francis	**M. MacKenzie-Charrington**
1st Traveller	**S. J. M. Ledingham**
2nd Traveller	**P. R. Salisbury**
Mistress Quickly	**A. D. Polak**

Produced by	**Mr. M. M. Gilliat** **Mr. J. C. Smith** **Mr. D. F. K. Welsh**
Directed by	**Mr. J. C. Smith**

Wardrobe Supervision	**Miss M. Grayson**
Lighting Direction	**Lt.-Col. W. H. C. Travers and J. H. White**
Set and Costume designs direction	**Mr. C. Wills**
Make-up direction	**Revd. B. Wilks**
Set construction	**Mr. J. Whittington**
Additional research and designs	**Major F. Blatchley-Hennah**
Stage Management directed by	**M. D. Smith**

Scaffolding kindly loaned by Mr. Frank Barham

We wish to thank also the many boys, staff, friends and parents who have helped in various ways with this production.

There will be a collection at the end of the play to help defray expenses.

There will be one interval of ten minutes.

end of them in 1968 by presenting the Governors with a detailed report. Typically of JDE it described material improvements and listed the things the school needed. As usual, a gymnasium featured on the list. Another feature of his report was a detailed description of the areas in which he thought the school was weak. He was always inclined to emphasise areas where he deemed himself to have failed.

The headmaster did not leave the boys out of this report. He emphasised to the Governors how an increasing number of senior boys made a noticeable difference to games and to the running of the houses. As long ago as 1965 the First XV won nine out of twelve matches against the Third XVs of bigger schools. The record of the First XI cricketers was also improving. It meant we could ask other schools for strong fixtures, but it would mean hard work in justifying fixtures when the school had a comparatively small Sixth Form. Certainly schoolboy giants were in short supply both on the rugger field and in the Boat Club. The one thing missing from this report was an account of the personal impact John Eggar had on the whole school during the period.

Between 1964 and 1968 177 boys left the school; 57 of them had attempted 'A' Levels in the Sixth Form, many more had had one year in the General Sixth. Since 1966 there had been a Sixth Form Society which David Welsh ran until 1982! A Junior Common Room Club began in September 1968 – JDE poured the inaugural pint – and a place opened where those over seventeen could have a pint of beer with their friends. Most problems of illegal drinking by our seniors outside the school thus ended. The difficulties the JCR has had in balancing its books are well known to generations of prefects!

A Games Committee, with senior boy representatives and the head boy acting as secretary, began in 1965. It has never failed to solve inter-house match problems, and contributed considerably with the development of school sports policies.

Building a sound Sixth Form tradition is far from easy. At Shiplake quite remarkable results have been achieved by boys deemed in the 1960s to be below the minimum required for Grammar School entry. They got their 'A' Levels and found very often that the polytechnics and HND courses suited their post-school academic needs rather better than universities. The Shiplake Upper Sixth has been less successful with the more able young man who has been easy-going since the age of about nine. Shiplake somehow manages to challenge the hard-working, determined individual who finds it difficult. John Eggar produced detailed figures for the first four years he presided over the school's academic fortunes; 57 boys attempted 'A' Levels, and obtained between them 64 passes. There were then about fourteen boys in each Upper Sixth year, and in the same period 54 boys left with six or more 'O' Levels and 23 with five. Lower down the scale, a large number had four 'O' Levels, and a handful left with none at all.

By 1968 our admission policy became fairly stable, and remained much the same during the rest of John Eggar's period at Shiplake. During David Skipwith's short period at the helm, the entry became largely one from the prep schools. There was quite a lot of selection, too. At least two boys labelled 'might play cricket for England one day' were turned down because their prep schools could not be equally optimistic about their work. John Eggar brought from Repton considerable experience of admissions, as a great deal of admission policy there had been in the hands of housemasters. He knew many prep school Heads, and had played cricket with more. The range of prep schools who sent young men to Shiplake widened considerably as a result. There was an increase in the number of boys who made Shiplake their first choice, and some remarkably good boys came to us as second choice, especially in January each year. John Eggar was very happy to keep faith with families who needed Shiplake. The need tended to be defined simply as a good varied school without a restrictively high standard of entry. Histories of many schools in the 1920s refer to a period when as many as 50 or 60 per cent of boys were never up to the old School Certificate standard. In the years since the 1930s, entry standards had increased and this excluded the kind of boy that Shiplake was now admitting. The non-academic schoolboy in any well-known school ceased to get in during the post-war 'bulge' years. The leaver without 'O' Levels was a fairly unusual product of Shiplake in the 1980s, but he was not an untypical public school boy of 60 years ago.

No boy has ever come to Shiplake without an interview; occasionally the interview has been at long distance, a friend of Shiplake asking in Hong Kong or Kingston, Jamaica the questions which would normally be asked in the headmaster's study. The great majority of parents were equally searching in their visits to us. It is a long time since we got a boy simply because we were close to Heathrow and the father wanted to choose a school in a hurry. Furthermore, not every parent reads the prospectus very carefully, and Shiplake owes a great deal to thoughtful prep school headmasters who sense that Shiplake will be better for a lad than his father's choice or his brother's school. Our greatest allies have been the satisfied parents, especially if a boy has caught up his gifted brothers during his time here. As far as Shiplake headmasters are concerned, the vital questions are these: 'Has he got something to build on?', 'Has he got something to offer Shiplake?', 'Will he survive?', 'Will he get a good, sound 'O' Level coverage within twelve months of his more successful prep school rivals?'.

Having let boys into Shiplake, John Eggar did not lose sight of them. He enjoyed teaching, and never gave it up. He loved solving the problems of a repeat 'O' Level set, and for several years ran a one-year 'O' Level Economics course for those who had given up a language. Under modern conditions it is not easy to be a teaching headmaster. David Skipwith did no teaching at all after March 1960, and in 1969 John Eggar had to cut down the fifteen periods he used to teach. Peter Lapping always found he was teaching one set too many.

The boys of the late 1960s made practical contributions to the growth of the school. The early generations probably knew about the unused space in loft areas long before authority decided to open them up to provide study areas for the more junior parts of each House. In 1968 Everett indulged in a great deal of back-breaking work to produce a rear extension in brick. This provided three 'three-man' studies and a hobbies room. The boys of the House made a big contribution to the cost of the work. At much the same time, Welsh House indulged in sponsored walks to finance the conversion of dormitories into study bedrooms. The Boat Club was constantly fundraising, with a boat house and a brand new 'eight' as their main objectives. It was a sign of stringent times in 1968 when the Governors appointed a young professional bursar and thus broke with a nationwide tradition of employing a senior retired officer. R.A. Alexander came from Dulwich, where he had been Assistant Bursar. A period of careful financial control began, and an organisation more suited to a bigger school was built up on the administrative side. A substantial amount of 'back-log' maintenance was started; a new national standard of fire safety had to be met. 'The whole school' in the words of MMG 'has been turned into a maze with fire doors everywhere.' Under Bob Alexander the cafeteria system began. However, we could not blame the new bursar for the disadvantages it introduced. You have to be a fairly old Old Boy to remember Shiplake meals when the prefects ushered in the latecomers, when meals began and ended with Grace and permission to leave was only granted when everyone had finished and gossiped for about five minutes. Under the new system you were free to choose the time you decided to queue up, you were free to choose from a range of dishes, but the main disadvantages were that meals were now rushed through, a sit-down and a long chat were no longer a part of mealtimes. The dreaded table monitor – the first promotional step in many a career – vanished for good. Many a crafty young man was, under the old system, able to consult with his housemaster at mealtimes. Now he had to make the effort to get to House Business.

The weather was particularly poor in 1968. Richard Devas, Old Vikings chairman in our Silver Jubilee Year, led the best cricket XI we had so far. Only eight of the arranged school fixtures were played; one of these was lost. In July 1968 Michael Duncan left the staff and moved to Tonbridge where he has since become a housemaster. He was the first young university graduate to come to Shiplake, gain his experience here over a five-year period, and then move on to an all-round schoolmastering career elsewhere.

1969 was our Tenth Anniversary year. It brought a long hot summer – the main celebration was a Tenth Anniversary Ball. This raised enough money to take the college into the minibus age. A brand new Transit was bought. It became a boon to the Boat Club, to visits, to Duke of Edinburgh Award projects, and it provided sound service for a number of years. In the end, it was forced off the road by a lunatic driver coming in the opposite direction. The accident took place at the Shiplake war memorial, and our minibus was a total loss; fortunately there were no boys aboard at the time. This minibus has had numerous successors.

The brilliant summer continued well into the autumn of 1969. While the weather was memorable, those who were in Welsh and Everett houses at the time may remember even more the everlasting mess caused by the conversion of these two houses to oil-fired central heating. This was also the summer when 'A' Levels for the first time seemed to be earlier than usual. We did not realise at the time that it would mark the end of an era. The summer terms would be shortened, and school would end early in July, the result, of course, being that the autumn term started early in September and became exceptionally – possibly unnecessarily – long.

Between 1965 and 1967 many new ideas that have now become part of normal life here were being put forward. House reports became a regular feature of the magazine from 1965 and House colours were first awarded in 1967. The open competitions for Essays, Poetry and Public Reading began, and Art prizes were introduced. The inter-house Music and Debating shields were presented.

In 1965 the total of full-time teaching staff passed the twenty mark. The staff were not without additional pressures. With the CCF came annual inspections. The Examination Boards began to use computers and the life of the master in charge of public examinations became more complicated. Since 1964 the post has been held by Richard Lee, Michael Duncan, Peter Bleackley – for ten years – Alan Butterworth and Mrs Cosgrove. The late Jim Kroth took Shiplake into the GCSE era and George Cassels followed just as Modular A Levels arrived.

In 1967 the outdoor summer play was abandoned as a concession to public examination demands. A rather obstructive stage in the Great Hall was erected so that the major production could be indoors each autumn. Even so, several of David Welsh's more memorable productions used other parts of the hall.

CHAPTER 8

Into the Second Decade

OF THOSE who left in July 1969 John Brown was the most notable. He is described in the history of Henley Rugby Football Club as one of the best wing three-quarters the club ever had. As master in charge of rugby at Shiplake he produced an excellent First XV in 1968/9. Many members of this team stayed on to help R. A. Esau's outstanding 1969/70 side.

Mr Andrew Southorn and Mr A. H. D. Barrow joined the governing body in 1969. They were soon involved in a significant decision. Mr and Mrs Waller offered to sell us the Red House. A chance to buy this house had been missed ten years earlier. To buy was eminently sensible as more accommodation was needed; there could be some expansion after a period of marking time. Expanded numbers could finance higher standards in a number of directions. In retrospect, this was a real turning point and led to the dramatic expansion of the 1970s. When the Governors considered the situation, they saw a sound basis for going forward. Full Ministry recognition in 1967 was followed by membership of the Governing Bodies Association in 1968. In the same year we joined the Independent Schools Careers Service. Some schools had experienced a drop in numbers in 1968, but Shiplake College remained pleasantly full at a total of 196 and the fees were £210 per term. Parents had made generous contributions to the swimming pool and to the firing point on the .22 range, and they supported individual fund-raising efforts by at least two houses. In the circumstances a fund-raising appeal to extend the college seemed justifiable.

There were other indications of parental support. Late in 1969 a Sunday paper headline announced 'Top school expels drug pusher'; it referred to Shiplake College. In a way it suggested that we had already achieved our aim of becoming an important school. However, drug problems in a school are never funny, but this publicity in fact did us no harm. It gave us a chance to reveal our policy, which was a certain tolerance and sympathy for the boy foolish enough to experiment with drugs, but at the same time total rejection of one who brought them into the school. We managed to devise a policy in 1969 which has stood us in good stead since and convinced parents that we had answers to a problem which became a national menace to school and community life for several years in the 1970s. It is never easy to build up in a community, a tradition that opposes current trends or fads amongst young people. However, sympathy for those who owned up and were willing to learn a lesson indicated that Shiplake was just as concerned as ever with helping young people to develop worthwhile standards and a positive outlook.

At first, the newly purchased Red House was considered as an opportunity to increase the number of resident staff. John Eggar was already aware of the problems of having two houses in the main building. He was moving towards the idea of giving Burr its own home when some Lower Sixth essays were passed to him. These had been set to discuss the case for and against a 'sixth form house' – then a current vogue – but the conclusion of the sixth form was 'give it to Burr'. The Governors then made a tour of 'congested districts' in the main building and they promptly decided to confirm John Eggar's view that Burr should have a home of its own. By June 1970 Burr was in a position to look forward to establishing its own separate identity at long last.

There was a substantial exodus in July 1970. The enlarged entry of 1965/6 – when Welsh house opened – left very much as a group. The school was not quite full in September 1970. There was space in Everett and even more in the main building because Burr had moved into the Red House. There was actually some teaching upstairs in the main building for the first time since 1959. John Eggar toyed with the idea of moving his study nearer to his sitting-room, but in the end, the headmaster's study remained where it was – in the best place to see from the window the general ebb and flow of school life. This room passed to the Deputy Head in 1992 when the new 'Admin' wing opened.

One fifth former failed to reach his new accommodation in Burr at the start of the autumn term. He also missed his first few days in the fifth form. P.D.M. Carson was a passenger on board one of the three air liners hijacked to 'Liberation air-strip' in the Jordanian desert. He and many other school children returning from the Gulf States spent three days on a diet of a tinned peach, a quarter of a biscuit each, and half a cup of water a day. Eventually the three aircraft were destroyed, but Carson and his travelling companions arrived in this country via Amman.

Carson's adventures in the hands of the Popular Front guerrillas were duly recorded in the school magazine and showed that the experience had enhanced his writing ability. With some official encouragement, Carson came to realise that his adventures could easily turn into an 'O' Level English essay on a variety of subjects. 'A long journey' or perhaps 'The end of the holidays' or even more appropriately 'Return to school' are all obvious stereotypes. When June 1971 arrived Carson managed to adapt his experiences to a suitable essay topic with some success. A good grade followed in August! There can be few English language candidates who had such positive help with their essay so many months before the actual exam. At the same time, of course, no one envied Carson.

The 1970 general election result gave a great stimulus to those involved in independent education. Since 1964 considerable problems had been posed for all types of fee-paying schools. The Labour government had set up a Public Schools Commission to report on their future. Shiplake, a very new school, had little in common with the seven great schools of the original Public Schools Act. Our problems and intentions were not the same as those of many others, especially the big boarding schools. Our entry was not particularly competitive. Unlike the direct grant schools, we could not help the clever boy from a family of modest means because our fees were too high. It was not our intention to be a refuge for the dull sons of the very well off. In fact one of the hardest things for a boy is to be the average son of a very successful father. Our high staffing ratio and our friendly approach were meant to be two answers to the problems of this kind of young man. While we were getting on with a useful job we felt needlessly threatened.

In the jargon of the period we were obviously in 'the private sector'. The expression 'public schools' was gradually dropping from use in favour of 'independent schools'. This approach suited Shiplake. We were far too young a school to have an 'old school tie' image. We had never had to worry about abolishing 'fagging' or ending the tradition of prefects being able to beat other boys. We never had a school cap. During this period many schools agonised over the abolition of their traditional uniforms and other hallowed institutions.

Shiplake was certainly independent in the sense that we could make our own decisions without having to wait a long time for local authority approval or for the next year's finances to be available. Nor do we have to wait our turn with other schools under the same authority for additional aid and extra buildings. Heads and staffs of local authority schools have traditionally felt secure and no one, ten years ago, would have imagined how rapidly they would have lost that security in a period of declining rolls and reduced financial provision. At a difficult time, the independent schools, with their ability to act freely and quickly responded well both to the prosperity of the early 1970s and the anxieties of the early 1980s. The head and governors of an independent school are free to act quickly and to appoint extra staff if there is a sudden and encouraging increase in numbers. A board of governors can deal with problems in the term they arise in: the Shiplake Governors were certainly able to respond quickly to new educational policies in South Oxfordshire. The virtual disappearance of selection in local authority schools helped us to increase our numbers – particularly of day boys. We went our own way, maintaining a flexible entry policy, when many boarding schools became over-selective. We were able to continue, on a small scale, providing a disciplined alternative both to the school with a narrow good ability range and to the big and very varied comprehensive schools. The talk in

Name .... *No.* ....

Number Sent	ALL TERMS	*Number Returned*
	†1 Regulation Grey Tweed Suit	
	†2 Sports Coats	
	†2 Pairs Grey Worsted Trousers	
	†2 Grey Slipovers or Pullovers	
	6 Everyday White Shirts, Collars attached	
	1 Black Tie	
	*2 Ties	
	12 Handkerchiefs	
	6 Pairs of Grey Socks	
	3 Vests	
	3 Pairs of Pants	
	3 Pairs of Pyjamas	
	1 Dressing Gown	
	1 Pair Bedroom Slippers	
	1 Pair Casuals with Micro-Cellular Soles	
	1 Pair Black Walking Shoes	
	1 Pair Wellington Boots	
	1 Navy Duffle Coat	
	1 Navy Raincoat (optional)	
	1 Pair of Gloves (optional)	
	1 Hairbrush and Comb	
	1 Toothbrush	
	1 Sponge Bag and Flannel	
	1 Pair of Nail Scissors	

† OBTAINABLE ONLY FROM HARRODS

Number Sent		*Number Returned*
	1 Travelling Rug	
	6 Coloured Towels	
	1 Linen Bag	
	1 Pair of Jeans	
	1 Coloured Shirt	
	GAMES CLOTHES—ALL TERMS	
	1 Track Suit (any colour)	
	1 White Sweater	
	2 Pairs White Socks	
	1 Pair Black Gym Shoes	
	*1 White Singlet	
	*1 Pair White Cotton Shorts	
	*2 School Games Shirts	
	*2 Pairs School Games Stockings	
	*2 Pairs School Games Shorts	
	GAMES CLOTHES (If Taking the Sport)	
	1 Pair White Cricket Boots	
	1 Pair Grey Flannels for Cricket	
	1 Pair Tennis Shoes	
	*1 Pair Rowing Shorts	
	1 Pair Bathing Trunks	
	1 Pair Soccer Boots (Rubber Studs)	
	1 Pair Jodhpurs	
	1 Hard Riding Hat	

* OBTAINABLE ONLY AT THE SCHOOL

In 2000 substitute 'the College Shop' for Harrods!

the State system was all about achieving smaller classes. We already had them; we were, although we did not realise it, well on the way to the situation we find ourselves in today when we hear time and again in encouraging tones the suggestion that 'there is nothing quite like Shiplake anywhere else'. How we come to establish our own individuality quite so certainly is hard to say. We have always been glad to borrow good ideas from elsewhere, but have never been interested in slavishly copying current trends or emulating any other school.

The 1970s turned out to be a wonderfully constructive period for all types of boarding school, but no one at Shiplake in 1970, unless he was John Eggar, had any idea of how far the school would advance during the decade. The present writer, who rejoined Shiplake College in the autumn, certainly did not.

The Boat Club got well ahead with their plans during 1970. Their fund raising efforts brought them close to the price of a brand new Donoratico eight. In response to their enterprise the Governors agreed to pay for a large boathouse of 'an agricultural type'. This was to be concealed in the quarry. The main object was to get the biggest possible building for the smallest possible cost – both of these boat club projects were completed during 1971.

The old year ended on a dark note quite literally. Due to industrial disputes there was a power cut which blacked out the carol service in Henley parish church. The result was that the choir and congregation sang manfully through the afternoon without organ accompaniment.

1971 proved to be the year of varied interests; early on there was a postal strike, but fortunately every house now had its own telephone call-box and the area had recently turned over to STD. Letter writing received a setback from which it has never quite recovered. A whole generation of boys took advantage of the up-to-date telephone system and learnt to arrange everything by word of mouth instead of by letter. Boys continue to welcome letters from home, but are less active in writing them. This was also the year of the British Standard Time experiment. In the long run, nobody cared for being two hours ahead of Greenwich Mean Time in the summer and one hour throughout the winter. The demise of the experiment was generally welcomed.

Mark Hayman, destined to preside over John Eggar's retirement celebrations as chairman of the Old Boys, was in 1971 captain of hockey. David Partridge had taken over the coaching and the First XI won 7 games, drew 2 and lost only 1 match. This First XI was probably the best balanced hockey side that we had before the 1980s.

During the Easter holiday the Great Hall housed a public enquiry into the line of a new main road from Play Hatch to Harpsden. The threat of the alternative proposals to our own frontage has already been mentioned. In the long run, the road enquiry had no impact whatsoever. The Inspector recommended the new route which had been put forward by the local authorities, but in 1974 the start of a campaign of national economy made fairly certain that a new road would probably not be built this century.

By no means everything started at Shiplake College stands the test of time – ideas are supposed to be more durable than people or buildings but this is not always so. For a number of years great importance was attached to Form Orders and these were read out at end of term assembly. One Harvard graduate reminded me recently that he had been bottom of the whole school at the end of his first term. There was an irritating system of scaling marks to help members of top sets to come above lower sets. From the mid 1970s, reports showed only sets plus the position and percentage in that set. Forms in each year are now arranged by house and run by a house tutor. Thus the form no longer indicates status or stigma and just survives as a convenient grouping.

In the 1980s cross country matches against other schools revived. Twenty years earlier we had great difficulty in producing senior and junior teams from our small number of endurance runners. At the end of the 1960s these people's needs were met by following the Farley Hill Beagles in the country south of Reading. This specialised activity ended when the spreading network of motorways forced the Farley Hill pack to move into North Oxfordshire and combine with an Oxford college pack.

Boxing fixtures with other schools died out in 1971. House boxing had stopped several years earlier. Fencing took its place for a while. For a few years there was the 'White Book' – a compilation of school, house and form lists in several permutations. It was the victim of an economy campaign – as were individual Sports Fixture cards a few years later.

Old Boys of this period would feel that Speech Day is now a shadow of its former self. GCE exams put paid to a whole day affair in the strawberry season. Soon we found ourselves in the position that there were only two possible dates – the Saturday before half-term or the last day of term. Neither of these has proved particularly suitable for a Service of Thanksgiving or large-scale exhibitions. The last occasion when Speech Day was on a grand scale was in 1977. Public examinations were postponed because of the Queen's Jubilee. Things are never what they used to be. 'The College hasn't got a siege gun place kicker like old Carlos Caralps.' 'Junior teams are not as tough as when Chaplain Wilks was in charge.'

In one area progress is consistent. We rarely have foul-ups on the grand scale of old. In December 1971 John Eggar and I were stranded at Twickenham after a memorable Varsity Match win by Oxford. Ours was the last coach in the park. Apparently every Shiplake boy was present except the Head of College, but he had the list of those supposed to be present. Unfortunately, he was the sole person unable to find the coach park. He deserves a mention in another context. A few years later he became our first Old Boy to teach in an HMC school. The school shop was badly damaged by fire on the night 16/17 April 1971. The blaze originated with a defective television set in the room next door. A good deal of out-of-date stock, mostly tiny cricket caps and under-size sports gear, was destroyed.

Looking back, it is fortunate that we got a proper house system going from an early stage. As the school grew bigger the house remained the smaller unit where the individual was not dominated by sheer numbers. In March 1971 we welcomed a parent to the CCF Inspection Day; General Dunbar, like many a helpful parent, was open and to the point. He did not conceal his doubts about some aspects of the CCF's work. Later the same year we were for the first time hosts to the meeting and social gathering of Number 10 District of the Prep Schools Association.

The Boat Club continued to make great strides and certainly projected the image of the school further than ever. The national press began to speak of Shiplake as 'a leading rowing school'. This was really premature praise, but none the less welcome. Certainly we were good enough when we entered the Princess Elizabeth Cup at Henley Royal Regatta for the first time to give an American crew from St Paul's, Concord, a good race. More than a decade later we were still having great difficulty with American school crews.

The rest of the story of 1971 is financial. A surcharge of £10 per boy had to be invoked for the summer term. This produced something over £2,000 – such a small sum by today's standards, but vital to a balanced budget! Rapid inflation was setting in. The fees were £255 per term in September 1971 and were planned thereafter to rise at the rate of £8 per term. A five-year review of expenditure from 1966 to 1971 had shown a 10 per cent increase in all directions. This itself caused problems, as keeping it down to 10 per cent had been achieved by postponing repairs and maintenance. One example of what had to be done in 1971 was the external restoration and re-roofing of Tudor Cottage. The cost of buying, adapting, fireproofing and extending the Red House was £28,000. This did not include the study extension to the rear, but the brick shower block immediately behind the Red House had to be built before boys could move in. The appeal produced a rather disappointing £26,000 during its first year: it did pick up later. The debt incurred by Everett House in the do-it-yourself extension was taken over by the Governors who now felt that the school was big enough to centralise all fund-raising. None the less, individual boy-based efforts to strengthen school assets did not come to an end at this point. The boat club has continued to raise money on its own account and in recent years the trekking club – particularly for their Himalayan expeditions – have raised considerable sums. The term came to an end in July 1971 with an impressive effort in the form of a mass sponsored walk to finance a badly needed servery. Little did we know when we buckled down to raising the £2,000 necessary what inflated prices we would be paying a decade later for a sports hall and new laboratories.

The July 1971 sponsored walk will never be forgotten by those who took part. About 170 set off and 64 finished. The course began three miles below Henley bridge and followed the river upstream to Pangbourne – that distance totalled 18 miles and 12 miles brought you back to the College. Among those who finished were JDE, who lost several toe-nails as a result, and the fittest member of the governing body, Sir Colville Deverell, then aged 66. Mr Stephen Oxlade ran the whole distance and Mr J.B. Wood finished it at a more sedate pace. The whole enterprise took place on a day of blazing heat.

During the holiday the servery was built where the gallery of the old billiard room had been: it involved the demolition of the strongroom of the original private house. The servery represented a great improvement upon mobile trolleys. Even so the project had not been completely paid for and those who had not walked in July were given a chance to do so in the spring of 1972. This time the volunteers trekked from the College downstream to Hurley and back. This walk took place in a continuous downpour: the financial objective was achieved. I can claim to be the only member of staff who completed both walks.

During his last two terms as bursar, R.A. Alexander saw the servery finished and supervised the construction of the single storey block at the rear of Burr house. The maths teaching block was built at the same time. Bob Alexander's rigid financial control had been invaluable since 1968. He was a realist, was frank, open and would smile widely as he pruned your financial demands to his way of thinking. He left us to become bursar at Bedales and this was undoubtedly a well-deserved promotion. He was replaced by J.A. Corbett.

The Independent Schools Information Service began in 1972 and Shiplake was one of its original supporters. More importantly John Eggar was elected a member of the Society of Headmasters of Independent Schools. This was a very well deserved honour and gave Shiplake an entry in the *Public Schools Year Book.* 1972 was a year when people rather than buildings made the news at Shiplake. The year had begun with a three-act play performed by the staff. JDE had set his heart on a staff play soon after he arrived. That we have not had another since 1972 is of no significance; suffice to say that everyone knew their lines and neutral observers said 'the casting was wickedly accurate'. Before and since this staff play, members of the common room have shown their dramatic skills in seasonal Christmas concerts and other burlesque activities.

In July Shiplake experienced its first two major retirements. Mrs Edna de la Praudiére and Captain Robert Byng CBE, RN both decided to give up full-time teaching. Edna had been with us since May 1960 and had already become our first lady member of the Old Boys Club. Robert Byng had arrived towards the end of 1962. There were other changes during the year. D.H. Drury left to join the staff at Canford; Skipwith had been the dominant Rugby and rowing house during his years in charge. The boat club made vast strides under his direction and in successive years he had coached Cambridge – producing a winning boat crew – and Oxford, who did not win! J.H. Ducker, who rowed for Oxford in 1958, also left the staff and was temporarily replaced for two terms by M.J.H. Charles. Like several other temporary appointments Michael Charles was induced to stay becoming Skipwith's longest serving housemaster.

M.W. Mash took over the timetable with the intention of computerising it, but the complexities of our system defeated the machine at that stage of computer development and things went on as before. There were six new members of staff in the autumn, which represented an actual increase of one. The Duke of Edinburgh Award leaders held a reunion of old boys who had gained the Gold Award; sadly the number of those attending was well below the total of 65 golds which had been achieved during the previous ten years. Charles Packer was the first of our cricketers to play for the Berkshire schools Under-Nineteen XI. Our own First XI won 5 matches, drew 4 and lost 3. At this stage the Under Fifteen XI was the only other regular side. It had been coached since 1964 by the chaplain who was now joined by Michael Charles.

On the educational front the early 1970s were years when 'integrated studies' were in vogue. At Shiplake new ideas had been carefully considered and we have often taken the best and left the rest alone. For instance from 1965 onwards the maths department took a considerable interest in modern maths, particularly the Schools Maths Project. On the other hand, Peter Bleackley considered stopping the school from buying a 'language lab' to be his biggest single service to the school! Project work – especially with history and geography departments working closely together – was a feature of the early 1970s; T. H. Jones was a moving force in all this. In 1970 the thirds did project work for a month in the spring. In 1971 it became one day a week: later it became part of one day.

Another approach to the problem of teaching was the organisation of work rather than its content. From 1974 to 1981 we divided the fifth and fourth forms into upper and lower groups. The differentiation was the speed in which they worked for 'O' Level and the number of subjects taken. The 1980s 'learning to learn' programme in the third forms had many of the objectives of the project schemes of a decade earlier. The growth of the school in the middle 1970s made organising project work for a whole year more difficult. In 1972 it was possible to take the whole of the fourth form to York for a three-day project in one 57-seater coach. This held the whole of the fourth form plus three members of staff, one staff wife – to look after health – together with one son and his dog! The coach for three days cost only £95 and another £150 covered all other expenses! A steel works, three museums, a battlefield, York Minster and a Shakespeare play were the main features of a hectic visit.

The retirement of Robert Byng allowed the careers department to move into what used to be Room 7 – though it was known for some years as 'the Captain's cabin'. This room could only seat twelve for teaching purposes and that was only because of the desks and benches that Robert Byng himself had installed. At the end of the last century this comfortable room had been the living-room for the resident stable staff. It was decided in 1972 to make it the home of the careers office and library. In the school's early days John Foster had made use of his RAF experience to get some careers guidance going, but the independent existence of the careers department really began in January 1966 when J.W. Whittington put up a shelf for the books and pamphlets that John Foster had handed over! With an attractive and permanent home the careers department began to make a big impact in the early 1970s. It soon required a busy, almost full-time, secretary and today only the headmaster's office and the bursary receive and send out more mail. JWW's long tenure in the post as careers master came to exceed even DFKW's years in charge of squash.

On 15 February 1973 the ever-popular head of science, George Wright, was rushed into hospital to have his appendix removed. On the same day, John Eggar produced an appendix of quite a different sort. In addition to his termly report to the Governors the headmaster outlined his ideas for yet more buildings. The Burr single study block and the maths labs had just come into use.

The Governors were planning to tarmac the courtyard in front of the main building, but as usual JDE was looking well ahead. The cost of using the Henley squash club courts was rising in terms of rent, light and travel costs. Our own courts might be self-financing – given the right scheme! There was a strong case for generally enlarging Sister's flat and the work was carried out in 1974. Everett, the most modern house, was short of single and double rooms; they were eventually added in 1977. A false ceiling for the Tithe Barn was first mentioned in this appendix. Behind the headmaster's thinking was the advice of the Master of Wellington College, Mr Frank Fisher, who urged the Governors to find space for the increased number of boys looking for boarding school places during the early and mid 1970s. The rooms in the main building that had been turned over to academic purposes in 1970 when Burr moved out once again were filled with boarders and Skipwith numbers increased rapidly.

Coming from outside, the new bursar saw to what extent the college office arrangements had failed to keep up with the growth in numbers. Miss Monica Tomalin was secretary to the bursar as well as to the headmaster. She answered both telephones and met every caller! The only other full-time help was Mrs Hinton who dealt with all the accounts single-handed while the school more than doubled in size. Visiting old boys were quick to notice the changes in the front office when, after fourteen years, Miss Tomalin handed over many and various duties and moved upstairs to become Skipwith house matron. Monica had a real affection for the main building from when it contained the whole school until her retirement late in the 1990s.

The other big change of 1973 was the arrival of a photocopier! The bursar could not see how the staff had survived for so long without the means of rapidly copying their own teaching materials. The old way had been to go through the office and have copies made by Gestetner. Although a great help to teaching, photocopiers proved a mixed blessing. Instead of the office producing notices and circulars everyone in charge of anything has been able to produce his own 'bumph' almost at will! The occasional economy drive has from time to time brought a temporary reduction in the amount churned out.

The rest of the year is soon covered. The First VIII beat Hampton Grammar School in the Princess Elizabeth Cup and then lost to an American school. Exceptionally rough weather brought about the abandonment of most of the Duke of Edinburgh Award adventure training in the Lake District. Charles Packer was awarded his Berkshire junior cap for cricket. Robert Esau and a team of sixth formers produced a literary magazine – *Contrasts* – which raised a considerable sum for charity. The hockey XI played a Hockey Association side for the first time. The Rowbotham Scholarship was offered to the school, and filled. Sister Grayson handed over the sick wing to Sister Noble. Two girl members of the Upper Sixth left and were not replaced. Looking back at 1973 it seems the quietest year since the school opened.

In 1974 the staff salary scale was from £1,830 to £3,310. The school was almost entirely a boarding school but in September Orchard House opened with R. A. Esau in charge of twenty-one day boys, including twelve who had just arrived. They occupied a two-roomed building. RAE broke with the tradition of having a new house named after its first housemaster. Perhaps someone had told him the story of David Skipwith who said on one occasion 'I don't mind shouts of "come on Skipwith" and quite like "well done Skipwith" but I absolutely draw the line at "oh beautiful Skipwith!" ' The name Orchard also avoided emphasis on the idea of a 'day boy' house. Those who arrived at 8.30 in the morning and spent a very long day here were to be fully integrated. This has been partially achieved by having a resident housemaster for Orchard. There has always been a problem in fixing a day boy fee; he has everything except bed and breakfast; the tuition cost is the biggest single item.

An extra 30 per cent added to teaching salaries and backdated suddenly pushed fees upwards to undreamed-of levels. In 1975 they were £370 per term for day boys and £525 for boarders; nine months later they went up to £410 a term for day boys and £590 for boarders. All this was very necessary as there had been, for instance, a 100 per cent increase in rates in the previous twelve months.

On one of the lovely May evenings in 1974 the catering staff served supper to the whole school on the river bank; the reason for doing so was a bomb scare. There had been many of these in the Reading area and we had no alternative but to evacuate all school buildings while the police searched. The sisters of a young man in Everett were apprehended by the police as they walked across the cricket field towards an empty school; the reason for police interest in their activities was a large cardboard box the girls were carrying. It contained nothing but tuck!

1974 was certainly a year for personalities. The director of art, David John, won a Churchill scholarship. In June at a 'no speeches' dinner Colonel Travers was the guest of honour; he had announced his retirement for the following month. His services to the school had been enormous, his energy and physical fitness were legendary, and staff and sixth formers involved in the early Duke of Edinburgh Award expeditions held him and Mrs Travers in the highest esteem.

Another link with the early days was broken when Colonel F.N. Richardson retired from the governing body. He had been a key figure in the first fund-raising efforts. Now that he had reached 80 he felt that he ought not to drive from Kent. Colonel Richardson enjoyed a lengthy retirement – he died in the spring of 1983. Mr Goodenough, having seen his successor firmly in place as chairman, also left the Board; his contribution to arranging the finance for our continuance in 1963 and to buying out Mrs Everett had been one of many vital services. He was replaced by Sir Edwin McAlpine.

A Gaudy was provided by the Governors and the invited guests were all those who had been at the school between 1959 and 1963. The sun shone beautifully all day, but while the turnout was a little disappointing the event was most memorable. We saw W.R. Hartley for the last time; he died suddenly at Easter 1977 while playing golf.

To cope with the record number of 244 boys in the school, five new members of staff arrived in September 1974. Amongst the new boys was Mark Gray, the Rowbotham scholar elected some time earlier. Briefly the terms of this award were: financial need, residence within fifteen miles of Shiplake College and all round abilities. The main public service feature of the year was raising the cost of training a guide dog for the blind. The total sum was raised in a very short time, mainly at a fete on the cricket field. A new four was presented to the boat club by Dr Gilbert Scott.

There were other milestones in 1974. There was the Fifteenth Anniversary Ball which has since been followed by an annual event of this type. In the light of experience we ended the eight-period day. We replaced it in the winter months by having one prep before supper. There was a welcome change in uniform; vee necked long-sleeved pullovers were permitted as an alternative to sports jackets.

More than once we had awarded Fifth Form prizes to a boy who subsequently had a disappointing exam performance. From 1976 Fifth Form prizes were awarded on 'O' Level results and the winners received their prizes when in the lower sixth.

The mid 1970s were exceptional for the variety of the weather. There was the very mild winter of 1974/5; this was followed by a sixteen-month dry spell which began in May 1975, and included the heat wave that covered England and western Europe during the summer of 1975 only ending after the hottest known June/July in 1976. During these dry spells the courtyard was tarred, and the shrubs and hedges on both sides of the lower drive were removed and lawn laid out in their place. Our many magnificent elms had to be felled during these years – all had fallen prey to Dutch elm disease. On the rare occasions when it did rain, the downpours were freakish. The 1975 Speech Day was the wettest we have known, and on 31 July 1975 – early in the summer holiday – the College was the centre of a freak storm that did considerable damage to the contents of the main building. Niagara seemed to flow through the front door and got into all the basements! The dry autumn of 1975 contributed to a high scoring rugby season. H. E. Alireza's First XV broke the scoring record of 1969, which had been another dry season. Three First XV members played for Oxfordshire schools. The dry spring of 1976 made levelling more of the front lawn for an even larger marquee a simple task, but it did little for the replaced turf. Mild springs are not necessarily healthy. February 1976 produced our worst 'flu epidemic so far, but it has twice been exceeded since then.

In retrospect, 1975 appears a quiet year just before the rapid but rather unexpected expansion during the second half of the decade. Mr E.P. Hatchett and Mr Charles Keen joined the governing body. The latter continued our well-established link with Barclays Bank. M.W. Mash left the staff after a long and varied contribution. At one time or another the maths department, Everett House, the Duke of Edinburgh Award Scheme and cross country had come under his management. Eight new faces appeared on the staff in September 1975: many of these were able games coaches and their impact on rugby and rowing was considerable. T.S. Morris handed over the physical education to one of the newcomers, thus leaving himself with only two major responsibilities – the school shop and CCF administration. Another administrative change was to divide the duties of the Head Boy completely from any responsibility in his own house. It had been increasingly difficult for one person to run the team of school prefects and administer the house in which he lived.

Building plans again came into the picture during 1975. John Eggar had been granted a sabbatical by the Governors and he, no doubt undistracted by other day-to-day concerns, had given thought to what the school really needed. In some cases the decision was made for us. The science buildings, an inspection concluded, had only five years of life left. The oak floor of the Great Hall had worn out; fire regulations obliged us to re-hang the library and terrace doors so that they opened outwards. Double doors had to be inserted into the bottom third of the bay window of the Great Hall and J.W. Whittington cleverly reproduced the style of the outside doors on either side of it. Towards the end of the year, John Eggar wrote, 'Enough has been said about an indoor games hall. We have done without it for seventeen years and in my view, though not in the view of the young games-playing staff, we can continue to do so'. This view was fairly quickly altered. Two years of fine weather were followed by three exceptionally severe winters. The Tithe Barn provided very limited scope for apparatus work and was not large enough for basketball. Growing numbers strained our games organisation to the limit whenever the fields could not be played upon and by 1978 relays of boys practised hockey on every available tarmac surface in January and February. Bus loads commuted daily to the Henley all-weather pitch.

The dominant factor in 1976 ought to have been inflation. In fact, it was the growth of Orchard House which gave the school a feeling of confidence that might not otherwise have been justified. The rapid rise in the cost of living was emphasised by the alarming fact that catering expenses in the long autumn term of 1976 almost caught up with what is normally the largest single item in a school's budget – tutorial salaries. The answer was to increase income as well as to economise: here the Orchard factor was important.

Orchard prospered from the outset and was soon taking part in junior house matches. As a result, in May 1975, plans were produced for a larger building and this was in use by November 1975. Shiplake has very few of its own local words but an 'Orchard boy' means someone who takes full part in school life and happens to sleep and breakfast at home. He is not often here on Sunday. An Orchard parent is a car driver running an early morning and late evening shuttle service. In January 1976, Orchard had 28 on the roll and school planning as a whole was based on 230 boarders and 30 day boys. Demand was such that the year ended with 234 boarders and 40 in Orchard. Orchard reached 51 by September 1977. In his autumn 1977 report, John Eggar wrote to the Governors, 'I never envisaged reaching 50 boys in Orchard within two years'. The rapid growth of Orchard had several fascinating aspects. The boarder whose home was close to the school disappeared: instead we had day boys living impossibly long distances from Shiplake as the waiting list to become boarders grew. The opening of the squash club made local parents more aware of us than ever and contributed to the growth of the Orchard entry. So rapid was the success of Orchard that the day boy became an expression in the accounts office only for fee payers who did not sleep in school. The use of Orchard as a label was encouraged wherever possible. During his period in charge of Orchard, R.A. Esau lived at Tudor Cottage. The principle that the Orchard boys spending long hours in college should be looked after by a resident housemaster has continued under D.S. Partridge, P.G. Hose and R.T. Mannix.

In spite of serious national inflation the school's finances were sound. In January 1976 it cost 76p a day to feed a boy – by June it had risen to 96p per day; the figure in 1966 had been the equivalent of l8p. The total the school had borrowed at this stage to finance improvements was £79,000 and interest had risen to £8,300. The capital sums owed were being reduced at the agreed rate, the annual turnover was fast approaching the half million pound mark, and the income from school fees did pass that figure early in 1977.

With temperatures so often in the nineties during the summer of 1976, it is surprising that Shiplake found the right answer to any of its problems. The exam candidates certainly found the hottest June for 300 years an extremely trying period. There was now no single place that could sit a large fifth form exam; the Tithe Barn continued to be used for large exams and many papers were now written in what the Old Boys newsletter unkindly called 'the Church hut'. This is, in fact, an excellent modern Church Hall seating up to 40 exam candidates. The building was generally empty in the mornings until harassed College administrators thought of renting it.

Another area of concern was the simple fact that much of the equipment bought when the school opened was now wearing out. Beds, blankets, chairs, even minibuses, had a limited life. The splendid oak dining hall tables also had to be replaced. The new tiled floor in the Great Hall, itself replaced in the 1990s, would not stand up to moving these tables when clearing the hall at speed. Removing the furniture in the Great Hall was a requisite for both school and community activities. The Governors had also approved a programme of re-wiring all buildings, and this was completed by July 1976 except for the stable block which was finished soon afterwards.

Since 1960, under the able management of D.F.K. Welsh, the College squash club had made use of the courts and facilities in the centre of Henley. However, rent, lighting and travel costs were making the use of the Henley club as expensive as the interest on a sizeable loan. If we could earn income from a squash club using courts in the school grounds during the evenings we would undoubtedly reap considerable advantage. An agreement with the sports and social section of Foster-Wheeler in Reading greatly helped. Such a club could be organised by the recently formed Shiplake Court Enterprises Limited. This was a separate company covenanting its profits to the school. W.E. Russell, the former England cricketer, was already here on a part-time basis and he was appointed full-time cricket coach and business manager from July 1976. His responsibility was to increase school income from non-educational activities. Thanks to the squash club which opened in the autumn of 1976 and the various activities of Shiplake Enterprises, the school has established closer links with the local community. We gained the convenience of squash courts on the edge of our own playing fields for boys' use during the day before club members take over during the evenings.

In the autumn of 1976, the school was four boarders above strength with an extra eleven expected in January 1977. There were already ten more Orchard boys than planned. Now dealing with these problems as bursar was M.C. Whicker who had come to the school from the P & O Line. Jim Corbett had left the school to become bursar of Haberdashers' Aske's School, Elstree: his last important contribution was to see the building of the squash courts going forward. The school was gradually giving up a number of rented flats so that staff could live closer at hand and was instead leasing property that could accommodate staff and a number of boys. Not everybody liked 'waiting' houses away from the school and parents and boys have to be thanked for helping to make these plans work so successfully. The result was that our fee income increased rather more quickly than inflation.

John Eggar reached his 60th birthday at the end of 1976. The wearing of reading glasses and the use of a hearing aid were totally out of keeping with his physical vigour. Mrs Eggar had managed to persuade him to give up playing hockey but he still managed several cricket matches a season. The Governors invited him to continue at Shiplake until he was 63. Looking back, 1976 was not a good year to have chosen a new head and 1977 was not a year for a new head to arrive. None the less John Eggar was now looking for every opportunity 'to get things right for my successor'. He also wanted to make things better for the boys here and now. Increased income was the only possible way. The approaching twentieth anniversary of the school would provide the occasion for an appeal to a larger number of parents than ever previously. In view of what was to happen, the arrival on the Board of Governors of a quantity surveyor – Mr L.T. Donaldson – was not inappropriate.

M.L. Woodcock had arrived as Director of Music and he took advantage of the magnificent 1976 summer to have an end-of-term summer concert in the marquee. The 1812 Overture was performed with fireworks released by the CCF, wine flowed and water music was played to those who had taken tickets for a summertime cruise upstream from the landing stage. The parents enjoyed every moment of it. Rather more conventional was an autumn term production of 'Oliver'. Over 100 boys took part. Quite suddenly school music was back at a level close to the very early days with the majority of the school involved and thoroughly enjoying it.

By 1976 the Remedial English Department had taken shape. For several years extra English teaching had been provided for new boys with reading difficulties. As far as possible we avoided use of the term 'dyslexic'. The GCE Boards were helpful in allowing some candidates extra time to write and spell as carefully as possible. Dyslexia is not easy to define. It is perhaps made clear by a fourth former's English essay, building to a climax on the subject of 'an emergency'. 'I decided to call the Fire Brigade and dialled 996.' Most of the older members of staff had not heard of dyslexia twenty years ago, but it is a matter of quiet pride that some of our most able entrants who had most serious spelling and reading problems have left us to go on to collect university and research degrees.

Tom Bishop – Head of Physics for all too short a time – rowed at the Montreal Olympics: his wife also rowed in the women's IV. The Great Britain VIII was stroked by Richard Lester, Captain of Boats and Head of Skipwith in 1966/7. His crew won the Silver Medal and actually led the Russians for part of the final. Another 1976 Olympic oarsman – M.H.G. Hayter – later joined the staff.

In the autumn of 1976 the First XV drew with our rugby bogy, Reed's School, Cobham, and the Second XV had an unbeaten season winning eleven matches and drawing one. The Second XV were again unbeaten in 1977 and in fact played 28 games before they lost a match in the autumn of 1978. The growth of school numbers made good second teams possible in all sports, particularly rowing, rugby, hockey and cricket. Certainly the Second XVs of the late 1970s would have done very well against our weaker First XVs earlier in the decade.

To a busy school one year is much like another. However, 1977 is an easy year to remember. It was the Queen's Silver Jubilee. The keynote was provided by the Queen herself. She asked that the jubilee should be celebrated not with vast extravagance, but with economy bearing in mind the nation's financial problems.

From 22 to 28 May, the week before the national celebrations, there was a joint Shiplake village/Shiplake College week of activity. There was a local history exhibition in the parish room, gardens were open and there were local activities almost every evening of the week, culminating with the gala attended by over 2,000 on the new field. The Chairman of the Governors was also at the time Chairman of the South Oxfordshire District Council and he was immensely pleased by this local venture of co-operation and team work. A plaque to commemorate local events was presented to the College by Shiplake Parish Council. It is now kept in the library.

Those who are trying to remember 1977 in relation to other years will probably remember it because of the RAF police dogs display during the Silver Jubilee gala, but there were many other milestones during the year. For instance, the Easter holidays saw the end of the 'pot-holed' back drive and the rutted gravel slope up to Burr and the classroom block. These areas were expertly tarred at enormous expense. Further expense during 1977 was another updating of our fire precautions; manually operated fire alarms had to be replaced by automatic systems. These included 'Banshee' alarms and most unreliable smoke detectors.

In spite of a rapid expansion, Shiplake College maintained a good safety record. There has not been any fire threatening pupils and no road accidents within the school grounds during three decades of increasing activity. The so-called 'sleeping policemen' were introduced on all drives during the 1977 Easter holidays and 'cycling' filled a page in College rule books. Overall, the community showed much commonsense, but given the dangerous character of the main road outside the school gates, car collisions were beyond College control. Members of staff elected to the parish council added their voices to frequent local requests for a speed limit on the A4155. Improved warning signs were cancelled out by road straightening and increased traffic speeds. Sadly the College record of student safety came to an end when a pupil was fatally injured early in 1994, the accident happening outside the gates. A 30mph speed limit now covers most of the highway from Shiplake to Henley.

1977 was the year in which the school had a really competent 'pop' group of its own. Those who lived in Everett during 1977 will remember it as the summer the House survived with holes in the wall, with the roof off the Lower Sixth studies and some gaps in the main roof as well. This was necessary whilst the extension went forward through flood and tempest. In the end, the Everett extension was finished with twenty-four hours to spare before the start of the autumn term.

The administrative history of the school in 1977 of course included the improvements already mentioned. From the bursar's point of view, the year began with the cost of a day's meals for one reaching £1.22. Not surprisingly an 8 per cent fees increase in May was the result; the boarding fee per term was now up to £680 and Orchard fees were set at £450. The Governors endeavoured to keep the fees unchanged for periods of twelve months in order to give parents some idea of what they were committed to. The Governors' fees policy was one instance of our attempt to plan effectively during a difficult period. Inflation made it vital to end each year with some kind of surplus.

To achieve this, income had to be increased, which meant trying to take more boys as well as asking the parents to pay more. More boys, of course, meant providing more buildings to accommodate them both by day and night. The Everett extension is an example of this. It increased the size of the House and over a five-year period paid for itself. By the end of 1977 we had 28 boys in 'out houses'. In order to keep faith with parents we had to provide proper accommodation for them as quickly as possible. Additional changing rooms for Welsh House, an extension of the art room and rebuilding the science laboratories were all priority matters. At the end of 1977 the terrapin laboratories had a life expectancy of three years at the most. The school had an overall development plan, but we tended to apply for planning permission as we needed each additional building. At this time, the Governors purchased Tigoni, a large house some way from the school. In the short run this proved a wise investment for accommodation and it was sold in 1981 to finance the permanent Orchard House buildings.

The First VIII has appeared more than once on the covers of *The Court*. The photograph of the 1977 crew suggests they were bigger than most. This is a reminder of the cry of Trevor Jones, our coach in 1974, who asked, 'Why are Shiplake crews so small?'. He then provided his own ambiguous answer by saying, 'We must ask our parents to do something about it'! There was no doubt about the commitment of the 1977 crew and it was appropriately stroked by the Head of College, J.R. Hardy. A photograph in the *Sunday Times* showed the agony of exhaustion and defeat when they went out of the competition to an American crew at Henley. Photographs of them remind us that we were still in a period of long hair. There is not an ear to be seen! However, the manifestations of current trends at Shiplake during the mid 1970s were more of appearance than attitude. Length of hair was very much a matter for choice in the sixth form and lower down the school authority ensured it was kept reasonably tidy. Two years later most ears were visible in photographs of the Himalayan expedition.

CHAPTER 9

John Eggar's Last Years

THE GREAT MILESTONE of 1977 was the school population passing the 300 mark: in the autumn we had 259 boarders and 51 in Orchard. We included seven citizens from European countries, ten from Asia, one from Africa and, curiously, none from North America.

On the personal side, Peter Caston joined the staff, and with his arrival the Remedial English department took a more organised form. In the summer, David Welsh had asked to be relieved of his House – feeling after twelve years that a change was needed. He handed over to R.A. Esau at the end of the year and D.S. Partridge became the Housemaster of Orchard. The previous Easter W.R. Hartley had died suddenly, and thus another link with the early days was broken.

The Combined Cadet Force had something of a re-organisation in 1977. The parade day was moved from Friday to Tuesday. The training programme was revised and more officers were recruited. The possibility of making the CCF voluntary was considered, but in a small school the official policy remained that every boy should take part for three years and thus a vigorous unit was a more likely result. By and large, the fathers were more keen on the CCF than their sons; the latter did not always see that the voluntary Duke of Edinburgh Award and the compulsory Cadet Force made a good partnership. One American mother of an English son happened to come down the drive on a CCF afternoon. 'Say, Mr Eggar', she enquired, 'do you have compulsory military training here?' Obviously not every parent reads the prospectus carefully.

At least one housemaster was well informed about a 'spin off' from these activities. Post cards arrived regularly from three members of the lower sixth who successfully attempted the Pennine Way in the wet August of 1977. Their subsequent account in *The Court* magazine of mud and north-east gales probably discouraged every reader.

Shortly before his 60th birthday, John Eggar – in close co-operation with Pam – had found an attractive home for his retirement years in Hinton St George in Somerset. There were many friends living in the area, road and rail communications were good, the countryside was pleasant, but it was by no means a remote place. Increasingly the Eggars spent most of their holidays in Somerset and in February 1978 John Eggar was stranded there by a snow-drift and missed part of the spring term Governors' meeting! While on the one hand having a country retreat raised tempting thoughts of retirement the same arctic weather and flooded meadows here at Shiplake gave JDE his first chance to don skates since he had left Derbyshire in 1963. The vigour and unexpected skill were revealed for all to see. In view of this energy, John Eggar's announcement in July 1978 that the school's approaching twentieth year would be his last took everyone by surprise. He believed that most of his immediate objectives would be attained during the next twelve months. He felt a little more tired than he expected to be and simply decided to retire just before he was 63 instead of shortly afterwards.

Other people were on the move in the summer of 1978 before John Eggar made his momentous announcement. David John was officially Director of Art, but he was also carpenter, stonemason, play producer, champion of the underdog, friend to all and impressive mimic of Rolf Harris! David John decided to return to full-time practice as a sculptor. He was a fine example of what a man of wide experience could bring to full-time teaching. The same could be said of Peter Bleackley, a distinguished former colonial civil servant. He came to schoolmastering in 1962 after a quarter of a century of public service. He tended to depreciate his own contribution: 'My most important service to Shiplake was to stop a lot of money being invested in language laboratories.' When he retired we all realised how he set a robust example of common sense against excessive excitement. His 'I wouldn't have thought that was really necessary' was an effective way of cooling any situation. On retirement he endowed a Bleackley Prize for Modern Languages.

Andrew Southorn had been Chairman of the Governors since 1971. He was proud of Shiplake College and his enthusiasm for the joint village-College Jubilee celebrations in 1977 has been mentioned. On Speech Day in 1978 he looked far from well and his own remarks were not without nostalgia. Over the years his genuine sincerity at Speech Days helped parents to adjust to the shock of substantial annual fee increases. When he spoke of maintaining essential standards and practising rigid economy, people really believed him. His quiet firmness, for instance, enforced an idea borrowed from other schools – that of charging interest on delayed fee payments.

By the time John Eggar had announced his own impending retirement it was clear that Mr Southorn would not be well enough to take much part in choosing the next headmaster; in fact, he died on 23 August 1978, leaving a legacy to the school. This bought a complete *Encyclopaedia Britannica*, and the balance was used to curtain the library, making it more comfortable during the winter months.

The Board of Governors was now fourteen in number. Air Vice-Marshal Alec Maisner had joined the Board together with John Turner. The latter was the first Old Boy representative on the Board. He had been one of the first generation of boys and an early member of the Boat Club. He was John Eggar's second head prefect and one of our first university graduates. The Board elected its senior member, Aubrey Goodwin as Chairman. He alone had served since 1959 and it was most appropriate that he should be in the chair 20 years and 86 Board meetings after the school began.

John Eggar took particular pleasure in all activities. Art, music, drama and involvement with the local community had played a small part in the education of his own generation. Many a boy who seemed unable to come out of his shell at interview expanded in some unlikely ways. This took place to the undoubted satisfaction of the Headmaster, to the relief of housemasters and to the delight of parents. The atmosphere of Shiplake had much to do with it. However, JDE was always quick to urge the need of any boy who continued to under-perform after he had come here. The frequent message was 'Should we be doing more?', 'Could we be doing more?'. JDE remained optimistic about those in his charge until the end of his years here and he taught many schoolmasters to adopt the same outlook.

An examination of results of first teams in major sports shows that there was considerable improvement in results during the second half of the 1970s. This was due, undoubtedly, to an increase in numbers in the school – especially at the top – and to the larger number of expert coaches on the staff in each of the major sports. Furthermore, this was the period when the 'squad' system took over. Each side now trained as a unit and practised from the outset of the season. A player making the squad in September, January or April was thus either elevated to the top team or relegated to a second team for the whole season. The old schoolmasters shook their heads. Housemasters wondered if competition for places would be reduced. Traditionalists regretted the disappearance of institutions like the First XXX or the First XXII. However, the results improved which was the most important factor in a small school.

The perfect cricket match ended the 1977 season. It was played against the Berkshire Gentlemen on a glorious July afternoon. All twenty-two players batted and the school XI matched their energy against the far greater experience of the visitors. When the last over began, all results were possible. The school won with a ball to spare: the bowler entrusted with the last over hit the stumps and removed the number eleven batsman, thus saving the umpires from any last-second error. This was just one example of a more positive and determined approach in all our games played.

On the river, the First VIII tended to move from novice to senior 'C' to senior 'B' status during the course of a season. The First XV Rugby fixture list was almost entirely against the First XVs of other schools, but two clubs were played

The staff in June 1979 at the time of J D Eggar's retirement

as well. The vast majority of the First XI cricket fixtures were now against other schools' First XIs and three club sides were also played. The majority of the hockey XI's fixtures were also against the First XIs of other schools.

The events of John Eggar's final eighteen months were very varied. There was a 'flu epidemic involving 190 boys on the one hand, and an appeal for £130,000 on the other! The main objective of the appeal was to build the Sports Hall. It was no fault of John Eggar's that the building was not complete until the term after he left. His days were spent negotiating with the planning authority, going to farewell social gatherings of all kinds and occasionally having to deal with the individual still unable to fit in.

The Sports Hall was completed 30 months after the initial discussions. Several of us had seen covered playgrounds and similar wet weather games areas, but few of us who went to a discussion meeting in May 1977 had a vision of what became a reality so soon afterwards. A real gymnasium, a hall big enough for all school sports to carry on when winter weather was at its worst, a room big enough to seat 100 examination candidates and a theatre/school hall were all suggestions made at this initial meeting. The last suggestion was ruled out almost immediately on the grounds that the building would probably be let during the evenings throughout the term. The shrewdest of those present at the meeting probably suspected that behind the general discussion was a real possibility of partnership with an organisation with a need to use something like a sports hall every evening of the week. We already knew who were our main partners in the use of the squash courts.

In October 1977 the Finance and General Purposes Committee of the governing body suggested that Foster-Wheeler should be asked to define their needs and their possible contribution to the enterprise. This meeting with Foster-Wheeler took place in November. The next vital step came the following February when the full Board of Governors agreed to submit their plans to the local authority. We had already moved a long way from the simple idea of a covered area to that of a complete building which would incorporate its own store rooms, changing rooms and a third squash court. Perhaps the most important piece of advice we received was from the Sports Council to make the hall one quarter larger than we envisaged. This meant a building with enough space for four badminton courts instead of three.

It was at this stage that John Eggar set his heart on the completion of the Sports Hall as his last big contribution to Shiplake College and to the community at large. He rather chafed at the delays as the plans went through their various stages at Parish and District levels. However, earth moving began in the winter of 1978/79 and by the end of February 1979 hopes were high that all might be finished by the following May. At this stage, unknown to JDE, the Governors accepted a suggestion that it should be called the John Eggar Hall. However, as is the way of modern enterprise, by the middle of June 1979 the

The Sports Hall – Opening Ceremony
Aubrey Goodwin (Chairman) Peter Lapping, Hector Munro (Minister of Sport) and John Eggar

project came to a halt through technical delays. There were problems about the amount of fire resistant material required between the hall and the squash court changing-room area.

Everything was complete a few weeks before Christmas 1979. Sadly, this was four months after John Eggar had ceased to be headmaster. He was present and spoke at the official opening ceremony on 13 February 1980. The whole school and 300 parents and friends who had contributed to the enterprise were present to listen to the Minister of Sport, Hector Monro, declare the building officially open. The parents watched a large number of impressive displays and they also remained for lunch. The size of the hall was perhaps underlined by the fact that only slightly more than half the floor space was needed to seat the 600-plus audience.

The equipment for the Sports Hall was paid for by profits from the annual Summer Ball, a regular event since 1974. The hall would have been an empty shell without the really substantial sums raised for fixed apparatus and moveable items.

It is surprising how quickly the Sports Hall has been taken for granted. It represents a magnificent achievement of the Governors in partnership with Foster-Wheeler and the parents. The planning had been co-ordinated by John

The Sports Hall – in use

Eggar and in November 1979 the cost added up to £152,000. Even at this price, heating and ventilation were not possible for several years and the result was problems of condensation during the winter months. The hall saw a considerable variety of use in its first three years. It housed summer concerts, was once used for Speech Day and saw the first of regular Parish suppers in connection with its Christian Stewardship Campaign. It has, of course, fulfilled its main function of providing indoor games opportunities during the worst weather of the winter. It has provided a base for a wide range of activities by the staff of Foster-Wheeler and later by Perpetual PLC. It looks most impressive when one sees 120 examination candidates working on a paper in spacious conditions. In 1983 the cricket nets, in conjunction with the new artificial practice surfaces on the field, were described as 'second to none' at a cricket school. Above all (or should one say below all) the floor covering provides a remarkably true and fair surface for playing all games, and if weather is chilly one only has to keep on the move in order to get warm.

The John Eggar Hall is a unique act of co-operation between independent education and a large industrial firm. Other schools have been interested to learn of the varied use and the imaginative exploitation of the hall during the evenings and during the school holidays. Visitors were able to take away a three-dimensional impression of the physical possibilities of a building which was above all utilitarian in its purpose. The visual impact of the sports hall extension has been softened by the Goodwin Building and the 1995 Pavilion. The trees planted in 1980 are now mature.

CHAPTER 10

Handover and Continuity

JOHN EGGAR'S final year began with 315 boys in the school. Fifty-one of these were in Orchard. Buoyant numbers were a considerable asset as inflation continued to rage. It was 9.3 per cent in 1978 and doubled to over 18 per cent in 1979; it was 13 per cent in 1980. The keynote of JDE's last three terms was planning. How his plans worked out is dealt with elsewhere in this story. The year went by with remarkable speed. Early in 1979 the Governors were able to announce the name of the next Headmaster. From the lengthy application list the selection committee invited twelve to visit the College. From these a final short list was chosen and Mr Peter Lapping, then a housemaster at Loretto School, Edinburgh, emerged as the final choice of the Board. The great majority of Mr Lapping's close rivals have subsequently obtained headmastership; this testifies to the quality of the field. John and Pam Eggar felt that their successors were so 'right' for Shiplake that the eventual wrench of parting became easier.

Peter Lapping had grown up in South Africa and had been a boarder at St John's College, Johannesburg. He read history at Natal University and carried off first class honours. He also played cricket for the university. He then spent two years at Lincoln College, Oxford, where he read for the Honour School of Philosophy, Politics and Economics. At Loretto he had been in charge of the history department and had run the First XI cricket for a number of years. It was the friendliness of everybody, especially the boys, that struck him during his first two visits to Shiplake. Untidiness in some of the boarding areas and congestion in others also caught his eye. At once he revealed himself as a man with an eye for detail. As no doubt was explained to him, the congestion in some areas was the product of inflation and the need to keep the school as full as possible. Peter Lapping believes in 'Fate'. From the outset, he felt that he and the Shiplake boy had a great deal to offer each other. He quickly realised that, while John Eggar would have been a successful head at a number of schools, Shiplake's needs in the 60s and 70s had been an ideal opportunity for John Eggar to display his business skill, exploit his hunches and instincts and provide the special kind of leadership that had been needed during the formative period. The two men, Eggar and Lapping, quickly became firm friends.

May 1st, 1979, was the school's twentieth birthday. The Governors' meeting nearest to that date was their 86th. The system of a full Board Meeting once a term preceded by a F. and G.P.C. meeting continued into the 1980s. The Governors' tributes to John Eggar included having his portrait painted and giving a dinner in honour of both John and Pam. A very well attended Old Boys day was another outstanding tribute. Speech Day was moved from the Spring Bank Holiday to the last week of term so that the parents' gathering and the speeches could be a real farewell. The prizes were presented by the Master of Wellington College. He was able to turn back to the post war years at Repton and amuse everyone with numerous tales of John Eggar as a young schoolmaster and also of Pam Eggar sharing in the transfer of Brook House from her father to her husband.

This is the best place in our story to pay tribute to Mrs Eggar's contribution over sixteen years. After the many difficulties caused by Mrs Everett it was clear that Mrs Pamela Eggar had a key role to play. As JDE himself said at his farewell Speech Day, 'few wives could have had a more thorough knowledge of boarding schools as a daughter and a wife'. It is to her lasting credit that her interest in everything at Shiplake was continuous, genuine and as keen at the end as it was at the outset. She took unceasing interest in the gardens, gardeners and grounds staff and knew the people in the office and the catering staff as well as anyone. The wide ranging interests of her three sons left her in no doubt about what young men's interests were during the 1960s and 1970s. Unlike older schools, housemasters' wives at Shiplake have played little part in the running of houses, but their unrewarded job of answering the telephone and boys' calls have as important a role at Shiplake as anywhere else. Pam Eggar tried to get the housemasters' wives and other resident ladies more involved in the life of the school and was, to some extent, successful. The biggest difficulty was that resident staff wives were either working away from the College or bringing up small children. Mrs Eggar's biggest single contribution was to make a wide range of friends for the school and she certainly played a notable part in ending our early isolation from the local community.

The weather was super-abundantly kind to the gatherings of Old Boys, parents and Governors in honour of John and Pam Eggar. Many felt that he was a remarkable headmaster, but the most telling remark came from a boy in the middle school – rather a troublesome boy – who told his Head of House on Speech Day that 'he was sure that Mr Eggar was a good headmaster and he was very sorry that he was going'.

The Duke of Edinburgh Award normally 'peaks' during the Easter holidays – its organisation, its efforts, its remarkable achievements are never publicised fully and those who go on the arduous training courses are remarkably modest.

In 1979 the Duke of Edinburgh Award organisation received overdue and well-deserved publicity when eight Gold holders and two members of staff made an August expedition to the Himalayas, as part of the twentieth anniversary celebrations. Other events in 1979, such as the arrival of a 'Carbocraft' eight for the boat club and bringing the art room extension into use, were overshadowed by the more dramatic events of the year. The new science laboratories and the replacement landing stage were other planning decisions taken by the Governors during 1979.

It was a good example of JDE's instinct for the correct decision that he suggested that the twentieth anniversary should be the year for an outdoor pageant. Outdoor productions ended in 1966, but we were left with the idea that the lawns in front of Shiplake Court were the ideal site for a major production. The summer concert in 1976 revived the idea and people's minds turned to consideration of a substantial enterprise.

Avril Lethbridge and David Welsh were asked to develop the idea to the full. They quickly decided that the lawns were not big enough and re-sited the enterprise on the river banks. The history of Shiplake Court is interesting rather than dramatic, and the idea of *Time and the Thames* widened the appeal of the enterprise to at least a regional one. Our producers ventured a great deal and we all gained as a result.

Planning began seven months before the production week and no one anticipated the 18 per cent inflation rate of 1979. As a result, the tickets were underpriced. However, we had to be modest and we had little idea of the quality of the final result at this stage. The weather was also a constant threat to an open air production. The publicity warned that 'the performance could go on in all but the most extraordinary conditions'. In the end, superb weather throughout Henley Regatta produced full houses but the sums donated to charity were disappointing. Soaring costs made a nonsense of early financial estimates.

At the end of the final performance, John Eggar invited everyone involved to come down to the performing area. It was only then that the vast numbers involved became clear. We had come a long way since April when a solitary bulldozer that was improving the site area stood isolated by floods! It was official policy that everyone in the school should be involved: as a performer, as a technician, helper or manager; this also applied to the staff. As soon as GCEs finished, other activities ceased and preparations plus rehearsals went on from dawn to midnight. It was felt that the boys gained as much from the experience as from the normal post exam work experience and industrial visits. The boys gained more than just a genuine feeling of achievement. They had experience of being part of a very large team and came to understand the discipline, patience and attention to detail needed for a big show to succeed. Working with adults and some grasp of real professionalism – as exemplified by the lighting and effects crew – were also novel experiences. One hopes that some of the

CHAPTER 11

Losses and Change

AT SHIPLAKE a member of staff could be a housemaster for fifteen years. This rule was introduced in 1965. M.M. Gilliat had been housemaster of Burr for a year before this regulation was introduced and the summer of 1980 marked the end of MMG's tenure of office (one year before the rule was introduced, plus his full fifteen years) and he was always a protective and persuasive housemaster. Twice during his years Burr dominated the inter-house sporting scene and generally managed to combine academic success with it. Mrs Heather Gilliat had, sadly, died in 1978 and she, too, had done much to make the Burr atmosphere a distinctly individual one. MMG also ceased to be second master in the summer of 1980 and handed over to me. 'Mike' as he was affectionately known, remained head of English until two bouts of ill health forced his resignation and early retirement in May 1981. However, he was secretary of the Old Vikings Society until 1982 and no one knew the former members of the College better than he did.

In 1979 the son of the groundsman of Bedales in Hampshire had a motorcycle accident which paralysed him from the neck down. Because of expert medical attention, he now has some movement in his arms and thanks to the efforts of the pupils at Bedales, he has also acquired a magnificient wheelchair (built in Germany but designed in England) which makes life more normal and acceptable. As 1981 was the Year of the Disabled, Neil Slatter decided to go on a 'Wheelabout Britain', which meant that he stayed at many public schools. Shiplake was on his route, and we were privileged to accommodate this remarkable young man. To celebrate his stay, the boys decided to raise some money. Accordingly, they offered their services to the local residents and managed to raise £600 through their efforts as babysitters, wine waiters, car washers, washers up, gardeners, window cleaners, etc. Neil's declared aim was to raise £100,000.

Having retired as Master of Wellington College, Frank Fisher decided to resign some of his governorships in order to concentrate on being the 'mastermind' in charge of the Independent Schools Action Committee. The aim was to counter Labour party policy, then hostile to boarding schools and to the fee-paying sector. Mr J. C. Wykes, formerly Headmaster of St Bees and subsequently Head of ITV Education and of ILEA Schools TV, decided to retire to Scotland. He resigned as Deputy-chairman and was replaced by Mr E.P. Hatchett. The Governors honoured their two ex-headmaster colleagues at a luncheon and suitable presentations were made. To maintain the tradition of having a leading headmaster amongst the Governors, Mr D.R.W. Silk, the Warden of Radley, was elected. In 1991 he was followed by another Master of Wellington, Mr C.J. Driver.

The College reassembled in September 1981 to hear that Mrs Everett, our Founder Patron, had died during the summer holiday; she had been seriously ill for some time. The College was represented at her funeral by the Chairman. It was eighteen years since she had moved away from Shiplake College and she was only a name to many of the governing body and to the majority of the staff. Only the very long serving had actually met her. We should not forget that she committed almost all her assets to the early days of the venture here.

The brick structure of the new laboratories was so obviously a step in the right direction that the Governors decided to enlarge Orchard and build the music school in similar materials. Work began in the autumn of 1981 but was held up for a long period by blizzards before Christmas and again just after the new year. As already mentioned, this work was paid for by the sale of 'Tigoni'. The science labs had been the last major item in the 1978 appeal and when the total promised had reached £144,000 in early 1981, the Governors had decided to 'rest' the appeal. Inflation had reached twelve per cent during 1981, but it did little to discourage an optimistic view at Shiplake.

One cannot be anything but surprised at the contrast between the austerity of the early 1970s and the enormous expenditure of the early 1980s. In 1971 a sponsored walk was needed to produce £2,000 for a cafeteria/servery. Ten years later nearly £350,000 was spent on developing the Orchard area. The comment on this by Mr Roger Goodenough is instructive. Our ex-Chairman of Governors expressed the view that every institution – like an individual – needs to go through a period of doubt and self-examination. Our period of tight expenditure control was rather like St Paul's years in the wilderness – a period of reflection before gathering certainty.

The months from November 1981 to July 1982 proved the most testing in the College's life as a community. The difference between a boarding school and a place where people are together from 9 till 4, five days a week, was emphasised by a series of tragedies which occurred in this period.

During his first year as a housemaster, Peter Caston had quickly earned the respect and affection of his House. On 5 November 1981 he was rushed to hospital for an immediate operation. Then, the Headmaster's Christmas holiday in South Africa was ruined by a fatal accident to his brother. And in the early weeks of 1982, the infant son of Mr and Mrs Christopher Collins died without warning a few days before he was to be baptised in the College chapel.

While these sad events were happening, Peter Caston appeared to have made a courageous recovery. Cancer had been diagnosed, but it was hoped that final surgery in February would allow him to return to part-time duty in March. He was able to speak to the whole school when he thanked them for their prayers and their good wishes. He emphasised the lessons he had learned during his illness. During the Easter holidays he weakened and he died early in the summer term. In spite of his long illness, his actual death still came as a great shock. The Parish church was packed for his memorial service. The boys of Burr House planted a memorial shrubbery in front of the House and the Common Room endowed an annual prize to be awarded for courage and determination in adversity.

Meanwhile, the Falklands conflict had begun. This caused great worry to boys who had fathers in the armed services. The reaction of public opinion in the college to these military events was striking. On the one hand there was a concern and sympathy for those who were directly affected and on the other hand a determination to support a policy of expelling the intruder. A good many house rules about late evening television were set aside so that senior boys could follow events.

Richard Southwood reported himself ill with jaundice early in June 1982. No one anticipated anything more than the inconvenience of having a colleague away from duty during a vital part of the summer term. There was hardly time to appreciate that he was incredibly unwell before his death was announced on Sunday, 20 June. Richard Southwood had been the old-fashioned type of schoolmaster insisting on discipline, industry and punctuality wherever work was concerned. He was a most helpful house tutor in Everett and gave any amount of time to help individuals over their work problems. On the shooting range one met an entirely different Richard Southwood, friendly, encouraging, challenging and humorous.

The loss of two schoolmasters in their thirties during one term overshadowed everything else. Richard Southwood died the day before the official opening of Orchard House and the music school by Lord McAlpine of Moffat. Orchard House parents joined recent subscribers to the appeal at the ceremony. Little did we realise that this would be the last official school function that John Eggar would attend.

During 1981 it was decided, in view of the size of the school and the increasing amount of administrative work, to separate the post of second master from that of senior housemaster. Tudor Cottage was to be the base from which the second master would, in future, operate. In September, 1981, it was announced therefore that D.S. Partridge would transfer from Orchard House and become housemaster of Everett at the start of the following academic year.

P.G. Hose was to take charge of Orchard. The illness of Mr Caston from November onwards meant that Mr Hose ran Burr for most of the year 1981 to 1982. One of the things Peter Caston realised during the spring of 1982 was that, whatever happened, he would never be strong enough to take charge of Burr again. He was delighted to know that Burr would be taken over by his personal friend and colleague in the Remedial English Department – Andrew Smail.

There were other, minor, challenges during 1981–82. The end of term blizzard in December meant that we had a carol service almost entirely bereft of parents. The choir carried on manfully, and maintained our traditional standard. The start of the holidays was particularly difficult for many overseas boys, with airports closed. Some boys travelled from Shiplake to Heathrow and back for several days before they got a delayed flight to some warmer part of the world! Much of the same kind of problem occurred in reverse when the next term began. However, it was interesting to see how helpful boys and families were to each other. One person's travel and holiday problems promptly became the concern of others who were able to help.

The Reverend David Dale and his family had taken up residence in Meltemi during the summer of 1981. The new Chaplain's previous experience as a serving army officer and a parish priest were invaluable during the many unexpected difficulties of his first year in residence. To overcome the increasing overcrowding in chapel, it was decided that each house should follow its duty week by having a separate early service in chapel an hour before the main service. In any case, a house coming together for a chapel service instead of just for routine administrative purposes was a welcome innovation.

Even before it began, we knew that the school year 1982–83 would be unique. For the first time there were no plans for major building during the year! Except for Mrs Trudy Wilson taking over Peter Caston's position in the Remedial English Department, and a replacement for RES, there were no changes in the teaching staff. The school returned to find central heating installed in Rooms 2 and 3 and extended to the barn. Apart from being the biggest structural shock the barn has experienced since its construction, central heating meant that winter lectures, video shows and play rehearsals were comfortable as never before. The plant did, of course, have its teething troubles. It failed to operate in the twelve hours before a parents' conference!

The fees in September 1982 were £1340 for boarders and £825 for Orchard boys. Due to internal reorganisation there were nine fewer boarders than the previous year. This was a step towards reducing the overcrowding in houses, although it has never been policy to take a static view of the accommodation situation.

The area enclosed by the new science labs, Orchard and the sports hall was landscaped and trees were donated by the architect, Mr Apps. Our major building programme had postponed a revision of the school prospectus rather longer than necessary, but in 1982 the school entered the colour photograph era. To Old Boys and parents used to the dreary documents of earlier decades, the Shiplake prospectus suddenly became an exciting and thoughtful document with many photographs of boys actually doing things! The wording was prepared by people comparatively new to Shiplake who were able to see its strengths and attractions with a fresh eye.

During the winter of 1982 the Headmaster found himself, with the encouragement of the Governors, investigating the possibility of having girls as boarders in the Sixth Form. A neighbouring property of exceptional quality was for a while on the market. On both ability and number grounds, there was certainly room for girls in many of our 'A' Level sets. The local girls' schools had no objection to our considering the possibility and the reaction of parents and boys was undoubtedly positive. There at the time of writing the matter rests. If a suitable property again becomes available and can be financed by fee income from girl sixth-formers, the Governors would undoubtedly go ahead with the project. Apart from the opening of Orchard House, it would be the biggest change of direction since the College began. However, Orchard has changed the basic character of Shiplake College very little except for the better and we believed that girls in the sixth form would have the same effect.

The start of the Upper Fifth/Upper Fourth system was mentioned briefly in Chapter 8. Before John Eggar retired, it was clear the system was not achieving the hopes we had of it. Originally, there was to be one small set working quickly to 'O' Level in up to nine subjects. All new boys would work a one-year general course on arrival, then selection would be made. The implication of having a 'fast' set was that other sets should work more slowly and deliberately towards their 'O' Level targets. As much as anything, it was the rapid increase in school fees in 1973 that distorted the whole experiment. Very soon, half the entry were put into the Upper Fourth and they were permitted to reduce their subject level by two. John Eggar felt very strongly that economic circumstances meant that all parents expected their boys to be able to attempt 'O' Levels after three years here.

Before joining the fourth form, four options were chosen out of seven subjects and these became the basis of a course to 'O' Level lasting at least two years. When a set or an individual was ready to take an 'O' Level was a departmental matter.

Peter Lapping persuaded parents that too early entry followed by disappointing results is a poor preparation for GCE success. The 1983 GCE examinations were the first test of this system and improved 'O' Level results were achieved both by three year candidates and by the older candidates who had postponed their entry until 6A. The number of boys starting genuine 'A' Level courses was in no way affected.

Looking back, it has been a consistent feature of boys' success at Shiplake that many who come here need a year longer to catch up academically with those who were their successful rivals at the Common Entrance stage. Shiplake's particular pride is that, in many cases, the same boys have eventually overtaken those who outshone them at the age of thirteen. In some cases, this has been done to a dramatic extent.

Apart from some schemes geared to establishing a friendly school around tutor groups, Shiplake started without an obvious blueprint. For much of the time, the staff have been carrying forward what they believe in. For a long time our scheme for work was over-simple: boys attempted 'O' Level after three years here and then either became 'A' Level candidates or joined a repeat 'O' Level group with a view to leaving at about seventeen. The division into upper and lower forms was a first attempt to cater efficiently for the wide range of ability here. The 1981 scheme was based on a very careful definition of the needs of boys. Peter Hose and his committee did not then know that 'O' Levels and CSE would vanish at the end of the decade.

'In the view of some knowledgeable people outside the classroom, Shiplake College is possibly the best school in England for the non- academic boy. We hope that our new scheme of work will strengthen our claim to be as good as any school in the land that caters for the group who are not outstanding at the age when they take Common Entrance.'

Thus one wrote for a 1984 readership. Since then, measuring added value to pupils' progress between 13 and 16 has confirmed our general belief that Shiplake has been well able to match methods to pupil needs. As indicated elsewhere, the 'Baker/Welsh' scheme for GCSE and other Shiplake successes were based on earlier experience – 'been there and done that more than once'.

CHAPTER 12

Pre-Jubilee Terms

A FEATURE of the 1980s was the greater involvement of the college prefects in routine and innovation. However, more systematic prefect training only began with Nick Bevan, who believed a few briefing sessions each September left too much to chance. While R.A.S. Pim (1980–1) and A.G. Baird (1982–3) set new standards, there was too much tendency to imitate the previous generation of prefects. John Eggar always intended to hand over to the prefects the duty of showing the school to future parents, but it was left to Peter Lapping to take this step. In retrospect one can see that the prefect body became more international during the 1980s, but it is only Heads of College who are recorded by name on an Honours Board.

If 1982/3 had a keynote, it was a boy-dominated year. Without the usual building programme they had no rival focus of attention. In the summer of 1982, Marcus Williams and Neil Russell combined with two Marlow oarsmen to win the Coxless IV Junior National Championships. This IV then went on to represent Great Britain at the World Junior Championships in Italy. They were defeated in the semi-finals, but only the Iron Curtain crews were superior to them. Marcus Williams remained available for 1983. He struck up an effective partnership with Donald Fraser at Henley Royal Regatta and they went as two members of the Great Britain IV to the World Junior Championships, this time at Vichy. They won the Silver medal – losing to East Germany by a quarter of a length. This was surely one of the best efforts ever to come from any British crew during the Iron Curtain era.

The 1983 First VIII again reached the semi-finals of the Princess Elizabeth Cup. They were the peak of the usual Boat Club pyramid – over a hundred ordinary members putting in a great deal of hard work between Lynch Island and Sonning Lock in every kind of weather. The success of the Boat Club was particularly pleasing as this was John Scottorn's last year in charge.

As many as five rugby players turned out for Oxfordshire under-nineteens. The First XI defeated the Free Foresters. The Upper Sixth concluded the year by getting the best percentage of 'A' Level passes so far.

Particularly striking was the efficiency of the prefects' ushering at the very crowded funeral service for John Eggar in May 1983. His death brought back many memories. Every letter from an old boy or parent to Mrs Eggar or to the school had its own particular memory of JDE. Early on (no one seems to know how or why) he acquired his nickname from the boys, 'Jack'; his sense of humour quickly made him many friends amongst them. No headmaster has an entirely easy first year and John's was complicated by a run of bad luck which lasted well beyond his first twelve months. He had to get to know the place; everything was unfamiliar after many years at Repton. At the same time he had to institute fairly rapid changes. He always believed that he was bad at staff management, but this was really only in the little things. For a man who expressed himself clearly on paper he occasionally gave a false impression by word of mouth. He once referred to a new member of staff as 'a real schoolmaster' somehow implying that the rest of us were not! He had difficulty in bringing conversations to an end and would sometimes be unintentionally abrupt. One always knew that with John disagreements resulted from his real concern to get the best answer and were not a matter of personality clashes. One could see from the outset that his highest priority was the well-being and progress of the boys as individuals.

His headship built up rather like a batsman's innings – cautious at first and then developing confidence. When first at Shiplake College, John Eggar was very worried about the size of our indebtedness, but later he took the cost of considerable expansion in his stride. Like a good batsman, he took time to play his shots; he was never a man for the quick decision, especially when it affected the boys. He was never put off by a wide range of issues before him. One should remember that a headmaster can be distracted by the needs of twenty or thirty colleagues during the course of a day. John dealt with one issue at a time, like the batsman playing each ball on its merits. He was always right behind the ball, he never stepped away from a difficult problem and was quick to accept blame when things went wrong.

John Eggar combined the old and the new in headmastering. He was very much the man in charge. It was generally reckoned by the 1960s that it was no longer possible for one man to mould a school in the way that Almond or Roxborough had done in earlier days, but JDE did achieve this in his own undemonstrative way. It became quite clear in the 1970s that headmasters had to be more businesslike and less scholarly than in the past. At Shiplake we were probably ahead of most schools in having a businessman headmaster who could easily define the school's needs, understand the necessary finance and carry the governing body with him. Throughout his headship, he left the boys in no doubt where they stood and many leavers were ready to admit that at a time of crisis 'Jack' had been right and they were wrong.

First and foremost, John Eggar was Shiplake's Headmaster. In some ways, it is a pity that his interest in young people was not made use of in a wider field. He would have made an admirable magistrate. John disliked headmasters who were too often away from their schools – 'absentee landlords' he called them. While a great believer in public service, John would have begrudged a day away from the college each week in order to do more public work. In the end, John Eggar provided an apt summary of his years in office. 'The aim', he said 'is to achieve the maximum results with the minimum of fuss.'

John Eggar is appropriately buried at Shiplake, close to the school which was his greatest achievement. At the funeral service, Basil Wilks spoke of John Eggar's Christian ideals, and at the memorial service arranged on behalf of the Old Vikings and others, Frank Fisher spoke of JDE's personality and all-round achievements. Even so, no tribute has really captured the essence of the man. A grateful parent's letter explaining her own experience of John's quick sympathy and ready help called him a 'very special headmaster' and somewhere inside those words is the real John Eggar.

In September 1982, Peter Lapping – actually Shiplake's fourth Headmaster – became for the time being the College's second longest serving Head. What are we to make of this? Shiplake's first two Heads were the victims of circumstance – they had difficulty in carrying the Governors with them as financial control lay in the hands of Mrs Everett. Their ability to choose the right policies was also questionable. One also has reservations about the ability of Alexander Everett and David Skipwith to sum up people correctly. Our first two Heads showed much ability to assure parents and they certainly managed to arouse the boys' enthusiasm. They shared with their successors a genuine liking for young people. However, since 1963, the destiny of Shiplake College has been in the hands of men who enjoyed good health and were possessed of an undoubted will to succeed.

CHAPTER 13

'Little Things are Important'

A SHORT DISCUSSION on how we have learned to organise ourselves and occupy our spare time may tell the reader twenty years hence more than any other chapter, especially since daily times and assembly days were thoroughly revised in the 1990s and new technology has made this prediction more valid.

ADMINISTRATION

Young men are always surprised to find that the key staff in a boarding school do not have holidays as long as the boys. There is a true story of a pre-1914 headmaster of Rugby who spent his holidays on golf courses well away from the midlands. He was always furious on return to school a day before term began to find that more letters had accumulated than he could answer in his own hand in twenty-four hours! To prevent a backlog of unanswered letters accumulating at Shiplake, the office is manned throughout the year except for Christmas week. Secretaries deal with the mail and there is always someone fairly senior on hand to make decisions if important letters have to be answered forthwith. Faxes and e-mail were almost unheard of until recently.

Until the mid 1970s, there was no fixed system about meetings; each department met to consider policy when the need arose. Housemasters met at the beginning and in the middle of term to make administrative decisions in conjunction with the Headmaster. The Headmaster met the Bursar and Second Master once a week. If necessary, announcements were then made to a full Common Room at break. All this changed. There is now a weekly staff meeting at break on Monday mornings and from 1970 the Headmaster and Housemasters began to meet at break on Fridays. These twenty minute meetings expanded into the fourth period on Friday mornings. The Chaplain, play producers, Director of Studies and other people join the meetings when their advice is required. The Headmaster and Bursar keep brief notes of any decisions made. To speed up the proceedings, an agenda was circulated beforehand and from 1979 minutes of these meetings have been kept. As the school grew, so did our system evolve. It was, therefore, quite amusing to attend one of the first conferences on the subject of the 'Senior Management Team in Schools' only to find out that what had been developing in the large secondary schools was also what we at Shiplake had evolved by rule of thumb. In the large comprehensive schools, deputy headmasters and other senior management figures meet the head regularly. They keep minutes of policy decisions and circulate information to the whole staff – just, in fact, what we were doing at Shiplake as a result of experience, but without any theoretical planning. Both independent schools and comprehensive schools have had to develop a workable system of week by week decision making in order to cope with the increasingly wide and, one hopes, interesting range of activities taking place in our schools. All decisions, of course, have to be reached with due deference to the Headmaster's legal responsibility as the person in charge.

While it is easy to blind the reader with figures, the fourteen things delegated by the Headmaster of Shiplake by 1983 to the Second Master had expanded to thirty-five within ten years. The responsibilities of the Director of Studies grew in similar fashion. This latter is, curiously, a post which Shiplake had during its first two terms and which was revived at the beginning of 1980. A Housemaster expects to chase up a different problem each day of the week and he probably has a list pinned up somewhere with about twenty vital administrative duties that he has to carry through each term. The outcome is nearly always a list to pass to the Headmaster or to the Bursar. In the spring term of 1982, there was a timetable of eighteen separate processes which senior masters went through in order to settle GCE entries and in order to arrange Fourth Form options for the coming year. The current list of staff responsibilities amounts to 160 items shared out amongst 37 full time members. In the first year that Housemasters' meetings kept minutes, some 340 decisions were listed in the course of three terms.

The real hero of administration in a modern boarding school is the Bursar and he would certainly not survive without his office assistants, who had, in 1983, to organise for the £5 or £6 a day per pupil then paid by parents, three meals, warmth, shelter, a place for recreation, pastoral care, a bed and medical services.

To the senior boys, and probably the resident bachelor staff, the Bursar is a hostel keeper. He may feel, as far as the Headmaster and Housemasters are concerned, that his role is hotel manager. One tends to think of the Bursar as paying salaries, supervising day to day services and ordering supplies. However, the Governors of most schools get a good deal more than this out of their versatile bursar. He is accountant, budget controller, building surveyor, catering supervisor, company secretary, fire officer, emergency control officer and personnel manager. The size of the Bursar's department only becomes clear when two or three days after the end of the autumn term his staff have their Christmas Party.

Mrs Hinton assisted a series of bursars for well over twenty years; while the school doubled in numbers, she continued to account for every penny. She helped numerous masters in charge of very many activities to get right the finances of their particular concerns. She had a remarkable memory: not only did she know what had to be accounted for, but also she was remarkably prompt to remind members of staff that as a result of activities away from Shiplake, the school actually owed them money! If it is any consolation to Mrs Hinton, her precisely kept ledgers may one day be of great interest to historians as Tudor and Stuart account rolls and vouchers are now, especially following the change from written entries to computer disks.

Long serving members of the Bursar's department included Richard Gapper who was Clerk of the Works for 19 years and Domingos and Celeste Carradina. These three helped to carry Shiplake through the second half of the 1960s, through the 1970s and well into the 1980s, to be followed by the two Manuels and Tina and Simon Brown. Furthermore, Mr Bill Brownbridge began his long stint as catering manager not long before the College Silver Jubilee.

If he ever pauses to think, the average schoolboy leaver probably asks of school records 'What have they got on me?' Parents probably ask themselves three or four years after the young man has left school, 'Will the school still be able to help him?' All we have on those who left in 1963 and earlier are sets of copies of the Headmaster's end of term report. These have been kept for all those who have left since then. For those who came from 1963 onwards, we have the original registration form, a record card covering all GCE successes and listing School and House positions held, together with crews and teams that the individual belonged to. His CCF record is also preserved. These records are all factual and no one could object to their retention. Copies of reports for university, polytechnic and other college entries are also retained. Otherwise, all other letters about him are destroyed soon after he leaves. We simply do not have room to store them. In fact, half a filing cabinet contains all the records we have retained about those who have been here. The Careers Department retains a limited amount of information about those who were members of the ISCO scheme.

STAFF GARDENS

While no one can approach the wonders achieved before 1914 in an age of cheap labour, the opportunities for successful gardening in the College grounds are tremendous. The southerly and sheltered aspect is a great help. By 1962 the school gardeners had to abandon attempts to grow our own vegetables and produce all the year round flowers from the greenhouses that stood where

Orchard does now. For a time, the greenhouses were taken over by Ievers – a distinguished dahlia grower even in his teens! For the past two decades, the school gardeners have been wholly involved in care and maintenance work.

New buildings mean new gardens and surroundings. Planting helps to conceal the stark newness of buildings. Pam Eggar originally declared she disliked gardening and yet, with John's help, she made a lovely one at Court Mead. The Lapping family enlarged the grounds of the Headmaster's House – taking in derelict orchard – and their careful planting made the area around Court Mead more secluded.

People forget that Meltemi was erected on the site of the incinerator! Heather Gilliat did wonders, with MMG's aid, on a very poor site. David and Jenny Welsh set themselves an enormous task with the amount they took in hand. Their work was spoiled by the loss of the elm trees at the back of their garden. At Everett, Malcolm Mash cleared and grew a lawn over a vast mess left by the builders. I continued his work by planting trees and shrubs to establish a mature garden. The only established garden was at Tudor Cottage and its size has defeated some occupants. All of us who have tried to do something with a marvellous site have been immensely helped by the natural warmth of the position. Our ground staff have always taken a tremendous pride in maintaining the lawns and trees to the best of their ability.

SCHOOLBOYS' CLUBS

Clubs are supposed to be guided by members of staff and run by the boys themselves. One of the longest lasting clubs was the Young Farmers which dated back to 1961. It was extremely vigorous under its first secretary Simon Stracey and in the early 1970s had another period of activity under Messrs Gore and Douglas. Old hands will remember the camping club which occupied Lynch island on Saturday nights until 1963 when it was replaced by the Duke of Edinburgh Award Scheme. Art, music, and playreading societies have tended to get submerged by College major productions. Electronics, photography, history, stamp and coin clubs have risen and decayed several times over the last quarter century. The Greek club had a very long run in the 1960s and into the early 1970s, but expired without any record. The Film Society had a long and successful career, but price cutting turned it into House-centred video clubs.

The most amusing club was undoubtedly the pets organisation which flourished a decade ago. It was really an off-shoot of biology and the master who began it moved to Pangbourne. During the holidays most pets escaped and took up residence underneath the terrapin laboratories. Occasionally members tried to renew contact with their disloyal pets. This normally took the form of borrowing staff dachshunds to drive the pets into the open. This club seems to have been perpetuated in more recent times by a ferreting club.

The Sixth Form Society began in 1966. It arose from the idea that the outlook and interests of 'A' Level candidates should be widened by a discussion/social organisation. It was run successfully by DFKW until 1982 when he handed over to PGH. The Society's annual reports show an amazing variety of activities although recently rising costs have limited theatre visits and social events. However, the Sixth Form Society may have deprived other clubs of senior leadership.

From its inception in 1968, the JCR has been a popular institution and it is hard to imagine Sixth Form life without it. The specially designed quarters high in the Jubilee Building gave the social life of senior pupils an extra dignity, never found in the original dark and dingy JCE.

SCHOOL DANCES

In the early 1960s, the school dance tended to mean persuading your father to buy you a dinner jacket and then persuading the school to finance a band and cabaret. The bands at these dances in 1961 and 1962 came from RAF Headquarters, as service bandsmen were allowed to operate privately in their off-duty hours. One of the school's prefects was the son of one of London's leading Masters of Ceremonies. He came to the 1962 prefects dance and gave the staff an example of how to use your personality to get things going. By the mid 1960s, the Christmas school dance had become something of a 'rag and bone' affair. It led a precarious existence as such and turned into a summer disco and barbecue in the 1970s. In recent years, the event made a welcome return to tradition. It survived the decade as a means of returning hospitality received at girls' schools. While our catering department made sure that our 'supper' was always of a high order, the dance itself was rarely memorable. The dance became part of a Social Day in 1981 and 1982.

Our guests from girls' schools arrived after lunch and took part in a number of activities during the afternoon. Shooting, canoeing and games contests in the sports hall were the most popular events. There was a break for tea in the Houses. On both occasions the March weather was most unhelpful. This was a great pity as the prefects had organised an excellent and varied programme and did their utmost to ensure that the visitors enjoyed themselves. This organisation showed itself to great advantage in March 1983. There was a genuine feeling that we had to get away from the well tried formula of a dance in the Great Hall. In fact, well over 100 people got away, literally. After a more gracious buffet than usual, hosts and guests departed downstream on a hired riverboat to dance the evening away. The weather was particularly springlike and it was felt that Alistair Baird and his committee had probably organised the best school dance anywhere for many a long year!

CHAPTER 14

The Old Vikings Society

TWELVE OF THE early leavers met on 2 June 1962 at the invitation of David Skipwith. The Old Boys Club was formed by this meeting and it adopted a set of rules which owed a fair amount to those of the Old Bloxhamist Association. The error about the connection between the name Shiplake and the Vikings was perpetuated in the name the club adopted. One tends to think of old boys clubs as being typically British or perhaps Anglo-Saxon. The more one learns about North American institutions, the more one realises that old boys organisations are at least transatlantic.

The club grew at much the same rate as the school. Two years after it began it had 80 members and six years after the start it had 230. The key 'OV' in the earlier days was Roger Hands who was secretary in the club's first year and then chairman from 1963 to 1969. Alastair Barron gave him considerable support in the first four years of the club's life, and the other real pioneer figure was John Osborne whose active connection with the club lasted until 1972 when he moved to Australia. A year after the start, the club was selling its tie at fifteen shillings a time and was sending out its first newsletter.

After he had been here a year, John Eggar realised that the key to the Old Vikings' future lay in effective liaison between the club committee and the college. The tradition of having the Bursar as a key liaison figure thus began and very soon afterwards he became the honorary treasurer. It was decided that the school office would prepare routine circulars. In 1964 the policy began of electing all Governors as honorary members of the club as well as members of the Senior Common Room after they had been on the staff for three years. The mistake of having an annual subscription was reversed and a £3 life subscription paid on leaving Shiplake replaced the annual hunt for renewals.

The first real milestone in the club's story was a reunion held at the Special Forces Club on 2 April 1966. This was David Skipwith's own club in London and a visit to a place with such interesting Second World War associations had an appeal of its own. It was, of course, the last occasion when club members saw

David Skipwith. This first reunion led on to a series of club dinners held at Shiplake.

Ten years after the school began, the Old Vikings Club could look back on a useful record. They had provided, as a memorial to David Skipwith, a lectern/pulpit and a clergy desk for college services, they had started producing regular newsletters. Until 1968 old boys received copies of the *The Court* and the school calendar.

There is the usual cry of anguish to be found in the minutes: no matter how hard the committee tried, it was very difficult to get answers from members. By now the club was in a healthy financial state. A premium bond was bought, and it won a prize in 1982! The committee voted Miss Tomalin an honorary member thus recognising the tremendous

Two trophies presented by Old Viking, Ian Baldry

The Baldry Trophy for overall best sporting house

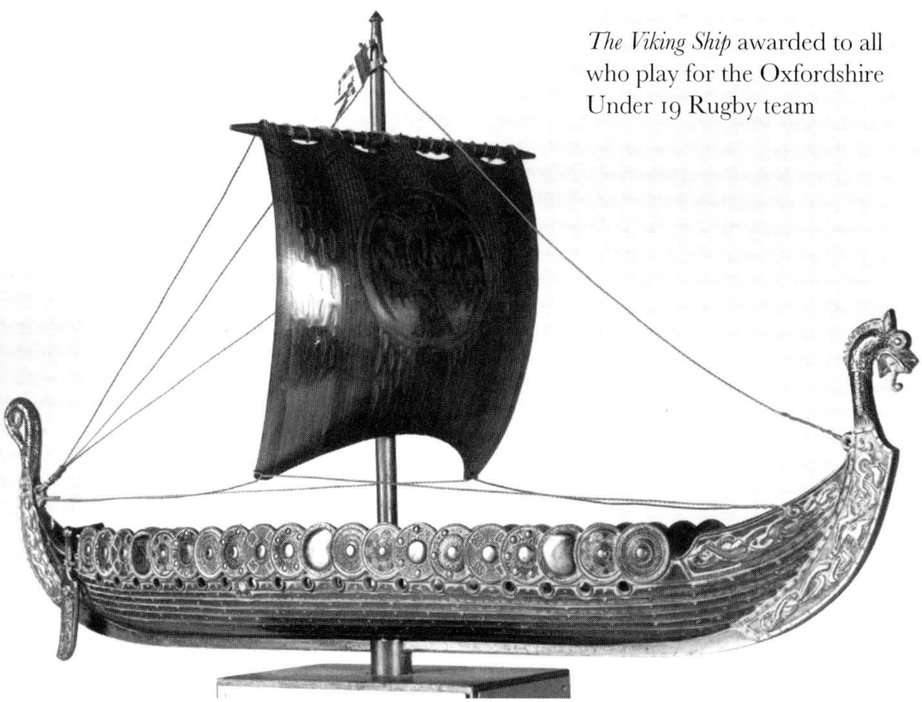

The Viking Ship awarded to all who play for the Oxfordshire Under 19 Rugby team

CHAPTER 15

'The Humour of it All'

'SCHOOL HUMOUR' dates very easily and it is with some trepidation that this chapter has been compiled. It is included partly because the lighter side of Shiplake life should not be forgotten. However, it is difficult to fit into the continuous story of the College's development and it is hard to convey the atmosphere in which the amusing events took place. For instance, at a well known College with a service background, not many miles from Shiplake, a housemaster asked one of the ex-regular physical training instructors to take evening prayers as he, the housemaster, had to be away. It is only when one knows the school background that what happened becomes truly amusing. The PTI called the house in question to attention and issued the following command, 'Lord's prayer, go!'

The outstanding 'laugh' in which the whole Shiplake community was involved dates back to the summer of 1962 when David Skipwith was in hospital. At morning assembly the chaplain was reading the collect for the day, 'Grant that this day we fall into no sin, neither run into any kind of danger'. At the same time he was looking for the prayer for the sick and therefore solemnly read aloud 'Grant that this day we fall into no sick'! Obviously everyone must have been listening because the result was a gale of laughter. With great courage the chaplain smiled broadly and said 'I hope God enjoyed the joke, I think we had better begin again!'

From the early days there is a story of a mother driving between Oxford and Reading and getting thoroughly lost. She made the best of the situation: 'Oh well, Charles,' she said, 'You failed Eton but there is a school somewhere in this area; perhaps we will go and have a look at it and see if they will have you.' They did!

Having started with 'school and parent' true stories, a selection of anecdotes dealing with all groups in the Shiplake story follows.

Unintentional ambiguity is often forgotten but one tale survived from the school's second term. Sister Black did duty in charge of health and acted as matron at the time. She was complaining to one fourth former about his badly made bed and announced loudly,

'Bernard, if you don't make your bed properly, you and I are going to fall out'.

Maths and English always cause problems. There has been more than one maths master who has sunk into a lunchtime armchair with a drink complaining that capitalism is doomed when the present Fifth Form take control of their fathers' businesses. Years ago, Sam Hall had a long argument with a young man who insisted that Blight was one of the leaders of the Corn Law League. 'Oh yes, sir!' the young man insisted, 'I am right; here in the book it says Blight attacked the Irish potato crop.' He had a point. As blight was the first word in the sentence, it was spelt with a capital B.

Events adults find funny, but Sixth Forms do not: a decade ago three prefects were guests at Sunday lunch in Lower Shiplake and they and the young ladies of the house volunteered to do the washing up. While doing so, they also finished off the pre-lunch Dubonnet. All felt rather tired after their endeavours and decided to take a stroll. The stroll ended back at one of the Shiplake boarding houses where the young ladies fell sound asleep. The prefects, now embarrassed as well as unwilling hosts, held a committee meeting to decide which housemaster to consult. When they had selected their man and explained their mid afternoon problem to him, he enquired with some curiosity, 'Why on earth did you come to me?' 'Oh sir', they said blandly, 'we thought you would understand!'

Christopher Pelloe (the longest serving member of the Old Vikings committee) was studying hospital management at Guys in 1969 where John Osborne, then secretary of the Old Vikings, was a houseman. Christopher developed a raging toothache which John only agreed to treat on condition that Christopher promptly filled a vacancy on the Old Vikings committee. At that stage he was in such agony that he was ready to promise anything. While at Guys Hospital John Osborne got stuck in a lift for several hours one Friday night. Unfortunately this was an evening when he was due to preside over an OVS dinner at Shiplake. He got out in time to telephone his apologies!

In the mid 1970s, the Yemen was one of the world's trouble spots. The son of Her Majesty's Ambassador there was at Shiplake at the time. A letter addressed to this distinguished diplomat 'c/o Foreign Office Private Bag Room' was returned to the office at Shiplake marked 'not known'. The address and name were, of course, clearly typed.

Satire in biblical style is an old form of schoolboy humour. Here is an example from 1965. 'The Bursar said unto John Eggar "I will build thee a cricket pavilion and I will build it cheaper than the boat house in the quarry". And the Bursar went forth and bought a kit and he studied the plans and with the aid of the maintenance staff he laid the concrete all wrong so that it had to be done a second time. And behold there was a great frost which damaged the concrete and for years after it crumbled continuously. From dawn to dusk the

Bursar and his men struggled with the construction and lo! great was the difficulty and much time and vast wages were consumed in the enterprise. When at last the work ceased there were various spare planks lying around but they were not the timber from which the balustrade should be made. "Oh well", said the Bursar, "the timber must have been built into the structure at some other point." The pavilion standeth to this day but so great was the expense thereof, that Shiplake bursars have never again attempted "do it yourself".'

The war between authority and school rules on the one hand and the whims of the young on the other frequently has a curious outcome. Somewhere in the mid 1970s a fourth former decided to combine an unapproved Sunday afternoon visit to Reading with the wearing of his unofficial best leather jacket. In a hurry he entered the ladies' lavatory and left it even more quickly only to fall into the arms of a policeman looking for trouble! Studying the young man's garb, the police officer decided on some questions. 'Where do you live?' – answer 'Brighton.' 'Show me your rail ticket' – 'Haven't got one.' Result, eventual admission that he came from Shiplake College. This did not seem particularly likely so our fourth former was invited to take a stroll to the police station. There he was asked to empty his pockets. The first thing that emerged was a large and illegal catapult. At this stage the police officer decided that a phone call would or would not establish this young man's connection with Shiplake.

In spite of events like these, the normal tenor of life at Shiplake is amusing rather than lawless.

Schoolmasters often get things wrong. Many years ago, Ted Gordon admitted that his biggest mistake when schoolmastering in Johannesburg was to tell Gary Player to get a move on and pass some exams as he would never be able to earn a living playing golf! In more recent times a newly joined member of the lower sixth was accused of falling asleep and snoring within five minutes of the start of the period. Unfortunately the master concerned had not met the new arrival – one of the school's worst asthmatics!

June 28, 1982 was the first day of a well publicised rail strike. Two lower sixth Skipwith members returned two hours late from town leave to Henley. They explained to their housemaster, 'We were waiting for a train'! The same generation a few months later discarded a table football machine from the JCR. They dumped it outside not realising that its great weight was due to the fact that it contained £120 in ten pence pieces.

A fairly recent captain of cricket contrived to lock himself into a pair of handcuffs. With great faith he went to Sister, of all unlikely people. She sent for the fire brigade, whereas a message to the maintenance department for a hacksaw might have been a more suitable step.

An aspect of Shiplake's history that is now almost forgotten, but was the subject of constant humour in the 1960s, was what was dubbed by those who remembered the years 1940 to 1943, the Afrika Korps. There were few members of staff not qualified to belong to it. First of all there were the ex-wartime soldiers. David Skipwith had been in the Sudan civil service and then the Long Range Desert Group and after the war had taught at Grahamstown. Ronnie Hartley had soldiered in Egypt. James Newell, the Bursar, and Jim Travers had been in Africa during their regular army service. Richard Lee came to us from the Forestry Service in Nigeria and when we appointed our first chaplain, naturally he had done his National Service in the Canal Zone! With the decline of the British Empire, Sam Hall and Peter Bleackley – ex-Colonial civil servants – joined us.

Then there were those who could, at one time, call Africa their home. John Foster (the first Second Master) had lived for some years in Kenya when his father was Director of Education there. Ted Gordon had grown up in South Africa, Mike Le Mesurier likewise. The changing political situation in Africa brought people to Shiplake: M.M. Gilliat had been on the staff at Grahamstown at the same time as David Skipwith, Margaret Reed was a matron at Grahamstown prep, John Wood had also taught in Africa, Robin Jenks (our third Bursar) had been in business in Rhodesia, and when we appointed a retired soldier – Brigadier Anstruther – as a temporary French master he, of course, turned out to be a sometime Chief Engineer of the British Army in Egypt. After Steve Morris, who had served in Libya, the African connection rather died out. Malcolm Mash, feeling rather out of it, took a tutorial job in Africa and climbed Mount Kilimanjaro in order to become an honorary member of the Afrika Korps.

Our headmasters knew the continent well. John Eggar had served during the war in North Africa and paid return visits more than once on extended holidays. David Skipwith was last there whilst driving from Capetown to Europe overland during 1958 and in the early months of 1959. Then there was a ten-year gap until John Worwood came, when the jokes about the Afrika Korps were almost meaningless. One ought to have known better. When Peter Lapping's appointment as headmaster was announced we heard that he had grown up in South Africa and had been educated in Johannesburg and at Natal University. This raised wry smiles amongst the old hands in the know!

Not surprisingly, when Peter Lapping had any crisis regarding staff appointment, he looked to South Africans. He appointed a lady Rhodesian Rhodes Scholar to take charge of art for two terms. David Reid, a Kenyan, was to help out in maths for a term or so. There, for the moment, the Afrika Korps saga rests. Perhaps one should wonder what P. T. Robinson, part-time maths master here in the 1960s, head of maths at Pangbourne for many years and before that, maths master at Milton College, Bulawayo, throughout the 1920s, would have made of the troubled political scene in present-day Africa.

I hope the lighter side of parent/housemaster relations is captured in the brief quotations that follow. I hope too, no reader will recognise himself after all these years! The letters from which these extracts come have all been destroyed and if a parent recognises a phrase will he or she please forgive me for making use of it?

The boarding houses increased in number during the 1970s. One of the resulting problems was to get to know the new boys. A housemaster might not teach the third form at all, or he might meet just a few of them in a team game he was still coaching. A partial answer was borrowed from another school. New boys' parents were asked to write a pen portrait of their son during the holiday before he came. The housemaster now got a report on the boy from home before he wrote one to the parents. This quickly became a useful exercise. It helped the parents too. With a maximum of five years of school education left, it helped them to list what had been done and what was still to be achieved. It helped to anticipate problems still to come. Most important of all, the housemasters learnt a great deal that never got into prep school profiles. These letters were not without their lighter side; 'How can a parent write an unbiased report on her little darling?' wrote a mother of three about her 'afterthought'. Another mother rejoiced in the challenge, and at the end of ten pages ended with a triumphant 'I bet you didn't expect to have to wade through all this lot!' With some information, the parents revealed themselves: 'His mother's ambition was to be a housemaster's wife' wrote one computer expert. 'He has walked to the top of most of the bens in Scotland, and done it without enthusiasm', wrote a mother about her tiny son, and a father confessed 'I am bored stiff by carpentry, electricity and technical things, but my son's inventions are positively Emmett-like'.

Many of the descriptions came well within the existing experience of the housemasters: 'Vague to the point of exasperation'. 'He is an individualist' was obviously not to go into the same new boy dormitory as 'gregarious'. This person might survive with 'prefers order to chaos'. An 'expects immediate answer to everything' would probably become a very bossy member of the house.

Often the new boy letter was more alarming than the boy himself: 'His money is gone before he has acquired it.' Housemasters must have wondered 'What shall we do at half-term with "He has never been on a train in his life"?' 'He has a habit of chewing his lip when he is under stress': we can see this at house business time. 'He needs standing up to', wrote a tiny mother of her tiny son. No warnings could be clearer than 'He ran away from his prep school on the second day' and 'He can't stand fire practices'. 'He is blessed with a strong sense of self-preservation', turned out to be, not surprisingly, a poor performer on the cricket field.

Three apparently different individuals were described as 'I warn you, he will soon become a character', 'Excels in tree climbing' and 'Rapidly accumulates money'. They soon proved to have one thing in common: all turned out to be excellent mimics of the staff, and were much in demand at end of term entertainments.

Many letters indicated success here or in the outside world: 'He is an optimist; West Ham will always win the Cup and he will always be top of the class without effort'. 'He is a realist, not a revolutionary and he likes making weapons – not usually lethal!' This chap later became an artist in wrought iron. 'His main interest is our dog which he grooms regularly' – this one became a hairdresser! 'His only interest is in heavy earth moving equipment', turned out to be somewhat solitary in his habits.

So many boys shared the same outlook. 'Not by nature the most industrious person' was very much like 'No schoolmaster has yet convinced Christopher that an amiable approach is any substitute for permanent effort'. We have all met 'Most of his reading is science fiction and horror stories'. A soldier wrote 'His great number of previous schools is due to his father being a serving officer and not to any allergy to headmasters'. Disappointed fathers wrote as follows: 'Why he dislikes sport is beyond me!' and 'His strong opinions rarely hold water'.

Most welcome of all to a housemaster was the following chap: 'His pet hates are girls, washing, cleaning shoes, anything effeminate, long hair and trendy clothes'. Surprisingly, looking back, parents do very little about their sons' smoking habits. An artist, who survived the minimum three years, left behind a poster which read 'Smoking can ruin your school career'. All housemasters have met parents who sit in their study furiously jabbing out one cigarette butt after another and saying 'I can't understand why my son wants to smoke'.

On a lovely summer's evening in 1969 a 'way-out character' – part flower power, part 'freak', clad in worn-out clothes and possessed of lank greasy hair boarded a train at Paddington. Behind him was an ex-Shiplake father who said loudly to the crowd around him 'Think – somewhere is a poor blighter who had the misfortune to be the father of this creature!'

A retiring housemaster's wife wrote to the *The Court* magazine: 'Answering the telephone is a major occupation for a housemaster's wife. There are anxious mothers at the beginning of terms, irate fathers who have just been informed of their son's latest transgression, and girl friends who inadvisedly ring the housemaster's number instead of the boys' call-box. Inevitably there are excuses for late returns after half-term or at the beginning of term, usually genuine (I think).'

Occasionally there have been calls from the police. In the early days when running away was fashionable, there was a call at 1 a.m. to say one of our lads had turned up at London Airport. The police were told they could keep him, and he was collected later that day at a more civilised hour. The message must have spread to other would-be absconders, because that was the end of running away.

One Sunday I took a message from a desperate grandmother, who had agreed to look after her grandson's pet rat, but drew the line at caring for six of them when it unexpectedly produced a litter. The rats were driven over and dumped on the door-step. They were donated to the biology department!

Housemasters' wives also see the look of apprehensive disbelief that boys have when a lady answers the door instead of 'the Boss': 'One Saturday morning in the early days, someone said he had "come about his trousers". It was in the days of drainpipe trousers which were barred at Shiplake, and this pair had been confiscated. I found it very amusing, but could not at first understand why this lad, who was one of the biggest thugs in the house, should look so apprehensive. Then I realised that he had interrupted me in the middle of dusting, and I was brandishing a ferocious paper-knife that I had just picked up from the desk.'

There must be many forgotten stories concerning the twenty-five or so staff dogs that have resided on the campus since 1960. The sick wing cat appears to have written two articles for the college magazine. One Sunday afternoon RAE took a stray Alsatian to Everett only to find to his surprise that the Everett Alsatian was already in residence.

What can beat the following dialogue? 'Sir' said a school prefect, 'I am in a spot of bother. I allowed X to ride my moped uninsured and the police stopped him.' 'I didn't know the police had second sight', sardonically enquired a housemaster. 'Sir', replied the prefect, 'He was going up a one way street the wrong way when the police stopped him!' The fine involved for this little escapade exceeded three figures!

The boys, especially the seniors, always triumph over the staff at the end of year concerts. The following verses came from the 1963 Christmas term concert and seem to be the only satirical work that has survived. 'The Vicar of Bray' was sung by Messrs Ferguson and Cowley during a performance of *The Hollow Crown* a few weeks earlier and the tune was adapted.

He came straight to the point and cured
Everything anti-social
With kindly smile and a demure
'I beg and I beseech you'.
All eating of food will forthwith stop
It gives a bad impression!
For he can spy through his window
Everything that needs redressing!
And this is the law we'll maintain
Until our dying day, Sir,
Exemplum Docet keeps your name
And Carter-Ruck to you, Sir!

A maths master got a TV set
In order not to watch it:
He'll work up enough courage yet
To just go up and touch it.
Meanwhile he'll send us all on runs
At six each misty morning
And if we leave off work for buns
He'll say we need a hiding.
Come up and see my skeleton
And all my bottled babies.
Don't mind the kids – just walk right in
They haven't got the rabies.
This school will be a first class place
When all the trouble makers go –
The only thing we have to face
Is that their fees will also!
Hells teeth! Don't walk on the cricket square!
Or by God I will cane you:
I'll swing you round just by your hair
And with a stump I'll brain you.
I hope by now you will understand
The glory of real Cricket
When mixed with History it is grand
There's nothing that can lick it!

Notes: The first verse catches the approach of John Eggar in his first term as headmaster. The refrain seems to have been put together more for the rhythm than out of any malice. The second verse refers to Malcolm Mash, then resident house tutor of Skipwith. The third verse refers to John Foster (then Second Master) and the last verse seems to say all that is necessary about me over thirty-five years ago. Furthermore, Shiplake has had three headmasters who believed that Cricket and History are an unbeatable combination of interests.

More senior old boys will remember a magnificient weeping willow standing halfway between the lawn and the riverbank: it blew down in March 1977. Eric Russell's prompt comment was 'I suppose we shall have to make our own cricket bats from now on'.

Many years ago, 'O' Level Biology practical was a very simple affair. There was a compulsory question 1 where the candidates had to cut something up and draw what they saw. Before them the candidates saw an apple. They cut it vertically, instead of horizontally as they were told. The result was, that what they saw and drew was rather different from the paperwork of the one candidate who had cut the apple the way he was told to. Looking round, the various candidates saw that they had done the job wrongly. However, they could not cut their apple a second time as all but one had now eaten their individual apples!

Mike Whicker has, in the course of years, become our longest serving bursar. Before that, he worked for the P & O Shipping Company and no doubt obtained some useful experience of dealing with all sorts of crew and of bailing them out in foreign ports. Being based so near the front door, the Bursar is frequently the first person to come into contact with the police when they arrive, either after a telephone call or totally unexpectedly. One of his more embarrassing requests for them to turn out was when he had to report that for a second time brand new cricket nets had disappeared overnight from the main field.

Twice in recent years the Bursar has had to fend off threats by the police to come and arrest boys over the age of sixteen. In both cases, the young men were highly anglicized citizens of Venezuela. Time and again they had failed to comply with the regulations that, as foreigners, they must register with the local police. One of the Venezuelans was also involved with the Bursar in another curious way. At half term, the Bursar wrote to the boy's father saying that the term's account had not been settled. A cable arrived promptly stating briefly that the young man had been handed a cheque for the sum just before he boarded the transatlantic flight at Kingston, Jamaica. Normally it is the Bursar who is looking into grouses from the Housemaster, but on this occasion it was the Housemaster looking into a question on behalf of the Bursar: the young man was interviewed and after a few moments' thought went off to his study and came back with the paperback book he had read during the flight. Tucked somewhere towards the end was a cheque for over £1000 which had been in service as a bookmark for some weeks. The other Venezuelan, incidentally, became our first Old Boy to join the French Foreign Legion.

Just before his last full year began, John Eggar rashly expressed the view that probably anything that could happen to a schoolmaster had, by now, happened to him. He never guessed for a moment that one of his newly appointed staff for September 1978, would run away before meeting the boys in class. The young man concerned was just taking up his second appointment. He attended the staff meeting, helped briefly with a new boys' rugger practice and then fled back to his lodgings, packed, and asked his landlady to tell the school that he would not be appearing again. John Eggar was nonplussed, but acted with his usual deftness and invited Mrs Cathleen Poole to become a full-time member of the science department. The other result of this incident has been a look of worry on the brows of the senior management team here if a new member of staff is late for his first-ever staff meeting!

During his first term, Peter Lapping attended the final briefing for a geography field trip. He was just stressing that informal expedition garb need not be matched by informal behaviour when a large ferret invaded the proceedings – behaving like the half-tamed polecat that it was.

Overheard after a talk on substance abuse 'I will experiment with drugs when I am older and more mature'.

Large plate glass windows in Everett became a problem as the weather-beaten frames aged. However this explanation was not accepted . . . 'the glass fell out while a large helicopter was passing'.

Henry Constantine Jennings (1731–1819) was the bankrupt last owner of the old Shiplake Court. Through the 'false, fleeting, perjur'd Clarence' and the Constantine family, Jennings had a claim to the throne of England. Late in the reign of George III, Henry tried to turn this claim into cash compensation!

Somewhat surprisingly this chapter of true and amusing occurrences was more often criticised than any other – as being out of keeping with a serious enterprise. It was, however, a part that former pupils contributed to and is reprinted with the last four tales added. Pickering College in Ontario has a four pillared portico, like something left over from Toronto Rail Station. The Head insisted they stood for Faith, Hope, Charity and Fun. How right he was. Furthermore there is the commandment for all Leaders and Instructors 'Never be dull!'.

CHAPTER 17

Pace and Confidence: 1981–1983

BY 1981 PETER LAPPING was in a position to write 'It is imperative we improve boarding accommodation' and in reviewing his first fifteen years as Head, Peter felt his destiny was to be remembered as a refurbisher of boarding houses. It is a paradox that the first major building project was the Jubilee Block – extra offices, an attractive shop, a new JCR and first rate accommodation for the resident catering staff. With this development came new architects, fresh advice and eventually a series of buildings in keeping with the Ernest George–designed mansion of 1889. More 'ambition' in our plans gained the confidence of the Planning Authority, gave a tremendous first impression to visitors and had an inexpensive element – a vast extent of used roof space! This continuity of design has now featured in five major buildings.

Parents were very tolerant and occasionally shared their sons' disappointment about study space and lack of privacy. It was sardonically said of me that 'he could not go into a room without thinking of how many boarders could sleep in it'! Peter Lapping's initial solutions were a combination of built-in furniture and fixed partitions in what had been dormitories. These proved popular with boarders and the fire authorities and pointed the way towards designs and plans for the new Burr and the subsequent reconstruction of Everett and Welsh.

Shiplake was a very full school during the early 1980s and the behaviour of some of the boys and the resulting atmosphere presented a few problems. In the interest of serious work, some adjustments were needed, but the balance between sport and work seemed right. Morale was high – the First VIII had lost to Eton in the semi-final of the Princess Elizabeth Cup in 1979 and apart from development in the Cadet forces and school music, there was a new Head with experience of most responsibilities – both academic and boarding. Peter Lapping described boarding care as 'Boosting confidence and repairing failure' and told the governors that during a typical evening a Housemaster 'wielded a busy pen and sat next to a warm telephone within ear of an active door bell and occasionally he needed a strong right arm'. The oblique reference to corporal punishment was a reminder that, by 1982, Housemasters had agreed to discontinue caning. No official announcement was ever made to the boys of that era. Replacements (such as estate work, rustication and close gating) involved Housemasters in extra work and created additional problems for parents – especially as by this time 50% of married women nationwide were working full time.

In 1981 the fees were £1,340 for Boarders and £825 for those in Orchard. Looking back from the start of the twenty-first century, it is hard to believe that headteachers of medium-sized boarding schools were paid little more than £10,000 per annum and the total of responsibility allowances paid to the five Shiplake Housemasters in 1981 was £8,627.

Boys at various stages of school life in 1981 may remember this as the year of the Royal Wedding – with Diana Spencer not a great deal older than themselves. The summer of 1981 was when sailing moved to Sonning and was the end of Mark Lee's all too short stay with the Boat Club. He went on to the difficult job of being chief coach to Cambridge University during their years of defeat. At one stage he made use of another Shiplake Coach, Mark Woodcock, who had migrated to Eton. Basil Wilks – chaplain since 1964 – left the staff but continued to be our neighbour at Fawley. The College saw a fair amount of him until lameness restricted his ability to get about. Apart from assisting in the Hambledon Valley group of Churches, a new venture for Basil Wilks was teaching painting to a ladies' group. He died in 1993.

Important arrivals at Shiplake were to be 'Viv' Daly to take charge of physics and James Johnson in Art. 'JLJ' was an Australian, married to a Dane, a sometime wool buyer and bush pilot. His considerable experience as a London Board 'A' Level Examiner in Art brought a cold draught of realism following the resignation of 'Crisis' Browne. Another 'stalwart to be' arrived a few months later in the bulky personage of Ian Lowry, who seemed to know a vast number of people through his days at TCD, with the BBC and while a hospital administrator. His skills were honed as a Territorial Army member of 'I Corps'.

Peter Lapping had found the staff recently strengthened by the arrival of all-rounders in their twenties. He saw the need to balance their contribution by bringing to Shiplake several men of proven experience and mature years. This was all the more important as our 'Elder Statesman', M.M. Gilliat, was only able to continue for a few months after he moved off campus.

At national level, 1981 was the year of privatisation's first appearance, the year of the attempt on the Pope's life and the first appearance of the ubiquitous 'Walkman'! At Shiplake, sporting progress loomed large. At Henley, the First VIII defeated Winchester *and* Groton – until then we had been unable to cope with American crews in the Princess Elizabeth Cup. In cricket, there was an exciting draw with the Free Foresters. Thanks to an undefeated century by Andrew Chancellor, the scores ended level. Most boys then in the school could say 'I was there' as this was the evening of the first of the Summer Concerts of

Massed Choirs, of which more in a moment. At the end of the autumn, large numbers were at Iffley Road to see the Under Fifteen Rugby side lose in the final of the Oxfordshire Cup. The First XV reached the semi-final – all these events were important in unifying a school now larger than ever and also to unite 'boarders' and 'day boys'.

Play production had been banished from the summer term after 1966. This embargo intended to give public exam candidates a clear run up to the 'O' and 'A' Level season. This was the situation when Malcolm Woodcock became Director of Music. His first summer-time venture was a concert in the marquee on the Sunday before Speech Day. Rehearsals had to fit into the gap between the end of GCE and the last days of term.

The previously described 20th anniversary pageant, 'Time and the Thames' was intensively rehearsed after public exams and was not intended to be a precedent in terms of a return to summer productions. It did, however, make the case for an end of year event involving every boy in the school. So, the Sports Hall became the venue for a series of concerts, giving 320 boys a chance to sing in a major choral work. Trebles and orchestral players had to be imported and I remember signing cheques for visiting instrumentalists. Some boys sang in five of these – starting with 'Carmina Burana' and finishing with a musical tribute to the Lappings.

Audiences had to make some allowances for limited rehearsal time before the final weekend of summer term performances. The Woodcock style was based on getting the confidence of boys, willing and reluctant, talented and unlikely. At least they all were able to have experience of singing in a massed male voice choir, disproving predictions of disaster. The part-time members of the music department provided unfailing, and some times unflinching support. Only one Woodcock event – a Spring Concert in 1983 – could be deemed a disaster. 'You did not miss much' was the verdict of prefects the morning after.

The May 1984 production of 'Jesus Christ Superstar' was one of the first by amateurs anywhere, but by no means the last at Shiplake. In using the front lawns and the main terrace it was another 'first'. The cast came from the three school years not involved in the public exams a month later. Even in 1989, when "Shiplake 900" was produced in May, most expected this to be a one-off, permitted because boys taking examinations did not have speaking parts. In 1990 the Music Department did not want to revive the Sports Hall concerts and a series of increasingly extravagant end of year productions became our main post-'A' Level activity.

CHAPTER 18

The Jubilee Year of 1984

STRICTLY SPEAKING, the twenty-fifth anniversary Jubilee Year of the College was the academic year from September 1983 and rugby gave the year a good start. Coaching was in the hands of three regular members of the Henley First XV. Paul Emerson's Under Fifteens won eleven games and lost only four. Peter Webb's Second XV won nine games in succession at one stage. Their final record was ten won and five lost with one match drawn. The First XV, coached by Tony Hooper, won five, lost five and drew three. Rugby was then played without replacements for injured players and the results of close games might have been different under modern regulations. The three draws were creditable performances against schools much larger than us.

In the spring of 1984, only one block of hockey fixtures was lost to weather so the First XI played thirteen games with an unchanged side winning six and drawing two. The Under Fifteen generation were particularly talented and their hockey side won six and drew two out of eleven encounters. The Under Fifteen cricketers had been undefeated as an Under Fourteen side and were again in the summer of 1984, with two high-scoring draws. They were overshadowed by the First Team who were undefeated by any school and tied their match with Magdalen College School. Six games were won and six drawn. Their spirit was excellent; five younger players, in a season of good wickets and fine weather, knew they would rarely bat. In the last home match of the season, the visiting school left us to get 195 runs in some two hours. They were obtained for the loss of three wickets. The team went on to defeat a strong Old Boys' XI, but a now tired side had much the worse of their final encounter, which was with the Free Foresters. Even so there was no disgrace in this result, but the team was bitterly disappointed. This cricket season marked the end of my close involvement with coaching and playing which had started in 1960, and there is no doubt that the standard of play in 1984 was as good as the results on paper.

By 1984, the Boat Club exceeded all expectations that we might have had a mere twenty years earlier. However, there was a trifle of the 'Early Days' about a Shiplake/Borlase coxless four winning the Visitors' Cup at Henley Royal

Regatta. James Blunt and Henry Trotter were the Shiplake members of this crew. They went to Sweden for the World Championships and reached the finals via the repêchage. The First VIII were third in the Schools Head on the Tideway and quickly attained Senior 'B' status. Of great value in the long term was Ian Baldry's decision to provide an additional inter-house trophy, weighted in favour of non-school team boys and giving most points to the competitions in which everyone took part. Ian's years in Everett – 1967/72 – convinced him that a competition spread over three terms would reward persistence ... and so it has.

Those who were in their third term at Shiplake in May 1984 are now in their late twenties, and the leaving generation of 1984, who were the last interviewed for admission by John Eggar, are well into their thirties. Nationally the picture was austere; this was the year of the Miners' Strike and the Brighton Bombing. The year saw the usual school events come and go. The Ski Party went to Austria for the first time and the French Department exchanged with a Paris school for the eleventh year. New to the scene was an RAF Section of the CCF, starting with twenty-two cadets.

The main summer holiday event was the Buri Gandaki Expedition – a follow-up to the 1979 expedition around Annapurna, and very much planned as part of the Jubilee Year. The figures are impressive: two years of planning, twenty commercial sponsors and help from a dozen individuals, twenty-four days walking by the nine boys involved and half the time at above 4,300 metres, not to mention the porters, sherpas and cooks – almost thirty of them. The weather was not as kind as in 1979 and on the twenty-first night, robbers slit the canvas on one tent to remove a camera and money belt and rifled the packs from two other tents without disturbing anyone. The account in *The Court* magazine is a fine record of an exceptional enterprise. In showing a film of the journey and in the whole process of reporting back, the expedition was as effective in its post-travel public relations as it was in the planning. Not surprisingly this success led to annual expeditions for the rest of the decade.

In 1983 several younger members of staff had moved to widen their experience. Chris Collins went to Allhallows and Steven Keen to Barnard Castle. Alan Butterworth, via Windsor Boys School, ended up at Oundle. Cheaper housing, away from the Thames Valley, influenced their planning. In the interests of boys' academic progress, Peter Lapping appointed the strongest candidates and among seven newcomers, Graham Vick and Eric Pollard were men of considerable experience and versatility. Graham Vick served with the R.N. Section before Eric Pollard resumed his connection with the CCF, taking charge of shooting. He had taken early retirement from Lord Williams', Thame, and was not sure how long he might remain. Eric was soon immersed in a familiar CCF-orientated world that eventually kept him here for nine years.

It had been policy in the early days not to start more than one new activity a year – rugby, Cadet Force, Boat Club and hockey had been part of an ordered progression. In 1983/84, no one thought about overload. The RAF Section (J.W.W. Whittington and twenty-three cadets) began without any of the earlier caution about taking on too much. However, there was clear evidence of a tired community by the last weeks of the spring term in 1984. Head races and the Sixth Form Dance came at the end of a term lengthened because of a very late Easter. Being in session when British Summer Time began, and losing an hour's sleep, came as almost the last straw for boarders and caterers alike. Shiplake did the obvious thing and continued on Greenwich Mean Time for ten hours longer, had a normal night's sleep and removed a midday hour between chapel and lunch. Ignoring what the rest of the Kingdom was doing inspired a certain amount of satirical verse, but seemed common sense at the time.

Another event of 1984 lasted much less than an hour. A Staff VIII raced the First VIII from the lock to the boathouses, losing narrowly. The combined ages of the staff was just under three hundred and while Mr Nigel Wells rowed at 'Two', his wife under her maiden name was at 'Seven'. Equally memorable to those present was an Evensong sermon by Alan Pyburn, Rector of Henley, who combined abundant humour with deep insight into the Christian life. Thus ended our seventy-fifth term, with the College running buoyantly before a favourable breeze.

Celebrations during the Jubilee Term extended from Tuesday May 1st 1984 until July 10th – another Tuesday. Everyone involved with Shiplake, except former parents, had some chance to be part of a happy term. The official birthday began in bright sun with a College photograph and was followed at eleven by a Special Service of Thanksgiving. The singing was magnificent and a full Sports Hall concealed any minor problems of acoustics, noticed during rehearsals. The Address was given by the Bishop of Dorchester. Immediately afterwards Mrs Eggar laid the foundation stone of the Jubilee Building. Guests for the day were current parents, the Governors and the staff. The boys acted as hosts. After lunch Mrs Goodwin named a new Eight, 'Jubilee'. Parents slipped away in early afternoon and by 4 p.m. Malcolm Woodcock had begun rehearsals for 'Jesus Christ Superstar'. The first night was only twenty-two days away.

A good economy during celebrations, and for all large-scale events in any year, is to use classroom chairs to seat audiences. Thus, for an event like Speech Day, we only needed to hire two hundred chairs. For 'Jesus Christ Superstar', chairs were put out every evening and returned to classrooms late at night. There was probably more humping of furniture in 1984 than in most years.

There had been a temptation to use the front terrace for a major production back in the 1960s but it was a good thing that we waited until we had the skill and resources to make effective use of the arena. The only problem was the limited number of seats with a clear view. Public exams excluded the Upper Sixth and the Fifth forms from leading parts and some key singing roles were taken by staff. Over three hundred appeared in costume, but wet weather marred the final night of what was an all-round success.

The sun, however, favoured a gathering of Old Vikings, wives and children. Five hundred came to lunch in the marquee and high spots of the day included 'It's a Knock Out', river steamer trips and the news that the Shiplake/Borlase Four had reached the final of the Visitors' Cup at Henley.

Our last guests were the heads of the prep schools who had sent us boys over the past twenty-five years. This had to be after the end of our term and before the prep school term ended. A few friends were unable to come, but a substantial gathering of heads and wives heard Ian Beer – then Headmaster of Harrow – congratulate Shiplake on how much had been done to serve the needs of boys and especially on 'finding a pace at which the entry could succeed'. The boys, having looked after so many guests this term at Shiplake, went off to their summer pursuits. A second Himalayan Expedition headed for Buri Gandaki; the senior cadets in the CCF went to Berlin and three boys had paintings accepted for the Royal Academy Summer Exhibition.

While all these celebrations went forward the Governors had been deliberating upon the starting date for the 'New Burr' and waiting for the Burnham Committee to revise teaching salaries. In the end the Board could not wait for Burnham and increased fees by some eight per cent. Boarding would be £1550 per terms from September 1984 and the Orchard fee was set at £970. The Chairman emphasised in his letter that the fee was inclusive and covered loan books, stationery, transport and laundry, amounting to nearly £300 a year for each pupil. Celebrating the Silver Jubilee was treated as advertising in the annual accounts and was something like £90 for each boy in the school. The Old Boys had paid for their big day out of savings and profits from their Jumbo Draw were given to the Buri Gandaki expedition.

Memories of summer 1984 did not linger long into the autumn. There will be some who remember being in an undefeated Under Fifteen Cricket XI which had also been undefeated as Under Fourteens. There may be others who remember being told that forty swans on the river at Shiplake was the highest for about ten years. 1984/85 was the school year of building, watching and living with development. The Burr Extension of the early 1970s was swept away in twenty minutes one September morning and McAlpines set about creating a new boarding house in twelve months. The building seemed to be from the centre outwards, and a tall beak-like crane lifted steel and building blocks. Concrete for first and second floors was poured from a dinosaur-like machine. Both soared higher than the Water Tower.

Meanwhile, the Jubilee Building had a roof by January 1985 and a huge rainwater soakaway was dug on the top terrace. Digging went into natural chalk and flint and there was no sign of earlier building anywhere near the Jubilee site.

The snags of two major projects going forward during the same winter were obvious. Every roadway had churned up edges and the busy delivery area at the bottom of the back drive overlapped with the Jubilee construction site. In consequence, a chalk white slime could not be contained. Throughout the winter Burr House showed the most tremendous spirit. The most senior boys had started with Peter Caston and rallied round Judy and Andrew Smail when Andrew took over after Peter Caston's death. The challenge of coping with the death of a young and popular Housemaster was followed by the duty of running a House during a complete rebuilding. Three able school prefects in Burr were supported by four others who would have been prefects in most years. Most of Burr lived in substantial huts on Burr's front lawn, took their showers in Everett and used temporary lavatories in the stable yard.

The year of celebration was clouded by the death of Michael Gilliat on October 14th 1984. We all knew what a burden his lameness, a result of polio, had become. As the funeral was private, the College tribute took the form of four personal appreciations. Miss Tomalin wrote on behalf of all the ladies; Burr and the Old Boys followed, along with biographical details. All the accounts agreed on Michael's successful marriage to Mrs Heather St. George, soon after he took charge of Burr House.

The most apposite tribute to MMG had been written by John Eggar in 1981 – just after Mike's premature retirement at the age of 56. Having emphasised MMG's previous experience and dedication, John Eggar continued:

'In January 1964, he became Housemaster of Burr, a difficult assignment for several years as it was in the wooden huts and half in the main building. His marriage to Heather took place in 1965 and no marriage could have been happier, particularly when they moved into Meltemi and Burr was united in the Red House. As a Housemaster, he was firm but fair, believing in discipline. Boys, as they got to know him, realised quickly his understanding and kindness. He cared deeply for all of them and was always upset when things went wrong. Heather was a tremendous help and between them they made Burr a happy and united house. In the classroom he was the organiser of the English Department where his knowledge was considerable and his teaching acute and well organised. He ran the Library for sixteen years. Shooting was a particular love and this he took over on arrival. Plays, play reading and debating were all part of his scene and his reading in chapel stirred everyone. From 1966 until 1980 he was Second Master and had the difficult task of keeping the balance between the enthusiastic, but often wild, ideas of the headmaster and the even wider views of the common room. For thirteen years we met regularly once a week and I would like to pay my personal tribute and thank him for his absolute loyalty, his willingness to listen and for his advice, so often right, but always given with a certain diffidence. He never complained of his considerable disabilities and all Shiplake will remember the incredible courage he showed after Heather's death.'

An entertaining postcript to the Jubilee year was provided by the Boat Club who had unfortunately quoted to the Governors the price of a new Eight from Empacher in Germany without adding the VAT. When the Bursar asked what the Boat Club intended to do about it, the money-saving plan to collect it ourselves was turned into a money-earning operation. Several boats bought by the ARA were brought back as well, thus earning the VAT needed.

No Second Master holding the fort on a November Sunday evening, three weeks back from a Sabbatical, is gladdened by a voice on the telephone saying 'This is the *Daily Mirror*'. The next words were more reassuring – 'Is it true that Shiplake boys have given up their Christmas Dinners to send the money to Ethiopian Famine Relief?' In spite of being given the details of exactly what was to happen, the *Mirror*'s five-liner next day was not entirely accurate. The story was also in the *Daily Telegraph* and the local press, but publicity was the least of the boys' intentions when the debate about what to do began. At the end of a long term, boys have little money to give away and a corporate gesture– reducing our celebrations somewhat – was looking in the right direction. The last school day of 1984 was not without Christmas Spirit ... the last lunch of term was enhanced in quality and quantity and the long drawn-out suppers were replaced by a hastily arranged and under-rehearsed Cabaret which many thought was more fun than the suppers anyway.

How we ended 1984 is an example of the wide range of things the boys did at Shiplake during the last fifteen years. They grew up, joined in team games, did as much they could have done at St Elsewhere's; they could row with more success than at many schools, but above all they could find their own ways of taking advantage of the atmosphere of the place, which has been called rich, interesting, unusual, special, distinctive and confidence building. What still puzzles those who know it best still is 'What is it about this place?' One part of the answer is that it is a school small enough for most boys to find something that they can do well.

Leavers from the Upper Sixth found employment in the Stewards' Enclosure at the Royal Regatta. When not at the beck and call of full-time staff or running any kind of errand, they could watch the rowing. *The Court* magazine captured Richard Maundrell, not many years later the youngest Captain in the Regular Army, 'cracking a joke' with H.R.H. Prince Andrew – not yet Duke of York or married. This was a very different kind of work experience from what the fifth form were getting post 'O' level via our Careers Department.

Kalpesh Patel wrote at length in *The Court* magazine on his seven years in England, starting with a small boy's exile from Zambia to a rural prep school ... 'somehow losing the person I was at home and quickly becoming an adult'. A sixth former from Hamburg enjoyed a year at Shiplake 'where fun and work were mixed up' and 'people did much for others'. Magazine accounts range from 'Why Cambridge?' to Ergo Testing for the J16 Crew, but Patrick Gubbins wrote with special perception about how his routine new boy medical led, within six months, to open heart surgery at the Middlesex Hospital. From a careful observation of Dr Tony Salmon – our retiring school doctor – at work to memories of post-operative intensive care, Gubbins was able to show in words the same skills he had later as one of our most distinctive school-boy painters.

Individual sports prospered alongside the major team sports. Our original founder, Alexander Everett, had hoped the way forward was through athletics, tennis, squash and sculling. David Scoins' management of athletics and cross country led to a raising of standards. He expected boys to take a substantial part in management and record-keeping and showed them how to computerise results. Cross country fixtures with Winchester and Charterhouse were new and popular. Improved facilities had their long-term results. In 1985/86, Charles de Lanoy Meyer and Ben Fitzwilliams spearheaded a squash First V that won all their sixteen fixtures. Twelve were won 5-0. From then on outstanding squash seasons became a regular feature of the Headmasters' reports.

Peter Lapping and Nicholas Bevan have always been proud of the number of boys away on expeditions. In the Easter Holidays, half the staff and over one third of the school could be away together. While most of these were voluntary, the problem of when to hold field courses – especially for Geography – in term-time and in competition with something else students might prefer to do had, and still has, no perfect answer. In 1987 the Paris 'A' Level art trips began – a week of viewing and sketching which eventually went further afield with JLJ.

HEDFAS, Henley's branch of the National Decorative and Fine Arts Association, had their monthly meetings in the Tithe Barn and senior boys were welcome at appropriate lectures – generally with JLJ as guide. A few years later, arranged by David Welsh at Nick Bevan's invitation, we began our own Tithe Barn Society – this time 'Shiplake Arranged' arts and music programmes open to the public.

CHAPTER 19

1985-1987: New Buildings and Steady Progress

THE FIRST TWO terms of 1985 had an 'after the party' atmosphere which meant the school was relaxed and happy and given to admiration of the way Burr continued to make the best of life in 'The Sheds'. Unfortunately 'O' and 'A' Level results were weaker than expected and came as timely warning against over-confidence.

1985 was a sad year for the maintained schools. 'Industrial action' in Berkshire schools meant that they cancelled 'Saturday fixtures' and two of our regular contacts were lost for several years. We first heard of GCSEs in 1985 along with 'Staff Appraisal'. This was promptly re-named 'Staff Development' to eliminate any 'element of threat'.

The commissioning of the Jubilee Building meant the long hoped for removal of the Green Huts. These had followed the Law of Temporary Buildings – if you put up wooden buildings for twenty-four months they will be used for twenty-four years. One was relocated in the Quarry as a workshop and extra store for the Boat Club and parts of the other were sold to a member of staff for use seven miles away! The loss of the huts attracted none of the sentimental regret that the 1971 extension of Burr was given. The open space was just large enough for a new tennis court.

The special Mountaineering Expedition of 1984 led to a series of smaller summer term ventures to remote parts of the world and in 1985 GSV provided an extra dimension by joining as a resident naturalist.

A Staff versus Boys Athletics match followed a week after the usual Sports Day. David Scoins (DJS) took the Head at his word – 'Schoolmastering is not worth doing if it is not fun' – and provided an afternoon where the senior boys outran the staff and the Masters had the better of the field events. In a tug of war the Sixth asserted themselves over the Fifth form only to lose two-to-one to the staff.

The end of the summer term 1985 began the process of turnover so that now

The Jubilee Building going up next to the Green Hut

only a small minority of staff and administrators remember the Silver Jubilee. Pat Noble moved to the school sanatorium at Shrewsbury and Dr Tony Salmon handed over his post of School Doctor – giving a prize for the performing arts as a momento of being with us from the outset in 1959. Mrs Cosgrove retired from the Maths Department and from running the Exam Office and Mrs Poole left the district. It was a sign of the times that boys with problems found it easy to open up to these ladies rather than through the traditional house structure.

Andrew Barclay left for a school with past connections with Horatio Bottomley and, on the domestic side, Mrs Dinnage retired after twenty-three years as Burr matron. 'Domingos and Celeste' retired to Portugal and the Old Vikings Society lost the services of Mrs Jackie Leigh, who had coped with a vast growth in 'old boy' activities during her years as a part-time member of the Secretariat. When the Old Boys were told that she had quietly left, Jackie was quick to comment that she was incapable of doing anything quietly.

In May 1985 the *Daily Telegraph* gave us some welcome publicity under the heading 'Shiplake in Ship-shape'. This was a review of our 'Facts Booklet' of seventy-two points about ourselves which was commended as 'making the case for independent schools in a way far superior to the usual glossy prospectus'. A number of schools asked leave to produce their own versions. No copy of this first edition seems to survive. The last two hundred and fifty copies went to the Industrial Society, where they were used in a manual showing UK industry how to improve its image.

A second edition of 'Shiplake Facts' came out in the election year of 1987 and, while not overtly political, emphasis was placed on the virtues of independence, the variety of our provision for young people and upon our contribution to the local economy. A seventh edition appeared in 1999 when Barry Edwards spoke of the 'affection and widespread regard for this little publication'!

Roger Harrold, Chairman of the Old Vikings in 1987, attended the summer meeting of the Association of Old Pupils' Societies. He hoped to find out more about how to get people to come to old boys' events, but came away muttering 'I had no idea how political it all is'. Not until ten years later was there a General Election Manifesto from New Labour accepting the right of independent schools to exist.

A list of 'Fourteen Points' drafted after a tour of Canadian independent Schools during the autumn of 1984 makes interesting reading fourteen years later. The Facts booklet issued by Pickering College had given the writer the idea for ours. Links with Pickering were developed following an invitation for one-year academic exchanges between recent leavers at each school. Three former students of Pickering spent time at Shiplake during their university years and about a dozen Shiplake old boys spent a gap year as Junior Masters at Pickering.

Other things which attracted attention included printed guides to all games staff and coaches and a wide contribution of tutors in support of Housemasters. We adopted a guide to games staff as a means of improving co-operation between coaches and the Sister in charge of the Sick Wing, but not until 1989. One benefit was that all aspects of sports organisation and care were already in print before the Children Act. Greater involvement of tutors in Houses also came in the early days of Nick Bevan's Headship.

In retrospect, the marketing policy of the Canadian independents foreshadowed our own methods and facilities in the 1990s. Canadian boarding schools followed provincial academic years, so pupils could move in and out of the independent world at will. Shiplake could risk losing pupils after 'O' Levels – attracted by Sixth Form College – and we thought it unwise to unsettle boys by too much emphasis on what lay ahead. By the late 1980s Shiplake was much better at briefing parents and boys about work and life in the Sixth. This was helped by the disappearance of 6A the repeat 'O' Level Year, and, far better study accommodation for sixth form boarders, a provision Orchard caught up with in 1996.

While people are more important than facilities, it was clear in Canadian independent schools that a visitor was looked after very well time and again, helped by the fact that a visitors' area was usually part of a modern administrative building, close to the centre of a school. Again, Shiplake caught up in 1992 with similar facilities.

1985 was the year that Gorbachev took control of the Soviet Union. In Britain, the Labour party was afflicted with its Militant Tendency and Clive Sinclair's battery car failed commercially. The proliferation of drugs amongst British youngsters had a significant impact.

Under the auspices of Narcotics Anonymous, three ex-boarding pupils – including one of our former captains of cricket – talked openly about their own drug disasters and subsequent escapes. Staff left after an hour of talk and questions. The discussion then continued for another hour and a half. PAL (Preparation for Adult Life) began at Shiplake in 1985. Senior members of staff had a party to mark forty years since Victory in Europe and Mr John Williams, the initiator of PAL, was a guest at this event.

Welsh House was directed for some time by Mr Mannix, as RAE was incapacitated by back trouble. Mrs Marjorie White returned for a second spell of temporary teaching here and then remained in other roles into the 1990s. Mr Welsh himself, twenty years on from founding the school's fourth boarding house, divested himself of the Maths Department, but remained as Director of Studies for the vital task of preparing Shiplake for GCSE and the new Baker-Welsh timetable.

Skipwith House was also facing up to change. Michael Charles relinquished his house after being in charge since 1972. Not every small boy could understand the elementary process whereby an ex-Housemaster becomes a non-resident yet carries on as a Head of Department. MJHC knew his boys very well indeed ... far better than they realised and while his pace was often deliberate rather than speedy, the whole community gained from his dignity and considerable stature. Michael and Elizabeth Charles were noted for the civilised social life of their house. Malcolm Woodcock, already well-established as a Skipwith resident tutor, took over and ran the House with the same style, but at a different tempo. With MJHC's change of residence came the end of our link with Shiplake House. With nine or ten bedrooms, the two wings of this mansion had at times housed two Housemasters and their families during the quarter century the Governors had leased it. Shiplake House was sold as a consequence of Colonel Phillimore's death, and in years to come the reader might ask why the College did not buy the house. The answer lay in how Shiplake House could earn its keep as a school investment. We were already spending half-a-million on a new Burr because an old house with lath and plaster walls and ceilings did not stand boy-created wear and tear. Ever more stringent fire regulations made Shiplake House far too expensive to adapt. Our experience of a repairing lease told us that Shiplake House would continue to swallow money better invested in modern college-owned housing. As a result of this policy, Harrison Cottages were built and a third cottage was bought.

The highlight of autumn 1985 was the official opening of the reconstructed Burr House. As a friend of Lord McAlpine, Sir Keith Joseph, Secretary of State for Education, was an obvious choice. However, his policies were not uncontroversial. National policies in the world of education had seen a wide measure of political agreement since the 1944 Education Act. Sir Keith's pursuit of change was positive, provocative or maverick, according to taste, and Peter Lapping was seen at his best in smoothing some ruffled feathers, especially among younger staff. Sir Keith's appearance among us was as modest as it was intellectually sharp. As the reception committee missed him at the gate, the prefects found him among the parked cars quietly reading a book. This was only about twelve months after the bomb attack on the Grand Hotel in Brighton, which had targeted the Cabinet!

We were rather late in realising that Burr's original Housemaster should be invited, but luckily he was free to come. Michael Burr had taught geography and been bursar during the school's early days and came over from Falcon Manor, his school near Towcester. He was given a warm welcome, especially from Aubrey Goodwin – our Chairman of Governors – who had known Michael Burr in 1959/60. Michael subsequently made a presentation to 'his' house and maintained contact with Andrew Smail, now four Housemasters on from him!

Mr Everett's return to Shiplake is described elsewhere, but this is perhaps the place to mention the third original Housemaster. By chance, in a military biography, the History Department found a few paragraphs about David Skipwith's last days in Special forces. He was a member of a party involved in blowing up a rail bridge behind enemy lines in Northern Yugoslavia. During their retreat, the party was pursued by pro-German Croats (The *Ustachi*). David Skipwith and a sergeant remained behind to delay the pursuit and were forced to surrender when they ran out of hand grenades. This late World War II incident aroused little interest among Skipwith boys and indeed, among younger staff.

The ill treatment David suffered as a prisoner of war was always known to a few, but became more understandable when the Croats fought the Serbs in the early 1990s and the Kosovo crisis became the background to Shiplake's 1999 anniversary. A sometime member of 'David Skip's' house at Bloxham decided in the later 1980s that Shiplake's Skipwith House was the place for his sons – a tribute not lost on those who had known DJS.

Philip Davey and Ivan Jacklin were newcomers to the staff in 1986, arriving just after James Kroth and Mick Llewellyn. The major departures were administrative. Eric Russell left after the 1986 cricket season, having arrived a decade earlier with the reputation of being the most smartly dressed of county and test cricketers... would that all schoolmasters had been equally neat in attire. Eric's last First XI were a fine fielding side, losing only three matches, but eight were drawn. The day-to-day running of the Sports Hall complex was based upon contacts Eric had made with Foster-Wheeler and other local organisations.

By the time Mike Whicker left the post of College Bursar, six major construction projects had been completed in ten years. These projects were evenly spread – Squash Courts and Sports Hall, an Everett extension and the new Burr, new laboratories and an Orchard House with much enlarged study space. Mike did much to establish local contacts through his informal style. He presided over commercial expansion in the holidays and brought in organisations that had their own staff and programs for holiday courses and foreign language students. Mike acted as Hon Treasurer to the Old Vikings Society and showed his public relation skills – acquired as an ocean liner purser – in dealing with former pupils who ranged from astute committee members through to thoughtless car parkers.

The new Bursar, Jim Mansergh, had considerable physical presence and a firm attitude to problems. He hoped that reasoned analysis could reduce "Bursar-bashing" grumbles but he was also the son of a pre-war headmaster, noted for firm attitudes. By training, Jim is an engineer and overseas postings had given him experience of negotiating with interested parties, and erratic suppliers. All this was most useful in the practical side of the three large projects of his first ten years – Goodwin, Everett enlargement, the Admin area, and then the Pavilion/Orchard development.

With the help of Mrs Hinton, Jim Mansergh embarked on small savings which added up to something between £30,000 and £50,000 a year. A sum like this was a substantial contribution to interest payments on new buildings. Drama and Music were encouraged not to exceed agreed expenditure and academic departments had found that improved budgeting did lead to more equipment and catching up with long postponed tasks, such as the Tithe Barn floor and replacing worn oak flooring in Shiplake Court.

While it was not until 1992 that the Bursar headed a department of secretaries and accountants in the same building, an obvious administrative structure had been created by 1988. This was doubly fortunate. The new Headmaster could see how responsibilities were delegated and we were ready to answer the questions of the wider world. By 1987, we employed 98 people, but only 40 were academics. The remainder worked under the management of Domestic Bursar, Clerk of Works or Catering Manager. Nationwide there was increased concern about the performance of Registered Charities for the purpose of Educating Children. Safety at work was another responsibility and the Children Act required vetting of all workers in resident education. Furthermore all inspections had always examined the proper management of school trusts.

Of special interest were two new Governors who joined the board in 1986. Richard Lester was a solicitor and joined John Turner as another distinguished former pupil. The boys knew of him as Olympic Silver Medallist in 1976, when he was stroke of the British VIII at Montreal. Some of the staff knew R.A. (Bob) Alexander as Shiplake Bursar 1968-72, who had gone on to far higher things in the world of school management. The possibility of a lady Governor was mooted and in due course Lady Camoys replaced her husband on the board. At the same time an old link ended: Hubert Beales, Bursar at St. Edwards, retired and Frank Fisher who had joined the Board when Warden of 'Teddies', died all too soon after he had retired from being Master of Wellington College.

1986 was a good time to consider progress made by the Old Vikings – our Old Boys Association that was now 25 years old. The College Jubilee had stimulated interest and a considerable reserve was spent on a OV Family Day. Nostalgia played a large part – we had some middle-aged old boys who contributed to a modernised newsletter and managed to impart news of five hundred individuals in some four years. The Old Vikings presented a main gateway to the school and paid for similar walls on the back drive some years later. A grand piano was donated to the Tithe Barn Society in 1989 at a Family Day to mark thirty years at Shiplake. During this successful period, Society finances were placed on a sound footing by a large and realistic increase in the charge for life membership.

Richard Devas and Christopher Pelloe, who had joined Shiplake in the early 1960s, were followed as OVS Chairmen by Roger Harrold and Rodney Davies who had left in the later 1970s. The latter did much to encourage recent leavers, especially in deciding upon a student rate for recent leavers coming to the revived Annual Dinner, which eventually moved to mid-September for the benefit of those going up to university. Tennis, cricket and hockey provided a series of splendid school versus OVS encounters during the 1980s but rugby went into eclipse due to insurance problems and fears about Men v Boys matches. Happily this problem has found an answer late in the 1990s at a time when OVS cricket and tennis are in the doldrums.

The successes of the 1980s were achieved through the sheer persistence of chairmen and committees. Unique reunions of the First IV of 1964 and of the two 1965 crews were of course small scale OV/Boat Club events which gave great pleasure to the former coach Sam Hall, and equal encouragement to Nick Bevan as new headmaster. Sadly, Sam died not long before thirty-fifth reunions became possible. OV expertise in computers produced a list of all former pupils, thirty-five years after the college opened, and the half-yearly newsletter then turned into a yearly glossy production in the capable hands of Bob Esau and later Michael Edwards. Financial planning is aimed at the first OVS bursaries or scholarships for sons, and eventually daughters, of former pupils.

On October 7th 1986 *The Times* sprang a pleasant surprise on us by including Shiplake among a list of 'Top Twenty' senior boys' schools. The information was taken from the *Good Schools' Guide* but the significance of the event lay in *The*

CHAPTER 20

College Needs and National Issues

IN RETROSPECT, the single issues of earlier years have clear connections. Traditionally in boarding schools, we all did much the same work and were paid on the one salary scale. The introduction of head of department allowances was a wise move ahead of the demands of the approaching General Certificate of Secondary Education (GCSE). The first academic allowances were paid in September 1986. At the same time there was a quiet determination not to pay allowances for games or rowing coaching by full-time members of the academic staff. These moderate additions to salary were a long way from the astronomical bonuses young graduates began to expect after the 'Big Bang' in the City of London in October 1986.

The last additional responsibility I acquired was to become 'Designated Officer' under the Children Act, to establish child protection procedures at Shiplake. In 1984 child abuse issues in Canada and New England vied for space in coverage of Reagan's Presidential re-election campaign. On the basis of twenty years work with children with special needs, Dr. Margaret Wells-Furby expressed a certainty that this would become a British issue. By 1987, we had our own 'Cleveland Gate' sensation in the northeast, associated with the now forgotten Dr Marietta Higgs. At Shiplake, a couple of breakdowns among very new staff led to the adoption of routine medical inspections to improve staff recruitment procedures. Little did we think we would soon be legally required to check the suitability of new staff for employment in solitary or sensitive situations.

The Secondary Heads Association (SHA) traditionally brought together maintained and independent schools. From the time the SHA included deputies, it was more easy for Shiplake to be represented at area meetings and annual conferences. It seemed important to keep in touch with maintained secondary schools at a time when we prospered and our neighbours faced exceptional strains. It was easy for independents to host meetings and offer hospitality. There was 'no such thing as a free lunch' when GCSE training days were held at Oxfordshire schools and it was sad to hear fellow Heads expressing the hope that they might find £40 per pupil for new books needed for GCSE, when at Shiplake the History Department had just spent a similar sum per boy for the one subject. Schools getting ready for local management or grant maintained status tended to ask us 'How do you find a bursar and how little can he/she be paid?' After her years at Henley's Gillott's School, Mrs Marjorie White was able to point out how fortunate we were at Shiplake to be able to devote days to careful consideration of any case of actual bodily harm.

1986 saw the end of the useful January entry into the third form which had brought many talented youngsters to us over the course of some twenty-five years. Large academic schools had a substantial post-Oxbridge leave after a seventh term in the sixth form. When the ancient universities changed their entrance systems, one result was that winter common entrance of any size faded away. This change happened when Shiplake was again over-full with two hundred and seventy-five boarders in September 1986 and sixty-two in Orchard House.

One exam system at sixteen-plus with coursework and the possibility of a national curriculum did much to bring Shiplake and other independents closer to the maintained system. Our links had become gossamer thin during the 1980s and we had been sheltered from problems of falling rolls, inadequate resources, staff cut-backs and low morale until heads of departments went regularly to area meetings during the terms preparatory to GCSE. Shiplake staff who had already entered sets for CSE found much familiar ground within the wide boundaries of the proposed system. We had been using CSE alongside 'O' Level for some subjects since the 1970s. Perhaps the best comment came in the early 1990s from Tim Wilson after he had obtained a First in Maths (with Distinction) at Newcastle University. 'At sixteen, Shiplake was so uncertain of my form in this subject that I was double entered for CSE and 'O' Level Maths!'

Our first Director of Studies in the 1980s was Peter Hose and he relinquished the task to David Welsh. Our response to change and David's solutions became known, as already noted, as the 'Baker/Welsh' scheme. It fell to Graham Vick, in charge of timetabling, to make extra subjects possible and to provide more double periods for course work and practicals and still staff 'A' Levels generously. In due course GSV replaced DFKW as Director of Studies and senior staff were given a permanent place in the management of change in monthly meetings of the Curriculum Committee.

While these changes were in the making, Shiplake was saying farewell to several senior members of staff who had joined in the early 1960s. All three had significant careers before coming to Shiplake, including membership of the 'Afrika Korps'. John Wood had arrived amid the 1963 snows and took charge of Geography and then ran hockey from 1964-69. He came to anchor at Medmenham where he was a parish councillor and churchwarden. John Eggar always remembered Steve Morris as the ex-regular soldier who joined the same term as he did. Richard Lee – chemistry graduate first and then forester – was to spend hundreds of nights in camp with the CCF and the Duke of Edinburgh Award. Retirement means a tribute in *The Court* magazine and a briefer mention in the history of a young school, but where long-serving school masters live on is in the memory – among the once young geographers, who were JBW's departmental colleagues, among CCF officers in other schools who learned much about cadet camps from TSM and all those once young golfers who went round the Henley course once a week with RML.

John and Betty Wood were regular supporters of Old Boys events until Mrs Wood became increasingly ill. Even so, John found time to help with the squash team. He competed against senior boys on the hockey field and at clay pigeon shooting, showing a fine sense of position in defence and a good eye and a steady arm. John decided to take early retirement, but sadly Mrs Wood died during the term John left us. All three received farewell gifts from the Old Boys. In particular they made sure that Steve's departure was not overshadowed by that of Peter Lapping. Steve had come with one Head and departed with another, twenty-five years later. Meanwhile, as OC of the CCF, Richard Lee remained Shiplake's representative at bases far afield for three more campaigns.

The amount that a small unendowed school could do to widen horizons in Arts and Music was limited by resources, as well as time and many gaps were filled in the 1980s by the endeavours of staff. Improved results at 'O' and 'A' Levels suggested progress in educational matters and it was only the Headmaster and a few staff who felt that as boys rose through the school, they became increasingly depressed by the WORLD PICTURE. The 'Cold War' was forty years old; the Berlin Wall seemed everlasting; the problems of the African continent got worse and worse. Disasters like the Herald of Free Enterprise shook confidence; there was another side to Scargill versus the constitution and IRA bombings came very close to the parents of some of our own boys. Peter Lapping felt that boys had little respect for the world their elders had allowed to develop. Other members of staff felt that young men were still remarkably resilient and we should not expect saplings to be trees. In the 1990s, some fresh approaches were tried in much the same areas of concern.

Boys of most ages did make a significant contribution, but not a long-lasting one, in a more traditional area – Chapel Services. Much energy was released when Peter Lapping raised his concern about the lack of religious conviction among many, indeed perhaps most, schoolboys. A Boys/Staff Committee ranged widely over what might or should be done. There were already some lessons from House Chapel – when once a week each House in turn took responsibility for a Service of ten minutes' duration. The value of these depended very much on the calibre of senior or junior boys involved, the time of term and the contribution of Housemasters and Tutors. In a few terms we ran the whole gamut from the very unusual and thought-provoking to the usual hymn, reading and prayers, from the under-rehearsed to the bizarre or well-planned. At this distance, the one significant new idea in the late 1980s was a Whole School Service on Friday afternoons, thus bringing in Orchard and leaving a main Sunday Eucharist for the confirmed and for confirmation candidates. There were some excellent services on Fridays; some mature addresses were given by senior boys with a gift for communication and all the staff who felt able to address a large congregation did so. The system ran out of speakers after two and a half terms. On arrival, Nick Bevan requested time to consider all aspects of school worship and we quietly moved to Services in the Great Hall on Sunday mornings as we had clearly outgrown the Tithe Barn. As one might expect, those who had doubts when John Eggar introduced Tithe Barn Services in the late 1960s, regretted the end of the Barn/Chapel era two decades later.

CHAPTER 21

Major Sports through the 1980s and Beyond

RUGBY FOOTBALL

In the autumn of 1984 a half-term tour to Devon proved to be the turning point of the season, as four matches had been lost and only two won during September and October. After losing to Queen's College at Taunton by just one point, the side won five matches and lost four. This was a young team and two members – Julian Buck and Graham Kuhn – were selected for area Under Sixteen trials and Buck went on to the final England trial. This was the first 'national' recognition for Shiplake boys. The Second XV season mirrored the Firsts – they won seven and lost six. At Under Fourteen level we saw the first signs of our 'Goliath' era, only the first fixture was lost and the new boys went on to win their remaining twelve games.

Several of our coaches were introducing up-to-date techniques into schoolboy rugby, especially in the matter of specialised positions amongst the forwards. This had a clear effect when senior inter-house matches were played; if one house had the specialist front row players a fair contest was hardly possible and questions of safety arose. This was all the more so as hard play in House matches was one of our earliest traditions. Seven-a-side tournaments replaced both senior and junior knockout competitions in the autumn term of 1989. For similar reasons of strength and technique, the Rugby Union came to discourage matches between schoolboys and young men, so in 1987 the twenty-fourth match against the Old Vikings was the last of its type.

Rugby football was strong at all levels in the autumn of 1985, but the Firsts disappointed their coach by failing to get going in the early fixtures – a draw with Bloxham was welcome but APH was delighted by an overdue, but thoroughly convincing, victory over Reed's School after years of trying. The College contributed six players to the County side. The Second XV won eleven out of thirteen and the Thirds, seven out of nine. While the Under Fifteens were not as successful as they had been the previous year, they did get to the semi-finals of the Oxfordshire Cup. The Under Fourteen's won all of their twelve fixtures and were the foundation of plans to strengthen further an already much improved block fixture list.

In 1986 the Second XV won eleven matches out of thirteen and the Under Fifteens 'A' Team won thirteen games and drew 10–10 with Radley in the Under Fifteen cup. Radley took the cup under the 'away' rule. The First XV played seventeen games, but an excellent season tailed away with four defeats. Overall they had scored 311 points against 105. The extra games beyond an average of one a week came through the Oxfordshire Under Eighteen Cup which we won at last. The semi-final hurdle was overcome when we defeated King James's (formerly Henley GS and now Henley College). *The Court* does not actually say it was Gosford Hill we defeated in the final, but it does praise an outstanding display by the three quarters and back row. The real merit of the season lay in five victories over schools larger than ourselves and of a calibre we could not have contemplated competing with at the start of the decade.

The 1987 First XV had five forwards over six feet three in height, but in his last season in charge, EPH again showed his flair and ability by filling problem places with players who had to master the demands of an unfamiliar position. This freshness of outlook had helped for several seasons.

Looking back several things are memorable. A first victory over Abingdon; Dan Richard's success as an Under Sixteen England trialist; the usual Second XV consistency and a diminutive First XV 'hooker' who was nephew to one of our 1960 scholars. In the Under Eighteen Cup we led Henley College at half time – the perfect local derby – but conceded twelve points in an injury-affected second half.

In bidding farewell to Shiplake rugby, Tony Hooper chose to dwell on the many hours of pleasure all his XVs had given. Dwelling on disappointments was foreign to him and he never sought victory at any price. His involvement with boys was year round. He was head of an effective Biology Department and also ran College Tennis. The boys knew he was a versatile athlete. They understood his sense of humour and his colleagues paid tribute to a man, invariably fair, honest and direct.

Over-high numbers throughout the 1980s coincided with a number of oversize all-rounders. Together these were the foundation of an era of rugby and rowing successes that continued into the early nineties, but could not last forever. These include the formidable 1991 First XV and the 'Goliath' VIII of 1992. Memorable rugby matches in 1991 include a victory over Merchant Taylors, a draw with Hampton School and the first Charlotte Starmer-Smith Memorial Match in which we lost by two points to Peterhouse, who were on tour from Zimbabwe. It was the first season we had encountered these schools and our First XV was largely Upper Sixth. It was this generation that gave us our first Henley victory over Eton – as described elsewhere. The names

Ostroumoff, Ouvaroff and Polansky were prominent in this era and implied adventurous family histories early in the twentieth century. The Charlotte Starmer-Smith Memorial Fund was a good example of Shiplake boys responding quickly to events beyond their control – the sudden and unexpected death of a young lady several knew. What can we do apart from listen to prayers in chapel? A one-off fund raising event for local medical funding became a tradition and a purposeful way of ending a rugby season.

Fixture policy at Shiplake could be the starting point of a Ph.D. thesis. The Boat Club has no problem – there are ARA regulations governing ages, crew experience and racing record. As a consequence, a coach can be overheard at lunchtime explaining to the unknowing why the First VIII has moved from Senior C to Senior B. In contrast, the First XV coach has to face the problem that behind his recent success against Merchant Taylors is a block fixture set up. The Second XV draw with Merchant Taylors, at Under Fifteen and Under Fourteen level we are outclassed to the dismay of watching parents.

Such a dilemma was outside our most optimistic thoughts during the 1960s when we were grateful to schools that found space for us at second team level in the autumn and summer. Hockey fixtures developed in the wake of the success of rugby and cricket. However, it must be stressed that hockey results have been the most even over almost four decades and inter-house hockey remains the best contested of all since a cramped summer term leaves little time for house cricket matches at any level and dare one say that, in an age of specialist scrum positions, inter-house rugby has been emasculated. Even in the mid-1980s, Peter Lapping was alarmed by the torrid tackling in a senior rugby final. In the 1970s we had to ask the question 'what was to be learned from fixtures with second teams of local HMC schools?' and while we gradually earned First Team fixtures, our ability to sustain them was a struggle.

By 1990, Shiplake rugby had replaced fixtures against three old, but no longer successful, rivals with three London schools treble our size, but their entry of eleven year olds had been together three years before they met our recently joined under fourteen sides. By 1996 this policy had been reversed. However, in bringing back former opponents and making fixtures with some smaller schools, the backbone of our rugby season is still matched with three schools considerably larger than we are and with three of similar size.

CRICKET

The cricket tide turned around Jubilee Year, in terms of good results. The flow of success was based on seasons of careful coaching at Under Fourteen and Under Fifteen level. However, one must contrast the strength in depth of the 1984 Cricket XI – unbeaten until the final fixture with the Free Foresters, with the very successful 1990 First XI which depended on three fine all-rounders and intelligent captaincy from a goal keeper/wicket keeper. On the basis of watching school cricket over four decades, I felt strongly that our cricket success at the start of the 1990s was due to an obvious near-collapse in the standards of our opponents, several of whom were bereft of the consistency shown for years after 1945. The brevity of the summer term and what was not happening in prep schools led to much discussion, especially as few cricketers were joining Shiplake at fourteen.

Shiplake's cricket resources have long been based on two fine grounds, but it was not until 1995, with the magnificent pavilion, that we have been able to offer the best of changing facilities through every season. As inter-school cricket is not played in leagues, Shiplake fixture-making has had, since 1993, to demote itself. Then we played five local HMC schools, two large grammar schools and four men's sides. In 1998 our cloth was cut according to means. In a cramped summer term travelling to Bloxham, near Banbury or Cokethorpe, near Witney was time-consuming and replacement with very local fixtures represents realism. The Firsts now play the Staff instead of a Headmaster's XI of club cricketers and two of the club fixtures have been replaced by very local schools. In the interest of a balanced fixture list we now play four schools we would have thought, in 1990, it was unnecessary to take on. Results suggest that standards have not recovered at the HMC rivals we still play, and we are getting good results against new opposition as well as bringing them to Shiplake.

THE BOAT CLUB

Increasing success was not only a subject of pride in the Shiplake College Boat Club but a contributor to all-round success. Taking a lead from one of our historians, who also had a public relations brief, the Boat Club became rather more conscious of the need to record its achievements and progress. 1984 had marked twenty years of regatta competition and a Boat Club Silver Jubilee year in 1988 began with a dinner at the Leander Club. By chance this event took place the evening before the Governors met to appoint a successor to Peter Lapping. Speakers paid tribute to the support John Eggar and Peter had given to rowing. The Bursar and I, sat quietly thinking that it was distinctly possible that the governors would the next day elect an Oxford Rowing Blue and distinguished Coach. This notion was kept to ourselves.

College rowing coaches were disappointed that it was difficult to get a large turnout of past crews for this dinner, but the Old Vikings committee was well aware of a general attendance problem. People only came back if they were sure they would know others. As a result, nothing was ever attempted to celebrate twenty-five years since the first cricket and rugby fixtures. At the 'May Day' bank holiday 1989, the first Coxed Four of 1964 returned to row again under the direction of 'Sam' Hall. This was indeed an affectionate tribute to Sam as a person and as a coach as the crew had lost little of its collective skill. In 1990, First and Second IVs returned for a similar reunion. The participants were delighted to be together again and were surprised at their surviving watermanship. Nick Bevan was most impressed by the technical competence that Sam Hall had instilled. Participants returned from as far afield as Western Canada. These reunions set the example for the 1972 VIII – to come back in 1997 – a quarter of a century after we first entered the Princess Elizabeth Cup at Henley.

At the Jubilee Dinner on January 29th 1988, the toast to SCBC was proposed by Ronnie Howard – in his time a winning Oxford President. He must have been wryly amused at a public disagreement between Sam Hall and Colonel 'Jim' Travers during speeches about when the Boat Club at Shiplake started. The retrospective view of most coaches appears to be 'gosh, we have some marvellous rows (disputes) in the old days but we got there somehow'. After long debate with any Headmaster about times and priorities, rowing coaches then debated loud and long with bursars about resources. After these issues were settled for a twelve-month, inter-coach arguments about club organisation and techniques seemed the driving force behind actual achievement. As a rugby or cricket coach, one respected the commitment of all involved on the river but we did know that in our sports you could have eleven or fifteen players who threw or passed the ball with different techniques and you still had a successful team. 'Try it this way – it will work better' was not aimed at uniformity in ball games. Even so, a clash between old coaches about 'when is a club a club?' seemed carrying riverside acrimony rather too far.

Rowing at Shiplake began as a summer activity and in 1960 there was an interhouse event in a clinker four – each house was timed over the course from the lock to the wet boathouse. Jim Travers joined the staff in September 1960 and looked after such equipment as we had and organised coaching during 1961. Sam Hall arrived in January 1962 and registered our club with the ARA during the year. As a result we appear in the 1963 Directory section of the British rowing Almanack. 1963 was the first season we competed against other clubs.

In 1990 we realised that Jim Travers was the only former master in charge of rowing who did not have a boat named after him. This was duly corrected in February 1991 during what was probably Jim's last visit to the College. Sam Hall died suddenly early in 1998, rowing regularly as a veteran until the end of an active life. After our victory over Eton at Henley in 1989, Sam was able to say he could die contented.

The Boat Club in 1990. Ben Hunt-Davis, later to win an Olympic Gold Medal in the Sydney Olympics, in the centre

The 'fleet' in the early days of the Boat Club

Weight lifting forms an important part of training for rowing

Ben Hunt Davis, Shiplake's Olympic Gold Medallist, at the launching of the eight named after him

Guy Jackson, cox of the First VIII for all his five years at Shiplake (1989 – 1993) and coach, Mark Hayter

RECENT GAMES PROBLEMS

At the end of the 20th century, the place of sport in British life (one almost wrote 'Brutish') is an endless debate. Many young people, along with some parents, think winning and image are important and reflect the distortions that professionalism has brought to motivation and training. If sport in independent schools ceases to be about young people having fun with a purpose, it will not be worth the endeavour. In the 1970s one tended to regret that able sportsmen at Shiplake did not take their ability far into club, County and national level. Today one is almost glad they do not.

Apart from two or three who have made some mark in motor sports, rowing is the main activity where Old Vikings have made a contribution. The few who have managed to row at a high level after ceasing to be full-time students have made sacrifices, not fortunes. Family financing, teaching at Shiplake, casual labour and sponsorship are among the expedients that our oarsmen have employed to get to Olympic or World Championships.

Rugby had the advantage of being the sport played at the start of the academic year and set several good examples – most boys could play for the school: there was a ladder to climb over the years, sometimes from Under Fourteens 'C' to eventual First XV – tremendous parental support and traditional cheering crowds. At the start of each year, the clashes with 'A' Level demands, the pull of minor sports and pressure from coaches all lay in the future. Season after season the most unlikely combinations of the raw-boned, semi-fit produced almost unbeaten Second XVs. However, the growth of specialisation amongst forwards brought to an end fifteen-a-side, inter-house rugby.

The foundation of rugby successes in the 1980s were to be found in a structure we had previously lacked. Coaching for new boys was so much better and, after three or four years together, the basic skills were established and more ambitious coaching produced confident sides that played with zest and sometimes a concert pitch brio. For several seasons we were fortunate in the size of our forwards and seeing last year's opponents again sometimes occasioned some confrontational forward play.

In the 1990s all this changed and several seasons were difficult simply because we lacked the schoolboy giants of the previous decade. We had great difficulty in sustaining the strong fixture list that had evolved before the lean years began.

During his time as Head, John Eggar moved from regretting we had started hockey, to believing it was the team game most suited to Shiplake. Over three decades it has been our most consistent sport and in the last fifteen years has gained from use of local all-weather pitches. It has rarely drawn the crowds and is the most affected by the weather. The Hockey Association match was always well watched, especially if a parent was among the visitors. Inter-house tournaments retain much of their importance and the First XI versus the Staff has brought each season to a happy conclusion.

Cross country and athletics are important because everyone takes part and counts so much towards the Baldry Trophy. Generally some unknowns come to the fore. While the Sports Hall should have led to improvements in athletics' training and techniques, this is an area where there has been the least advance. In an overcrowded summer term there is little room for expansion. Senior boys showed skill in being the managers of Staff v Boys athletics. Sports Day itself attracts little support from parents.

Shiplake cricket in the early 1990s demonstrated some essential truths. The 1990 XI had remarkable results and was an example of a team being stronger than its parts, with shrewd captaincy from an Upper Sixth scholar who was an adequate wicket keeper. In 1991 and 1992 serious weaknesses were covered up in part by the performance of two exceptional schoolboy players, Hall and Caston. In 1993 Caston was unable to reproduce his form with the bat and results were grim. The following summer, the traditional start-of-season questions found no answer – there really was no one to make the runs or take the wickets.

We had turned out weak XIs at other times, but a season that used to last three and a half weeks into July allowed for lessons to be learned and results to improve. House matches also suffer from a nine-week term. In spite of many difficulties, Wanderers' cricket survived. Under the management of Andrew Smail, staff and boys continued to entertain local clubs on our excellent wickets.

The Cross-Country and Athletics squad under David Scoins in the early 90s

Athletics in the summer term

and Hockey on the 'astro' in the Spring

Parental support at Under Fourteen and Fifteen levels makes cricket on the new field look as good as ever. After two decades of coaching and umpiring at junior level, Michael Charles retired in 1992 and Andrew Smail left Shiplake after eighteeen years involvement with Colts' cricket. The completion of the new pavilion was good for the morale of Shiplake cricket and the 1998 fixture list – much modified – included only three schools we were able to take on five years earlier. By contrast, in 1997 the First XV still played six of the twelve schools we played in the successful 1991 season.

CHAPTER 22

Summer Holidays and an Unannounced Visit

ALEXANDER EVERETT, a fit looking sixty-seven year old, visited Shiplake in August 1987. Pursuing various interests from a home in Oregon, he was out of touch with former contacts in England. I had to tell him that Mrs Everett had died in 1981; this was a great surprise as he had no inkling that she was no longer alive. Although they had been long divorced, this was a sad moment. Our surviving founder went off with a copy of *Wish and Fulfilment* (Part One of this volume) and a few days later requested a private chat about some aspects of the information it contained about the period before he started the school and in the very early days before he and Mrs Everett separated (see Appendix 1). After he left, I made some notes of the main points, together with my own observations and some subsequent checking of my sources.

Alexander Everett began by stressing his own school experience and his reaction to the critical years 1939-45. The war had been such waste of young talent and some of its causes could be tackled in schools. He had been unhappy at prep school and at Aldenham, 'where seniors bullied juniors and masters thought nothing of it'. (The Aldenham register shows he was a day boy there between the ages of fourteen and sixteen.) By the age of twenty he was keen to change the character of schools, but some years of ill health delayed him. As a result he began to teach in prep schools unqualified. He subsequently started his own prep school and here he first met Mrs Richardson and her son Richard. By his account, Alexander was pleased at her interest in his ideas and surprised by her offer of partnership and marriage. They both went to work at Ashfold while the search for a property began. Alexander had sold his own prep school and was keen to stress that he invested in 'Shiplake Court School. It was not all my wife's money'.

In retrospect he wished he had done more research into the policies of innovative schools. He had visited Gordonstoun but regretted he had neglected the theoretical side of pioneering ventures. Important steps had been taken quickly;

he had little idea of Mrs Everett's state of health and he failed to find the Director of Studies he needed, someone who could be an innovator and academic leader. David Skipwith was the third person he had to turn to in the first term. Alexander never saw himself as headmaster of a senior boys' boarding school. At least, that is how he felt in 1987.

What he wanted was a school where boys could compete against each other as individuals, sculling, riding, playing tennis, squash and golf. He wanted a school without team games. In our discussion he repeated this more than once along with his regrets about lack of research. At this point it is worth adding that while riding and golf have been minor activities, these sports have always contributed to the growth of individual self-confidence, but where does one draw the line between the usefulness of competition and help given by the coach or instructor?

Whenever we discussed particular issues I felt I had the advantage of having studied the minute books of the Governors and some of their early meetings, some indeed, written up in Everett's own hand. He made the frequent comment 'It is a long time ago and I don't remember exactly'. He remained convinced that 'One of the press barons had arranged for the free article in the *Daily Mail* because his grandson was at Shiplake in the first term'. The Minute book confirms that we paid for this leader page feature and Debrett shows there was only one press baron grandson of the right age and he was at Stowe in 1959!

Everett was disappointed at the bullying described by Stewart Cowley (p. 26) 'I had no idea there was any ...' He felt I had called him a bad teacher; he felt he was 'gifted and inspired'. The actual words used were 'Alexander Everett was an ineffective schoolmaster and by no means a leader of men'. Having just said across the table the he 'never wanted to be a headmaster' and descanted upon prep school experience, I am left a decade later thinking he never defined the term 'good schoolmaster' in a way John Eggar had done. Of his brief return at the start of 1961 he said, 'this was part of my plan of twelve months earlier to resume a place at Shiplake if my marriage could not be rebuilt'.

Alexander Everett spent a long day at Shiplake in company with the hundreds who came back for the Old Boys' 'Thirty Years After' reunion in 1989. Few present actually knew him. He was disappointed that it was planned to be a 'no speeches occasion'. Many who had heard or read of him were interested to meet him.

From 1963 onwards the printed list of Governors and Staff was prefaced by the note 'Founded in 1959 by Mr Alexander de Morley Everett and Mrs Eunice Richardson'. Some twenty-five years in the United States produced the streamlined 'Alec Everett' whose talents had flourished in a more expansive society. In some ways his career had been the mirror image of the Episcopalian clergyman known to Shiplake GCSE historians as the educator of the future President F.D. Roosevelt. Endicott Peabody had become a missionary in Tombstone, Arizona and friend of Wyatt Earp long before founding Groton School in Massachusetts. When President, FDR made his old headmaster chaplain at the White House. In his own inimitable way Everett had moved from Founder/Head to success in the western states.

CHAPTER 23

The Lappings Move On

AT THE START of the twenty-first century, Peter Lapping's nine years at Shiplake, take on the appearance of an interim management between two headships of a longer length. Having arrived at Shiplake in his late thirties, Peter knew he either had to remain at Shiplake for twenty-two years or move elsewhere after ten years or so. Naturally he argued that it might be bad for Shiplake if he was in charge for two decades. Lightheartedly he claimed that the location of the headmaster's house and the hours he and Diana had put into the gardens of Court Mead made it difficult to leave. His list of the schools he would like to move to was quite short and he began to look around at a time when governing bodies of large schools were appointing heads who had gained experience as heads of smaller schools.

While the Lapping years appear a short reign, they were successful and stimulating. Furthermore, the school was stable and secure, the momentum of John Eggar's later years had been sustained and twenty-five years after John and Pam Eggar first came to Shiplake the Lappings could feel Shiplake was firmly established. Everyone could see they enjoyed their involvement and, as a result of promotions, staff expansions, retirements and two sad deaths, Peter had appointed a dozen men to the staff as well as three lady members. People who have just arrived at a school tend not to speculate about the plans of a young head who has recruited you and everyone involved with a busy headmaster hardly gave a thought to the notion that his all round success would be of interest to governors of several large schools. Peter used to joke that the only things he had not attempted were conducting an orchestra and running a Cadet Force.

I was involved in Peter's plans to the extent that his absences at usual times had to be covered. Peter Lapping's new appointment was announced simultaneously at Sherborne and Shiplake and letters went to all parents concerned on the same day. The unexpected nature of the news caught Shiplake by surprise as it came hours after the 'Great Gale of October 1987' when minds were focused on damage which seemed to be greater the further one lived from

Shiplake College. In many subsequent conversations with parents and friends, Peter was able to say that the roar of the wind had kept him awake, forcing him to ask himself if the elements themselves were protesting against the change.

The actual announcement to the Shiplake staff produced one of those hushed pauses that stay in the memory. When Peter had finished it fell to me to make appropriate comment on behalf of the staff: a not unfamiliar duty after important announcements – and on this occasion carefully prepared – but never to a more unprepared group of academics. The moment of surprise turned to a mood of congratulation and genuine pleasure in the success of one of our own.

It is never safe to generalise about the outlook of young people. Peter Lapping was concerned about a groundswell of pessimism in his regular discussion periods with sixth formers. Their confidence in the security of a familiar world could be jolted by any event from the wreck of the Herald of Free Enterprise, a family divorce, fathers becoming redundant, to a family manufacturing business begun by a great grandfather becoming the victim of Thatcherism. What they read in papers of Africa and Asia, of famine and persecution was at variance with what they heard in Sunday Chapel. The Litany could be endless – Was university worth-while when the seemingly unqualified amassed serious money in the City? – Will I be able to compete? – Do I want to compete? – Who is there to respect? Peter Lapping naturally did everything to make his final year a success, but instinctively boys speculated about what the next head would be like and how many changes he would make.

John Eggar became accustomed to the parental question 'Will you be here to see my son through five years at Shiplake?' He used to joke that he must be looking older than he felt. This was a question rarely put to Peter Lapping by parents who valued his understanding of their sons and were conscious of his warm welcome. Most parents were in management and, naturally, understood the world of promotion, change and moving on. They congratulated him upon his move and accepted his assurances that all would be well.

When *Wish and Fulfilment* (Part One of this volume) was published, Peter Lapping understood the need to appraise men still alive and active when recent years were described. In his case there is no question of 'weighing in the balances'. The practical improvements of his years and his manner of working are sufficient tribute to a headship that was never dull or muddled.

Peter Lapping was a good listener and open to ideas; he was patient, calm when things went awry and preferred conciliation to combat. Colleagues were allowed their say and the curmudgeonly and unhelpful were tolerated and then persuaded. Much ground was covered at meetings – sometimes at inordinate length! Peter was convinced this was better than cutting corners. However, undermining others doing a job properly was not permitted. Those who conferred regularly with Peter Lapping found him open to suggestions and willing to modify his own proposals. When colleagues were occasionally unhelpful, they found themselves disarmed by a clear and restrained analysis from the Head. Staff and parents found Peter Lapping unwilling to meet anger with anger. Difficult decisions about boys were made with some speed but without haste. Staff were listened to more than in the 1970s and parents felt that all aspects of a pupil's misdemeanours had been carefully considered. This had to be the case if parents were at the other end of a telephone in Iberia or the Far East.

T.H. White had been Head of English at Stowe before acquiring fame as author of *Sword in the Stone*. White once advised a pupil who had broken a Heal's lamp as follows 'only by observing these civilities could much emotional wastage over trivial things be avoided'. This takes us near to the Lapping approach – to look carefully at new ideas, to listen at length and with care, to be clear without heat or ire and finally gain co-operation with a smile. Words were translated into action – many private kindnesses were shown to those new to the staff or recently ill. At any briefing or when reviewing yesterday, Peter was constructive, never resentful and sought solutions rather than confrontations. 'Openness and charm' said the late Professor Raymond Wilson, 'were ingrained in his character'.

By way of farewell, the Old Vikings presented a teak garden seat to Peter and Diana in the hope they might get some time to relax in their next garden. Of particular pleasure to Peter was the dinner given to the nine former pupils who had been his Heads of College and had led each year's prefects. The school's own farewell was intended to be a one-off: a College Dinner in the marquee the night before Speech Day. Including staff and ladies, well over four hundred sat down together. Julian Buck of Burr House, just over two years later to be on active service in the Gulf War, presided and made the presentation. Afterwards, Orchard House went home; the juniors to bed and parties of seniors then set out six hundred chairs for speeches thirteen hours later. A few finishing touches were needed next morning. For the first time since the mid-1960s the whole school was able to sit down together. The event looked impressive and was voted the greatest fun. During the summer holiday in 1988, the Governing Body gave a dinner in honour of Peter and Diana Lapping. On behalf of boys, parents and staff the Chairman emphasised the many little kindnesses, going well beyond the call of duty, that were so natural with Peter and Diana. In reply, Peter hoped that the governors would continue to help the families that had needed Shiplake over the last three decades.

By a curious chance, the announcement of Peter Lapping's retirement from Sherborne came during Shiplake's 40th Anniversary celebrations. Peter would leave Sherborne after that foundation's 450th commemorations.

The Court magazine covering PHL's last year at Shiplake was a remarkable compilation. It departed from the traditional publication of record and set a pattern for several years, almost ignoring speeches, guests of honour, prizewinners and recording first team results only erratically or not at all. The merit lies in a remarkable range of articles, a description of which follows:

Paul Emerson contributed an article on 'Safety in Sport' and along with this, the Bursar gave details of insurance arrangements. The School Sister wrote on 'Fitness to Play' and two 'rugby-watching mothers', one with three sons at the College, outlined their emotions.

The student view of coursework was printed alongside a staff explanation of coursework from Chris Foster, whose Geography Department was much affected by this fresh emphasis both at GCSE and 'A' Levels.

James Welsh reported on his first month of VSO work in far away Jakarta, while from six miles away, Angela Drinkwater-Lunn wrote a sympathetic account of her holiday break from our Ceramics Department as a volunteer art tutor at Reading Gaol.

From the father's viewpoint came a light-hearted contribution from Colonel Donald Lear. He estimated he had signed cheques to cover sixty-four lots of school fees during the fifteen years his four sons had been with Michael Charles and Malcolm Woodcock in Skipwith. The entire Lear family came to Speeches in 1988 to mark the end of a worthy connection.

In contrast, a thoughtful obituary paid tribute to Doug Wilson, one of the volunteer coaches the Boat Club attracted. He had actually died while rowing with three veteran friends. He had rowed for fifty-seven of his sixty eight years and last competed at Henley in 1951. Ten years earlier he had led a group to safety after the fall of Crete. Doug was one of those versatile people attracted to Shiplake. His career had moved from radar to banking and accountancy and then on to modern languages and computing.

Amongst those starting a career as an Upper Sixth leaver in 1988 was Sanjeev Bakhrania, one of those delightful young men who contributed as well as received during years at Shiplake. From the Indian subcontinent, he was so prematurely grey that he could be mistaken for a member of staff. A delight to teach, unfailing and courteous as a school prefect and Chapel choir member, Sanjeev came into his own as an agreeable companion on the cricket field. Not surprisingly, he joined the 1988 summer expedition, travelling out to Srinagar to trek at 13,000 feet and above in the Zanskar Valley.

Peter Lapping got to know a number of staff through playing cricket and helped and encouraged others through his own experience of coaching rugby. Like his predecessor, he was converted to the pleasures of supporting college rowing in all winds and weathers. Every boy who tried his best was encouraged with a smile and a chat ... 'The school is small enough for the Headmaster to know every boy' was his watchword. As a person, Peter disliked gossip, but welcomed being kept in the picture. He could defuse a situation through tact and humour and declined to be depressed by pessimists. What did depress him was failure to be as thorough in essential paperwork as he was. He found time to produce measured judgements on one side of A4; furthermore, Peter found the unorthodox approach of value when it helped boys to succeed. Visits to boys in hospital, kindnesses to staff families, sympathy to staff in sickness, prompt letters of thanks, numerous little kindnesses are the actions remembered after meetings and speech days are forgotten. Being quick to bring support to boys, parents and colleagues was important to Peter and Diana. Peter could be caught unawares by unexpected resentments, bouts of intolerance and lack of sympathy for anyone in need. In contrast, Peter could be firm. Indeed he found no difficulty in reaching decisions for the benefit of the boys. As a result, some colleagues were disappointed over promotions and the allocation of our most scarce resource, staff accommodation within the school grounds.

CHAPTER 24

Admissions – Who Came to Shiplake?

BY 1987 SHIPLAKE had taken boys from one hundred and ninety-one different prep schools but, with a trend for boys to board within an hour's drive of home, our links became more regional during the 1980s. We were perhaps slow to see changes in the schools dealing with the early years of fee-paying education. Some were becoming more academic, but we seemed to get far fewer well-coached thirteen year old games players. Some were aiming increasingly at day school places in the former Direct Grant (and mainly day) schools with entry at eleven years. At one time, most boys coming to Shiplake after common entrance had already been boarders for up to five years. Now, at thirteen, some had never boarded, others only briefly, so our housemasters, tutors and prefects could no longer assume that newcomers 'knew the ropes'.

In 1982 Frank Fisher warned us in a lecture that senior boarding schools could no longer assume that prep school leavers were as well drilled in basic skills as traditionally they had been. Knowing how to set out work, knowing how to address an envelope and being prepared for a morning's timetable were not as widespread in a new entry as in the past. Schools should provide a 'Learning to Learn' programme for first year pupils soon after arrival. Michael Charles, our senior housemaster, needed no convincing of this. His early experience of teaching had been in a leading prep school and he took charge of this project. He was quite prepared to sacrifice history teaching early in the Third Form to push home basic skills. Subsequently there was the usual debate about how much improvement came from an intensive course. Eventually 'Learning to Learn' merged into teaching sets how to work on their own for GCSE coursework purposes.

Irrespective of problems boys might have on arrival, 'O' Level and 'A' Level results improved during the 1980s and Peter Lapping was keen to emphasise the academic destinations of boys with a CE average of between fifty and forty per cent. By 1988 there were as many as twenty applicants for each place at Shiplake. Graham Vick, as Director of Studies, felt most were youngsters who would not prosper at Shiplake and when these were steered away, there was admission standard in 'ex Direct Grants' and would provide a new market for prep schools. Furthermore there were more day places available for feepayers at a time when there was a drift from boarding.

Shiplake's admission policy in the 1980s was to look for boys capable of a sound GCE coverage at 16 plus. Three out of four who came could manage this and the fourth would need a good deal of support – amongst the most able were members of the sixteen per year admitted with some English difficulty – the word dyslexia was deliberately underplayed.

In 1988 we disappointed a large number of potential parents (and some prep school Heads) by not admitting boys who had no reasonable chance of reaching our targets at sixteen-plus. They would not be able to keep up with the right pace we set for the bulk of our entry. In September 1990, Shiplake was still the slightly over-full boarding school it had been for twelve years, but during the year a number of boys withdrew during their first three terms. If he can manage the work, a boy will put up with the inconveniences of boarding. If every subject is a constant struggle, it becomes very hard for any housemaster to help parents and their son through the first terms of boarding school. It was a case of every member of staff at Shiplake giving to themselves the encouragement offered to boys – 'try harder'. This was at a time when young people had immense difficulties with the word 'No'.

CHAPTER 25

More Plans and New Buildings

WHILE THE HISTORIAN sees several strands of thought and action going forward side by side, he has to write about them one after another. Boarding house improvements were taking place alongside planning to extend and modernise teaching areas and alongside the transition from GCE 'O' Level to the new GCSE. Some Shiplake pupils spread 'O' Levels over two years, but the GCSE was clearly an exam for everyone at sixteen. These strands interlaced. Modernised boarding houses made Shiplake more attractive for summer holiday letting and would contribute to the cost of new academic buildings. Improved Arts and Craft areas would make holiday courses more interesting. If new buildings contained flats, more teaching staff on site would reduce expenditure on rented accommodation, improve our 'pastoral provision' and help out-of-class activities. However, none of these benefits by themselves reduced day to day problems of verbal bullying, homesickness or alleged boredom.

There was no simple process for investing surpluses in new buildings. Fire regulations changed and health and safety at work was the subject of legislation. Furthermore, the plant wore out. There were five kitchen modernisations between 1964 and 1993 and three servery updates after 1970. All had Fire and Safety considerations as well as efficiency and hygiene in mind. Most facilities never last as long as is hoped. Telephone systems last somewhat longer than computers, redecoration is almost part of public relations and the architect was surprised at the attrition on building materials by boys, bags and furniture moving. The copper ducting that housed the wiring of Everett House succumbed to corrosion fifteen years before the date predicted in 1961, but the replacement system was scrapped within seven years when Everett was remodelled in 1991-92.

One senses that our planning had improved post-Silver Jubilee, almost as if the era of improvisation was over. We were no longer caught out by unexpected spending of the type mentioned. They were budgeted for. Even the Summer Ball committee changed policy. By 1988 members decided that enough had been invested in the Tithe Barn project and that future Ball profits should be divided between small schemes and medium-sized projects. The first result was the fitness room addition to the Sports Hall.

The Old Boys, through the Old Viking Society, contributed in two ways. An improved main gateway was mooted as something that could be opened ceremonially in 1984. The untimely death of the OVS President, John Eggar, postponed the project for a year. The final, simple but effective, result owed something to the low brick and stone wall entrances to Commonwealth War Grave Cemeteries. Subsequently the Old Boys provided similar walls for the back drive. The second objective of old boys was to provide something that would enhance school life, but was not something that the Governors felt was an urgent educational need. The grand piano in the Tithe Barn is an example of this stage of Old Boy support. A decade further on, their planning now involves scholarships for children of former pupils.

Improved gateways and modern, easy to heat and clean, buildings are not easy to value when assessing how Shiplake College maintained confidence, kept up numbers and encouraged boys to stay for five years instead of three or four. Occasionally it was possible to delight everyone by a surprise move, rapidly executed. In the Summer holiday in 1988, the tarmac tennis courts were replaced by an all-weather, all year round 'artificial grass' surface. The work was done by probably the most objectionable contractors we ever used and was subsequently floodlit – somewhat to the concern of our neighbours. This scheme was the last planned in the Lapping era. However, Peter Lapping had spent part of his final year preparing a long list of outline schemes for the 1990s and all members of staff had been able to contribute to estimating future needs. It remained for a new Head to decide priorities, once he had time to study the requirements of the new exams, additional teaching areas and, as yet, incomplete updating of boarding houses. If that was not sufficient, Orchard House could not cope with their shortage of studies for senior boys much longer.

Peter Lapping was more aware than anyone of the problems caused by our scattered office arrangements (as already mentioned) and secretaries had to move to and from our one computer terminal. He also shared with colleagues the assumption that we ought to replace prefabricated buildings – the largest of which was the Maths block.

The solution advocated by Peter Lapping was imaginative, but in the long run it found no friends. A central office area had to be near the old Shiplake Court – the ground floor of Everett would be large enough and the upper floor of this boarding house could convert to the needs of the Maths and Computing departments. An entirely new boarding house could then be built in our one unused area, the quarry. This would be reached by a new roadway through the orchard. Although the existing Everett was only twenty-five years old, it had dated rapidly. Rebuilding on the one unused site would be expensive and not the best answer to any academic needs. While moving 'admin' and offices out of

Shiplake Court would release some rooms for new uses, the school would be no nearer to finding answers to several other problems. Art and Ceramics were in cramped former stable accommodation with a Technical Drawing office above. Woodwork was confined to a basement area and we were several laboratories short. The need to modernise was driven by the coursework theme in GCSE – especially in Science and Design subjects. Socially the day boys survived in a prefabricated building and changing rooms for visiting teams were woeful – here embarrassment was the motivation for reconstruction and expansion.

The sweeping changes of the early 1990s were planned in rooms that would soon cease to be our collective headquarters. Visitors still came to the small front office – once described by the original school secretary, Monica Tomalin, as 'built round me like a nun in a cell'. The Bursar met architects in what had been Mr Harrison's business room in 1891. The Head and Bursar together then looked at drawings spread out on the large table of the only reception/meeting room we had, at one time the sitting room of the pre-1914 nursery wing. The Head's secretary worked in a former bathroom – another narrow room, while potential parents gathered on the landing and stairs of the mansion, just outside the Head's study, a room which had been a bedroom in the house's early years. Outside teaching hours, boys circulated past every office door. To generations of boys, those running the school were visible and all too accessible.

CHAPTER 26

Departures and Changes by the 1990s

TWO SENIOR LEAVERS have already been mentioned alongside John Wood. John Eggar always had a soft spot for Steve Morris, who arrived with him in September 1963. Steve was involved with the CCF throughout his years at Shiplake and was one of the last of our pioneers. He gave up responsibility for Physical Education just when the Sports Hall opened and had only three years in the purpose-built College Shop before retiring the same term as Peter Lapping moved to Sherborne. Other key figures moved within a few years, in particular, Richard Lee, who had been OC of the CCF through the 1970s and 1980s. He retired in 1990. In the Laboratories he was the friend of those who found things difficult and always placed the emphasis on what boys *could* do, long before this became an objective of GCSE. An old boy totalled up the number of nights RML spent in Summer Camps and in support of Duke of Edinburgh Gold Award expeditions in the Lake District or in Wales – an average of three weeks a year over twenty-five years. The Old Vikings knew Richard well enough to present him with two individual teak garden chairs so he could talk over the day's golf (one of his many Shiplake responsibilities) or discuss the Stock Market over a beer.

In the early 1990s David Dale left the college. He had been Chaplain since the early 1980s. Towards the end of the 1980s boarding schools began to appoint Chaplains on short-term contract and since 1991 the post at Shiplake has been held by four clergymen.

David Partridge left Shiplake at the end of 1991. His particular vision had been in his response to the question 'What comes after Duke of Edinburgh Gold Awards?' His answer was a series of expeditions for the very well qualified going to Nepal or Kenya. This involved David in giving up much of his summer holiday to travel in remote places and much of his spare time to planning every detail of each enterprise. Year after year he obtained good Economics results for his 'O' and 'A' Level sets. Hockey prospered for a decade under his control and after some years as Cricket Master he continued to coach at Junior level. His Colts rugby sides were equally well drilled. David worked hard to make sure that his charges in Orchard House made the fullest possible contribution to a mainly boarding school. Orchard had a special part to play; its members were never spoken of as 'day boys'. David Partridge concluded his Shiplake years as Housemaster of Everett.

One of David's disappointments was that his subject Economics lost ground following the arrival of GCSE. It was not a core subject and was taken by fewer fifth formers. This had an impact on the number of 'A' Level candidates. David was a dominant figure on any hockey pitch and a trenchant rugby player among the forwards. In the cricket nets one could see how he helped boys solve problems in the Economics set. I was among many colleagues and senior boys who spent summer days in the Wanderers' XI, playing cricket against local clubs. Many a captain badly underestimated David's ability to increase the scoring rate in an evening run chase. He frequently plundered fifty runs when his side needed to score rapidly in those last twenty overs.

Fortunate is the headmaster who can tell an incoming housemaster 'just concentrate on two things, your timetabled subjects and getting to know your House' adding 'set aside sports and societies for the next four or five terms'. In the nature of things the staffing provision at Shiplake, though generous, did not permit housemasters to forget about their extra-curricular activities. In the 1990s, Shiplake housemasters remained in charge of major sports but they ceased to be heads of departments. This gave more scope to the Curriculum Committee to respond to academic planning without finding housemasters 'wearing two hats'

'D of E' in the Brecon Beacons, 2000

joined the governing body in 1985. Mrs Cosgrove retired in 1985 and handed over to Jim Kroth. Phil Davey strengthened the English Department and Ivan Jacklin replaced another lady, Cathleen Poole. Henry Trotter maintained the tradition of Old Boys helping out in various ways. James Blunt of the 1984 Visitors Cup crew was about to graduate from Reading University while Henry was pursuing international Rowing Honours. During the severe floods of 1987 he sculled all over the water meadows and through farm gates – something not done since the floods of 1960. In spite of the departure of outstanding players such as Ben Fitzwilliams and Charles de Lanoy Mayer, squash remained of a consistently high standard.

In 1987 Christopher Foster took charge of Geography. He proved a good listener at meetings and provided the shrewdest of comments at a time when we knew GCSE and 'A' Level 'projects' were coming. As a sailing Blue, he missed salt water and in a few years we lost him to his old school, Lancing. A neighbour, but not a rival, of ours disappeared when the Divine Mercy College closed. A few years earlier we had been envious of their connection with the sister-in-law of J.F. Kennedy.

In 1988 we survived the first Comic Relief day. This was also the year when we first became aware of 'Crack' and 'Ecstasy'. The Soviets evacuated Afghanistan and JWW and Mrs Margaret Orr organized the fourteenth successive exchange with one of Paris's rougher arrondissements.

CHAPTER 27

A New Headmaster's First Year

NICK BEVAN had rowed for Shrewsbury at Henley in 1960 – in a victorious Princess Elizabeth Cup Crew – and thirty years later was firmly established as Shiplake's fifth head, but only the third since 1963. He continued the Oxford tradition, but was a 'first' for Shiplake in three ways. His knowledge of rowing went back to his winning place in the Boat Race crew of 1963 and he was the first 'trained teacher' to be HM, having done the Cambridge Cert. Ed. after five years as an army officer. In addition, he was the first son of a schoolmaster to assume the post. Tradition has it that his father joined the Shrewsbury staff for a year and remained forty-two! Sons of schoolmasters have been fairly rare at Shiplake – DFKW and PE being two. Like his successful predecessors, Nick Bevan was a Housemaster at the time of his appointment and came with the reputation of being one of the most effective Housemasters in the country.

The Governors were not lacking in expert advice in appointing a new Headmaster. The Warden of Radley, Dennis Silk, made a considerable contribution in helping to shortlist candidates. Warden Silk had replaced Frank Fisher as our Headmaster-Governor, responding to our invitation with 'Shiplake is the kind of school I would like to be a governor of'. In due course, Dr. Jonty Driver, Master of Wellington College, replaced Dennis Silk, in turn to be succeeded by Keith Dawson.

What were boys doing that made Shiplake an interesting school to join in 1988? They were showing much maturity and more inventiveness than earlier generations – this is not to belittle the originality of earlier generations. A much larger Sixth Form contributed to variety of activity and television and the press had much more impact. During the 1960s and 1970s charity collections were very much a house matter and community service was staff led. By the 1980s the contribution of senior boys was much greater; some showed real ability in free time to work among handicapped children and staff had little to do with our participation in events like Red Nose Day – apart from saying 'Yes' when many would have rather said 'No'. Boys spoke regularly in weekday chapel and with an enlarged entry had more experience of day-to-day living with boarders who were themselves partially handicapped. Much as usual, Societies flourished or dwindled as enthusiasts came and went. Various initiatives – 'Preparation for Adult Life', – come to mind and were very much senior boy organisations. When Business Studies advanced to 'A' Level, commercial activity seemed endless. There was a stage when many boys were much more computer literate than many staff.

In bringing Nick and Annabel Bevan to Shiplake, the Governors kept to the well tried policy of a family man with good housemastering experience. Nick had been a regular army officer and an assistant master at Westminster. An exchange year in Australia, together with managing an appeal at Shrewsbury School, were further recommendations. It is by no means certain that finding a head from among housemaster applicants will continue. Under modern boarding school conditions, the job of housemaster has become more specialised and leaves little time for preparing for headship. In 1978 Peter Lapping had some formidable rivals among fellow housemasters, but candidate Housemasters a decade later were less impressive and in 1993 the strongest candidates for my position were not among housemasters. Increasingly, a house in a boarding school is a destination rather than a stepping stone. Writing as one 'who has done the state some service', there is a feeling that running a boarding school has changed as the young have altered. Four decades ago newcomers to the school were children till fifteen or more, yet at the top of a house they were young men who might be on active service 'East of Suez' fifteen months after leaving. A House had rules that established understood boundaries for twelve weeks at a time. In matters such as smoking, a housemaster was a gamekeeper and hopefully the main influence on a boy at school, especially in matters of getting the balance right between work, sport and general employment.

A new boy in the 1990s needed more help in adjusting to boarding than those with prep school years behind them. Entrants now are more concerned with weekends and parties than the hobby and pet-minded boy of 1970. Even before the Children Act, housemasters were increasingly divorce counsellors and social workers. Drink and drugs had long joined smoking as problems. Outside pressures on young people, more complex ways of supporting individuals, punishment that was remedial, all made housemasters and their spouses busier people with little time to prepare for headship. Housemastering was increasingly specialist at a time when heads were more and more busy keeping up numbers. In the 1960s one learned one's trade through frequent and informal chats with an expert like John Eggar and often imitated one's own housemaster. The once-a-month twenty-minute Housemasters Meeting of the 1960s became all break every Friday in the 1970s. The day changed as opinions varied about when was the most difficult part of the week to prepare for. If the difficulties we overcame at Shiplake were any guide elsewhere, running a boarding house alongside a demanding teaching programme was by no means an all round training for school management. At Shiplake the five houses retained individual styles of formality or otherwise. Not every boy or parent got on with his housemaster, but an extension of the tutorial system well beyond supervision of work and progress was well established before the Children Act. In a school small enough to keep in sight the really important, a housemaster who knew his boys could also be a housemaster whose returns and paper work were habitually late. As maintained schools became larger and fewer, Deputy Heads proliferated. In 1984 I was impressed by the part played by 'assistant headmasters' in Canadian independents and it was no surprise when British boarding schools began to create the post of Deputy Head later in the 1980s and to promote them to Headships in the 1990s.

The Bevans found a happy and relaxed school and the new Head was quite contented to give eighteen months to finding his feet before any in-depth discussions about new academic directions. As the first Shiplake Head able to play a musical instrument, Nick Bevan was disappointed at the lack of response to an energetic Music Department and felt that each year zest for drama had to be restarted among boys. The end of any production was greeted with relief rather than any cheerful chorus of 'splendid, what shall we do next?'

The list of things that the new Head noted for longer term consideration also included fresh objectives for Orchard House, a new pattern of chapel services involving the end of Tithe Barn services, reducing the time boys spent in the CCF and finding more time to achieve our current objectives. Partly as a consequence of earlier and earlier public exams in the summer term, the Shiplake year had become shorter in the 1980s, dropping from almost thirty-seven weeks – including Saturday teaching – to little above thirty-four. From autumn 1989 four days each were added to the September and January terms. This was not a perfect answer as the Autumn term was already overlong and the Spring term was often beset by minor epidemics.

All schoolmasters are influenced by their first teaching post and Nick Bevan had begun at Westminster in the early days of John Rae's headship. One aspect of Westminster was recognisable at Shiplake: the need to use space for a variety of events by moving furniture! At Westminster, the problem was caused by ancient buildings on a confined site. At Shiplake it was because our Great Hall continued to be cafeteria, assembly room, concert hall, debating chamber, Sunday chapel and main hospitality area. Changes from one role to another were the responsibility of the Duty House, with House tutors and Second Master giving support. The Tithe Barn and the Sports Hall were also multi-functional.

The variety of life at Shiplake was brought home to the new Head at Easter 1989. French students residing at the College decided upon night operations in the churchyard. Boredom rather than preparing for compulsory military service seemed the excuse. This rowdy event was snuffed out by an unplanned pincer movement; the Second Master coming from the direction of the school and the Headmaster emerging from Court Mead. As a former Light Infantry Officer, it was N.V. Bevan who spotted the element above in the giant cedar tree. This was the last 'Easter let' to residents as major building projects thereafter restricted letting opportunities to the months of July and August.

By his first Summer term Nick Bevan had made half-a-dozen internal appointments, found replacements for two colleagues who were leaving and kept the school full for autumn 1989. As any modern Head must, the position on drugs, drinking, smoking and theft was made clear. An isolated incident was thus summarised: on the returning train from Paddington a boy produced a packet of cannabis and rolled a cigarette in the buffet car. He was asked to leave the College, and three other boys involved were suspended for two weeks. The incident had been reported by 'an alert and responsible prefect' and proved well within the competence of someone who had been described as 'one of the country's most effective housemasters'.

The fact that 'many things are slightly disconcerting to the newcomer' may have left NVB with the feeling that events might run away with him during his first summer term. There *were* 'many things' to get used to from 'one's first Speech Day' to one hundred and twenty maths candidates in the Sports Hall. He had met the Old Boys committee and was 'committed' to welcoming up to seven hundred guests, old boys, wives and families just before the end of term. Furthermore there were the disruptions in May 1989 occasioned by rehearsals for 'Shiplake 900'. This Pageant/Commemoration of local history will be discussed in due course but having agreed to replace the end of term Summer Concert in the Sports Hall, the Head found himself faced with escalating production costs and night after night of not very successful rehearsals. Nick Bevan had come to Shiplake believing that 'Drama was the best of all team sports' and he had noted in January 1989 that 'I am led to believe that many Shiplake productions come together at the last minute'.

After the 'Shiplake 900' he was able to write 'it was a great challenge to the organisers and a great educational experience for the boys taking part. This enormous success has done us a great deal of good with the local community and I only wish it could have been more widely publicised'. In retrospect, our failure to achieve the widest publicity was due to us only realising at the last moment that this was an absolutely 'Alpha' event.

The Old Boys' Thirtieth Anniversary gathering took place during a spell of brilliant weather and Old Vikings were able to depart knowing that the College was in good hands. Certainly Nick Bevan showed his ability to welcome so many people who were new to him. The same fine weather continued for the best run Shiplake has yet enjoyed at Henley Royal Regatta and the narrow defeat in the final of The Princess Elizabeth Cup owed something to the Head's part-time coaching.

Shiplake Summer term continued into the vacation with CCF camps and treks in another continent. In September 1989, the Head paid tribute to the meticulous planning by D.S. Partridge of the Chulu East expedition to Nepal, when twenty-two boys had a testing month, 'an experience they will never forget, never wish to have missed, but which they will never want to repeat'. When Nick Bevan also described a modern corps camp as 'far removed from the unpleasant experience of his youth', one wonders if some of his words were selected with relief as describing his own opening year at Shiplake College.

CHAPTER 28

Centenaries and Commemorations

THE DATES 1889 and 1891 appear at various places on the facades of the late Victorian Shiplake Court. So, the centenary of the Victorian mansion was the starting point of the 1989 pageant 'Shiplake 900'. It was possible to capture some of the certainties of a century ago, but some of the Victorian attitudes inherent in the style of the 19th century mansions could not be brought back to life via *Son et Lumière.* Shiplake Court shows a desire for privacy. An inconspicuous Lodge is at the start of a long drive. Trees provide seclusion and shelter from the English weather. Large windows admit what little sun there will be. Internally Victorian mansions are much alike. The continental system of communicating doors was disliked in England – though the early nineteenth-century Shiplake House had them. The large fireplace is the focal point of private rooms in Shiplake Court. A business room near the front door meant that callers who were not personal visitors were kept from the inner house. When there were no guests, the man of the house was to be found in his library. From a drawing room the lady of the house controlled her staff and here guests assembled for dinner. Best clothes were a ticket of admission for children's hour in the drawing room. At Shiplake Court a two-by-two processional route from drawing room to dining room is still obvious. The dining room is close (the present staff room) to the domestic wing. The Great Hall never had a real purpose in a private home. Imitations of minstrels galleries and mediaeval roof trusses aroused scorn as a two-story waste of space – even from their architects.

The English attitude to food and children perplexed foreigners – roast beef and mutton alternately throughout the year and visitors could stay and go without realising there were children in the house. The Nursery at Shiplake Court was in the present sick wing and adjacent bedrooms.

Some nineteenth century rooms at Shiplake Court have been lost through reconstruction. The billiard room – a male refuge from boredom and rain – is divided between the servery and staffroom cloaks. The butler's plate room and the housekeeper's rooms are now part of the kitchens. However, the servants' hall and the wine cellar are still identifiable. A cynical schoolboy might feel that

Malcolm Woodcock – devising his next musical extravaganza

the spirit of the place has not changed. The unvarying routine for inmates and servants, and the status-dominated regime, continue in the clockwork punctuality of school routine. In the same manner there was a routine of feeding, grooming and watering in the magnificently appointed stables – with obligatory courtyard – dominated by a clock tower which we have imitated atop the Pavilion roof.

Some of this Victorian and earlier detachment could be recreated in a spoken prologue to the open air performance, but our real scope was to be found in the comings and goings of Englefields and Plowdens, Jennings and Harrisons and our stage was the ground they once owned. I took on the task of drafting scenes based on written sources and Malcolm Woodcock quite rightly felt that if we started with one national event we could invoke others by using themes associated with Falstaff, Alan Bennett and Noel Coward. Malcolm chose the music, with one exception, and elected to stage the most recent centuries on the front terrace, having set the bulk of the performance in the courtyard. His brief to a professional sound and lighting expert did make this production 'Woodcock's finest hour'.

From the Harrison family arriving at the new Shiplake Court via conflicts with the Abbot of Missenden and the 'siege of Basing House' – transported to Shiplake in 1644 – we sat from dusk into night. *Son et lumière* and the spoken word brought us via the Edwardian era and the family heir killed in action, to the BBC's Second World War use of Shiplake Court. With the centre of London only thirty-seven miles away and the blitz then within sight and sound, the terrors of the time were recreated in light and fury.

With the arrival of a new school in 1959, the final big scene had to be with the boys of 1989. I was quite convinced that 'West Side Story' – a London hit in 1959 – said something about the world of young people to the young people of every generation. Sondheim and Bernstein's 'Gee Officer Krupke' made for a perfect dance routine. Lines dealing with drugs and human degradation were a little controversial, but sheer youthful vigour was the perfect antidote to emotions built up in previous scenes and put the Sixth Form centre stage at the end of a long evening.

Teamwork was tremendous during performances after erratic progress in rehearsal and not infrequent crises. The courtyard had been made safe for cavalry by a last minute decision to scatter tons of oak chippings on the tarmac. Borrowed horses were inclined to stray, a vintage car ran on time, borrowed costumes and weapons eventually got back to owners and the school went to bed at 2 a.m. more than once during this time.

Years later, when confronted with sixteenth and seventeenth century portraits at Plowden Hall, one suddenly realised how successful 'Shiplake 900' had been. Somehow Shiplake's past – the very spirit of the place – had put the breath of life into our enthusiastic efforts. After three decades we had truly related to our ancient home.

CHAPTER 29

Pressure and Resources

JOHN EGGAR argued that the most disappointing of academic reports should offer some hope of improvement. Most boys felt that things got better during their years at Shiplake, thus more buildings and improved facilities made sticking it out worthwhile. The Boat Club had a pioneering spirit, and a combination of DIY, fund raising and parental gifts hastened expansion beyond the annual funding from the Governors. In the early days of computers, expansion depended on the ingenuity and the scrounging skills of staff as well as upon ability to get value for money. However, in many areas young staff were in much the same situation as boys; there was the hope that facilities would gradually improve as money became available.

Wisely, Nick Bevan chose to open a debate about future building by asking 'what ought we to build next?' The consensus was substantial. The next development should be academic, geared to the next century, should deal with the demands of the new examinations and hopefully bring Design and Technology, Computing and Art closer together. The case for bringing Maths teaching and Physics into the plans was strongly urged.

Hopes were turned into reality between 1988 and 1990, when the Goodwin Building was opened and named after Aubrey Goodwin. He had been a Governor from the outset and was Chairman from the late 1970s and through the 1980s. While his death marked the end of an era, his name is commemorated in an ambitious scheme, entirely forward-looking, ample in provision and not part of an existing structure.

The development owed much to the architects. This was their third major project at Shiplake and repeated the style and design that had already worked (use of roof spaces, similar materials and external stairs) and had gained the approval of South Oxfordshire planners. The main architect, Andy Nicols, argued that a scheme costing £1.2 millions should contribute to first impressions of Shiplake. For twenty-five years potential parents had driven past a long brick wall before they saw anything of merit. To our surprise, the Berlin Wall's demolition was followed by the demise of the sacred wall that planners had insisted on preserving. Half of it was swept away and the Goodwin Building stands astride it. The condition of planning approval was that the timber Cricket Pavilion and garden sheds should be redeveloped in similar style as soon as possible.

The architect also advised the retention of the Maths Block in a new role as the home of Art and Ceramics. The Examinations Office was retained, ample storage provided, work areas for both painting and pottery opened out and an exhibition gallery added to the frontage. All this cost an unintended £70,000 above the budget for the Goodwin Building. The former home of Arts and Ceramics was taken over by the English Department. They found the former Technical Drawing Office in good order but were warned in 1991 that there was no money for modernising other spaces! Five maths rooms had cost £10,000 in 1971. Ten years later the one Technical Drawing Room alone absorbed £10,000.

The completed Goodwin Building offered several improvements beyond its obvious brief. There was space for ground staff to maintain equipment as well as to store it. The roof space contained the usual flat and offered further ample storage space. In earlier decades the problem always was 'If we buy it, where can it be safely stored?'

While the Goodwin expansion was the start of a new era, some staff who had waited so long for modern facilities, enjoyed them briefly and then retired. One or two who had kept subjects going to 'O' Level moved on when we began to offer their subjects at 'A' Level. Parents often mentioned that their warmest welcome was in the Art School or in the Drawing Office and JLJ and BB continued to break off teaching and explain to visitors what was going on until retirement caught up with them in the mid-1990s.

Nick Bevan hoped that every member of staff would have his or her own classroom by 1992. Ironically, the Second Master then offered to give up his large and draughty Room Six. This had been a History room for twenty years after an earlier life as a two-storey loose box, Chemistry lab, and tiered lecture theatre. It was converted to a Careers Centre with two offices, study area and library/gallery. Back in the 1970s when the Sixth Form was small, this room was cramped enough and sordid enough to be a dance hall with the Barn used for sitting out and refreshments!

Nineteen eighty-four had not turned out to be the year of George Orwell's Big Brother, but the end of the school year on July 6th showed that the monster of the exam-dominated summer term truly had taken over. In 1960 the Shiplake Summer Term had ended on July 28th – the last Thursday of the month – while in 1998 the chosen date was the 1st July! There are a few schoolmasters still active who may recall teaching all through the hot July of 1959 and rather more who paced the classroom in the blazing July of 1969. Even in the early 1970s, public examinations ending earlier in the summer created the problem of what to do later. 'A' Levels which once began around June 18th – prompting jests about candidates meeting their Waterloo – now start almost three weeks earlier.

What has been lost remains a problem for most schools but has become a distant recollection for parents and lies beyond the memory of many of those who teach. What standards of tennis and cricket might some of Shiplake's gifted players have reached in a season spread over three months? A day at Wimbledon was once easily fitted into a summer programme. A tennis tournament for staff, families and boys, all day cricket fixtures, CCF camp during the last week of term, and even time to watch home fixtures are now memories of a distant past.

There are other elements to these changes. By June in any year all involved in a boarding school are weighed down by burdens reaching back to the very long Autumn term spread over four months. Sixth Forms are larger and it was much easier to manage a house of forty-three than it is to keep up with a house of sixty plus – thirty of whom have little to do after public exams confined to June. The proliferation of exams and the growth of Sixth Form numbers have contributed to increased problems in what used to be the best term of the year. At the same time, the ways in which young people expect to use their leisure time at weekends make it hard to resume a school routine on any Monday morning and almost impossible to return to any kind of routine after the public exam break. It is only rowing crews who keep up their training pattern to the end of the school year. Perhaps this is why their out-of-class activity is still as successful as we think cricket and tennis used to be.

It seems impossible to make a sensible mnemonic from the main secondary school issues of the 1990s. CABQP covers Curriculum, Atmosphere, Behaviour, Quality and Provision. The nature of the curriculum required some decisions by Nick Bevan in his early days. David Welsh took charge of examining all ways in which Shiplake should respond to GCSE and core curriculum issues. At Shiplake, these issues were dubbed the 'Baker-Welsh' proposals in ironic tribute to a not very popular Secretary of State.

GCSE brought to an end a long-standing problem at Shiplake – a division between first time 'O' Level success and those repeating some subjects. Indeed we had several very successful nineteen year-old 'A' Level students who had postponed some 'O' Level subjects for one or three terms after the age of 16. Once GCSE arrived, the demand for repeats in anything other than English and Maths just faded away. Almost everyone undertook some 'A' Level work, especially in Media Studies and Design-related subjects. As GCSE was an examination for everyone at sixteen, it was not possible for some departments to postpone a first entry until after the Fifth Form. Every member of a set was entitled an attempt.

The pleasant atmosphere at Shiplake was one of the things that had attracted the Bevan family to the College and while the behaviour of the boys was impressive, the new Head felt there was more need for prefect training and he doubted the wisdom of an unselective system of boy guides for visitors.

I was confident of the all-round strength of the staff in 1988, but a new Head will see uneven performances more clearly. From the position in prep schools we all knew that a 'shortage' of boarders was impending and parents would expect value for money when they had a choice of places at six schools. There could be a gap between a teacher's quality and his ability to teach a new or much changed GCSE subject. The provision for Arts, Drama, Music and Sport would be clear to any parent looking at the 'termly calendar'. Shiplake is almost perfect for outdoor drama, but other facilities varied from good – the Sports Hall complex; to interesting – the Tithe Barn; to doubtful – visitors' changing rooms. How CABQP issues were tackled during the 1990s is a long story.

As already mentioned an area in which 1990s caution did not apply was in outdoor summer productions. The embargo on major outdoor events lasted over twenty years and through the 1970s and 1980s little happened that cut across the public exam term. The 1979 River Pageant was rehearsed after 'O' and 'A' Levels and Jesus Christ Superstar performed at the end of May 1984– in Jubilee Year – and tried very hard to be a Lower Sixth and Junior form production. No one thought that staff rehearsals and performances would affect their performance in the classroom. The energy of Malcolm Woodcock, his production team and the whole school went into end of year Summer Concerts in the Sports Hall – every boy was in the Orchestra or in the massed choir until 1988.

The May 1989 'Shiplake 900' had much the same effect on Shiplake summer terms as the fall of the Iron Curtain and a series of Summer Spectaculars followed the public examinations season, using the front of the school or the lawns above the Thames or the Stable Yard. While this revived memories of the early 1960s some were left feeling that every other year might be better. Since 1990 there has been an unlimited commitment from all concerned and much less dependence on staff to play leading parts.

After coping with the very expensive 'Shiplake 900', the Bursar quickly dubbed each summer production 'another Malcolm Extravaganza' partly because each production almost deprived him of the aid of the Domestic Bursar, Mrs Elizabeth Cooke. One might say that the summer production began the busiest part of the year for Mrs Cooke, as she bore the main burden of dealing with summer holiday tenants which was soon followed by supervising preparation of the school for the Autumn term after some or another major building project came to an end.

Alongside Malcolm, several generations will remember the persuasive Mrs Marjorie White, who came early in retirement to help in the English Department and has remained in a multiplicity of roles for over fifteen years. Few people can have found such an active retirement one mile's cycling from home.

Coming at the very end of term, post exam productions have been somewhat neglected in *The Court* magazine. The 1990 revival of 'Jesus Christ Superstar' is not mentioned at all. This production featured a very original interpretation of Herod Antipas by Ivan Jacklin and a further revival in 1995 saw his son, Seymour, in the same role. In 1990 and 1995 the part of Christ had been played by senior boys, whereas in 1984 the key roles had mainly been given to members of staff. One particularly remembers in 1984, the five tallest members of the Common Room being cast as High Priests – excessive headgear emphasised the whimsy of Malcolm Woodcock as producer. Summer productions with a substantial musical element got the success they deserved and the 1995 'Superstar' production in particular caught the imagination of everyone involved.

Many older readers know what it is like to have a much-loved grandparent's rambling home demolished and the large garden covered with 'town houses'. It comes as a shock when bulldozing a slope means you cannot even recognise a once familiar landscape. Some changes bring a wry smile ... 'would you credit it, there are girls where we used to be as third formers!' New buildings and adaptation to new uses are as inevitable as is the gradual retirement of long serving staff. Since 1987 other familiar reference points have been moved. For a long while, Common Entrance papers looked just as they had in 1960. To an older generation 'O' Levels and Advanced work in the Sixth was just a variation. 'School Certificate' and 'Highers' and CSE was the part of the examination system that needed some explanation. GCSE, the National Curriculum and a range of fresh subjects at 'A' Level, with a move away from long examination papers as the sole form of assessment, all mean that parents have become strangers in a 13 – 18 world, just as Shiplake Old Boys find themselves semi-lost among our new buildings.

In the Silver Jubilee photograph of May 1st 1984, there were fourteen members of staff appointed by Peter Lapping and eight who had known the school in the 1960s. When he retired in 1998, David Welsh was the last representative of the 1960s and, thus, of the survivors of a solid core of masters appointed by John Eggar. Peter Hose, Malcolm Woodcock and Peter Webb became the senior group. Looking remarkably youthful in 1984, 'Dick' Whittington and Brian Burgess have retired. Ian Lowry and Mark Hayter have been promoted elsewhere and Richard Mannix together with Peter Gould are housemasters of some standing. The sad fact is that anyone who left Shiplake before 1974 will come back and find no one he knew then. However, Bob Esau, as Old Vikings' Secretary, was always about the place and has met most of those who have come to Shiplake since 1965. In terms of gathering news of Old Vikings, he was one of the most successful of secretaries until retirement in 2000.

While it was always clear that the 1990s would see the retirement of several who had spent most of their working lives at Shiplake, there were other unexpected reasons for change, especially shortages in some subjects, and redundancy. Traditionally, any Arts vacancy produced a flood of graduate applicants, but suddenly the flood of applicants in many departments dried up and Shiplake lost well qualified youngsters in promotion moves. Furthermore, the opportunities to coach on the Thames was no longer attractive enough set against high property costs forty miles west of London.

Expansion at Shiplake had tended to ignore staffing costs, especially in the time of small sixth form sets. If there was a demand for a subject, someone to teach it was found and a fresh examination subject appeared in the timetable the following September. Much of this was paid for by the school being very full, at around 330. No one wanted to drop back to a less crowded 300. Anyone who wanted to attempt 'A' Levels was allowed to stay and newcomers at post 'O' Level were welcome. These sometimes disguised the entry figures of those who came at thirteen and stayed five years. However, in the 1990s numbers did drop to 315 and then to below 300, and some retiring staff were not replaced.

Nick Bevan never doubted that Shiplake gave value for money, but in the difficult early 1990s he felt that we must provide full value for fees paid. In this, he had the full support of the Bursar and the expertise of the governing body in making difficult decisions. Suitability to teach new or much altered GCSE and 'A' Level subjects had to be the main consideration and three or four established members of staff, with the help of their employers, stepped aside and took some form of early retirement. These adjustments were spread over several years and were part of a new realism which included the future of successful subjects such as Economics and the decision that Classical History would not continue after the retirement of David Welsh. Another kind of 1990s realism is considered elsewhere: our inability to sustain the very strong fixture lists which the Rugby and Cricket Clubs had built up in the 1980s and which were affected by a smaller Shiplake coinciding with changes in admissions policies at rival schools.

CHAPTER 30

Change and Routine

IN MANY WAYS the new buildings of the 1990s speak for themselves, a continuing style, involving matching the original 1889 mansion's plum-coloured brick and tile, plus timber gables with dormer windows to use fully every roof space. As a result, Orchard has been rehoused and Everett remodelled with administration taking over the ground floor of the 1962 Everett. The Pavilion provided long-needed visitors' changing rooms and the large multi-purpose Alan Massey room. Maths, Physics, Design and Technology – at home in the Goodwin Building since 1991 – will be joined by other subjects following improvements to the early 1980s Chemistry and Biology laboratories. Soon the John Eggar Sports Hall will be almost the sole reminder of an earlier dependence on prefabricated structures.

Aubrey Goodwin had been a Governor from the very early days and there were few aspects of his work – especially as Chairman of the Board – that were unknown to his widow. The opening ceremony in September 1990 of the Goodwin Building revealed Mrs Goodwin as the most adept of open air speakers. Her charm and humour made many of the assembled donors to the Appeal even more pleased that they had contributed.

Mr Edwin Hatchett opened the Administrative Wing in September 1992. From his riverside home at Lower Shiplake, he had been an on-the-spot adviser to three Headmasters and was now stepping down as Vice Chairman. The official opening, on the same evening as that of the reconstructed Everett, was entrusted to me, as its longest serving former Housemaster. He pointed out to the Bursar that the old house had been a real bargain in 1992 terms. The twice-extended Everett had cost a mere £42,000 – including £25,000 in 1962 when the pound was really strong. Over twenty-eight years, the capital cost had been £100 per boarder.

In 1965, John Eggar had persuaded Lord Cobham, a Shiplake parent, sometime Worcestershire Captain and ex-Governor General of New Zealand, to open the original Pavilion. Thirty years later it was John's eldest son, Tim Eggar, Privy councillor, MP and Minister of the Crown, who opened a far more

The new top floor for Everett taking shape

elaborate new Pavilion. The proceedings were more cheerful than the weather. The First XI defeated the Old Boys and Welsh House had a gathering to mark thirty years of activity.

The new Orchard House was completed shortly after the Pavilion and more than any other shows, step by step, progress in five years at Shiplake. With proper provision for day students becoming an issue for many boarding schools, Orchard was, for the moment, the last word in what parents, boys and Housemasters looked for and became 'the cynosure of neighbouring eyes'. As is sometimes the case, gain is accompanied by loss. Alan Massey, a parent Governor, had directed the Pavilion/Orchard Appeal until his sudden death, so the Orchard opening ceremony was entrusted to Mrs Merrill Massey, and a splendid upper chamber in the Pavilion was named the Alan Massey Room.

From such a close perspective, one cannot lay down what the future observer may think, but the 1990s are already a decade when Shiplake College became physically unfamiliar to those here in the first twenty-five years and, by 1998, became a school without any of the faces familiar to pupils from the 1960s. The familiar landmarks were almost dwarfed by new buildings. In some ways the routines endured longer than the early staff or the temporary buildings. Until the mid-1980s, parents and pupils could feel they had shared the same public examination experience. GCSE has changed all that and times at Shiplake – much the same for three decades – are not what they were. An Old Boy driving along the A4155 thinking 'it must be break, I'll drop in' might just be lucky, but he would struggle to recognise the rest of the day. Even more would he be surprised at the changed Shiplake Sunday. Saturday school may be the next thing to adjust to rapid change. Retired staff would have the same feelings of lack of recognition and we must now examine these in more detail.

In 1989 Miss Monica Tomalin completed thirty years of service. Her ability to put a name and a House to every face was legendary. While 'revenants' did not know the present Head, they did know 'Miss T' and she was always about the place during vacations. (During the 1980s, summer vacation visitors often found J.W. 'Dick' Whittington on site, planning careers programmes or restoring the Tithe Barn.) In term-time David Welsh, Bob Esau and I were known to those here before 1975, even if not as swift as Miss Tomalin to feed career news to the OVS Newsletter. Between 1994 and 1998, the last of the founding decade all retired, but the very early days are still represented on the Governing Body by Old Boys: John Turner, who entered in September 1959, and Richard Lester who came four years later.

From slow beginnings in 1985, teaching space doubled by 1991. However, during the 1990s most Arts subjects were still taught in the Stable Block. Here the hastily created rooms of the 1960s were a link with our early years. The fortieth anniversary developments will remove History, Geography and Modern Languages from their 1960s location and leave the Stable Block to English, Learning Support, Media and Business Studies and Careers. No doubt some of the late Victorian woodwork that caught the eyes of inattentive school boys in the past, will be torn out and the Stable Yard will be less busy, as indeed the Victorian mansion itself is. With the migration of reception and offices to the ground floor of what is now a three storey Everett, the main building has been left to Skipwith, Sick Bay and the caterers, with the Clerk of Works hanging on in one corner. In this far bigger school, signposting has come into its own.

The use of the terms new and old in education is dangerous. Fresh subjects are in the timetable in the Sixth Form and traditional ones are giving ground. Indeed how ambiguous has the word traditional become! Talking of 'new' public examinations had a limited value even in the 1987 transition period. The pupils had not taken any other exams – changes were new only to parents, subject teachers and examiners.

While those who retired in the 1980s would approve of public exams probing what pupils can do, they would be surprised by how structured everything now is – not only within departments, but between them. Through the 1960s and 1970s, we stressed 'no set is larger than sixteen and a boy may be in a top set for one subject and in a lower one for others'. Opting for subjects created larger sets even before a sixteen maximum size became very expensive. In History, two sets began a four-term course towards 'O' Level but rarely kept pace with each other. A third set began perhaps a five or eight-term course in a more straightforward Social and Economic History. With a national examination for all at sixteen, all must show knowledge of the same prescribed material and all emerge with internally moderated coursework completed at the same agreed date. It is now vital that departments cooperate to spread completion dates between different subjects over several months. In 1998 we found out that the Directors of Studies in other HMC schools had considerable powers to prevent boys having to complete six assessments in the last six weeks of a Spring term.

Former staff and Old Boys would, until recently, have found daily times much as before. Some adjustments were made ten years ago to introduce many more double periods below the Sixth Form. These were needed for coursework as well as in the Science laboratories. Several factors have recently brought about the biggest changes since 1960. The Head felt boys were ready for chapel and assemblies well before 8.40 a.m.. Was there a fifteen minute slot that could permit the start of teaching well before 9 a.m.? Earlier lunches would help away teams and the winter routine of classes starting at 4 p.m. was most unpopular. There was a further anomaly – Thursday afternoon had long since ceased to be used for inter-school fixtures, but had survived as a Shiplake half day. The answer to these issues is now an eight period day and a much better use of late afternoons and evenings. Preps, periods nine and ten for the Sixth, Utility Time, Music and Drama rehearsals take place in a slot before supper or after 7.05 p.m. The official working day ends at 9.05 p.m., much as it ever did!

Out of class, Old Boys would notice other changes. Schools show less interest in playing Squash, we now have the use of pitches on the large field below the boat houses, an ex-soldier is no longer employed to run CCF Admin, and the shop manager is no longer a part-time member of the teaching staff. Credit items in the shop are at the Manager's discretion. The Housemaster's 'chit' – 'do you really need this? have you checked with your parents?' – is a thing of the past.

It was clear from the earliest days that flexibility was a Shiplake strength, and this continued willingness to adapt swiftly to problems has been valuable in the 1990s. In so far as an extended Housemasters' meeting is the senior management team (only Malcolm Woodcock was a long standing member before 1990), so it is a fresh team that has adapted to circumstances that may change again. As a result, Houses vary more than previously. Burr is fully boarding – with an international flavour – Welsh works in close liaison with Orchard and the Lodge accommodates Sixth Form 'day girls'.

Any school career has a framework of routine in which the remarkable can become central – especially when well recorded in *The Court* magazine. The Easter holiday was always one in which to be proud of the forty per cent of pupils who were away on staff-managed expeditions, and a number were inevitably engaged in fund raising for ambitious summer holiday or gap year ventures outside Europe. In spite of school fee increases, parents, more than ever, seem willing to support holiday events in which schoolmates want to participate. Ease of travel and greater affluence have an impact, because one remembers, a life time ago, spending holidays earning money for optional equipment for voluntary events for the next term ... not the next vacation.

The concept of a duty week for staff and Houses was rooted in a wish to know 'what was what' for the next seven days, in which Sunday differed only through no teaching, a major Sunday Service and school suits for half the day. A hectic week of special events could turn a House and its tutors into a task force, dealing with anything from an early breakfast to late night furniture moving after a conference. Reform of this enduring set-up means that full boarding houses share the weekends between them, assisted and encouraged by staff whose other responsibilities make a full week's duty very difficult. Each House is on duty the same day each week and the duty week for staff runs from Monday to Saturday.

It is a relief to pupils when their opinions are heard and encouraging when their suggestions bring improvement. The Games Committee, well over thirty years old, was one of the first to involve senior boys. The Chapel Committee was less well known but has been vigorously revived by Robert Prance and meetings between Bursar and Catering Manager on the one hand, and House representatives on the other, improved when the minutes of regular meetings were published.

A School Council, inaugurated in 1997, stresses communication, awareness and suggestions from all year groups. The Head of College and his deputy are Chairman and Secretary of this council of twenty elected members. The Headmaster or his representative is in attendance. The brief is to look for better ways of doing things, rather than to attack the unpopular.

CHAPTER 31

Progress, Preservation and Confidence Building

THE BACKGROUND to the Bevan family's early days at Shiplake were the two years of momentous change in Eastern Europe when the Berlin Wall was breached and one-party systems were abandoned. The early months of 1991 saw several Old Boys on active service in the Gulf including Julian Buck, head prefect in 1987-88. The autumn term of September 1991 began against the background of Yeltsin defying the Soviet Old Guard from the top of a tank. The background to Shiplake's first thirty years was the Cold War. By contrast, the secure progress of Shiplake College emphasises how fortunate we have been and how manageable have been our difficulties.

The Welsh House Appeal ended in the autumn of 1988. Bob Esau had directed it, and his committee was, in the main, composed of parents and well-wishers. Once again current parents were the main donors with a little support from Old Vikings. Only the most local of industrial or commercial concerns were likely sources of aid and an invitation to parents from the 1960s – 'just to come and look at us once more' – faltered through fears of being asked for money. The extension to Welsh House had been officially opened by David himself at a pleasant Sunday evening gathering of parents and Old Boys. No one deserves more to have his name inscribed in stone near the centre of his endeavours.

The school year 1988–89 was not wholly low-key. The all weather pitch/tennis courts came into use and the two Harrison Cottages meant more resident staff. The acquisition of a cottage across the main road, our third property there, produced jokes about the A4155 going through the College. Lady members of staff began a campaign to make the Library more user-friendly and a wide range of magazines was introduced while senior boys took charge of all involvement in the innovative 'Red Nose Day'. Two December events came under scrutiny in 1988: they were the Christmas dinners and the mass exodus to Twickenham for the Oxford and Cambridge rugby match.

By 1970 two Christmas dinners of equal size had become necessary and with the growth of a fifth House – Orchard – one of the dinners required an overflow into the Skipwith day room. Houses held some kind of party on the evening when they did not dine. In 1989 all was changed. Every House had a party, supported from the catering department, and Houses in rotation could have a more formal event in the Great Hall. A turkey and 'pud' buffet lunch was provided for all on the last full day of term. A more united celebration was then planned for the last evening of the academic year. The 1988 Marquee Dinner had been thought of as a once-only farewell to the Lappings, but it had proved possible to sit every pupil together with academic staff, wives and matrons for a three-course meal and have the tent ready for Speech Day twelve hours later. Arrangements used in the early 1990s have stood the test of time. Nick Bevan moved the presentations formerly associated with an end of term assembly to the Marquee Dinner. At first these end of year dinners were complicated by senior boys having to get back from work experience, or from the Henley Regatta, but dates and times have changed.

A Varsity match expedition had somehow grown from a privilege for First and Second XV's to a mass jaunt for anyone who had played for any rugby team. This sporting occasion had been a good introduction for boys to a national institution. One went for many years before the concept of 'corporate entertainment' produced a game where watching the first ten minutes of play was spoiled by numerous late-comers who were not infrequently also semi-intoxicated and who barged to and fro during and after half time – their need for the public lavatories being greater than any consideration for those intent upon eighty minutes of rugby football! Increasingly one sensed that the Varsity match was no longer worth attending – at first our party was much reduced in size and now this event no longer figures in the end of term calendar.

Dermot Cowper proved an excellent motivator as cricket captain in 1989 – playing under him was the 1988 skipper, Tim Wilson, who had decided that 'A' Levels came first. Peter Lapping was convinced that the fully committed could combine good 'A' Level work with being in the First VIII, which was an issue that arose again in the 1990s. It is a particular problem for a rowing coach who has candidates who must get A grades! Tim Wilson later became an outstandingly successful junior master at Pickering College, Ontario 1989–90 and subsequently became a schoolmaster. He felt that pressure to get results on the cricket field was less important than success in the examination hall. He personally proved his point, obtaining a First (with distinction) in Mathematics while at Newcastle University. Colleagues, parents and Old Boys will see something of their own need to adjust to the situation that he faced a decade ago.

James Welsh (just senior in Orchard to Tim Wilson and the son of DFKW) spent a VSO year teaching English in Indonesia – his adjustment being to work in third world conditions far removed from the prosperity of the Thames Valley. He was one of very few to provide much feedback to others planning a gap year.

If the only way to understand a country is to live in it, Shiplake's contribution to international awareness is an improving one. We have always had boarders from every continent and gap-year schemes for sixth form leavers have been well used. Senior boys from Germany and France have been good value as boarders, but only since our financial position became stronger in the 1980s have we created significant opportunities for young Australians, Canadians and Americans to be working members of the Senior Common Room.

Nine Shiplake leavers have spent a year as junior masters at Pickering College, Ontario. Reports from Canada made clear that our 'volunteers' showed great maturity and were willing to do anything asked. Two monitoring visits by me showed that a school with a Quaker tradition found aptitudes in our young men that we had not been able to spot during their years at Shiplake. In return, Pickering sent us, after their university courses, Oliver Gomes for a year and Chris Campbell for three!

Nick Bevan came from Shrewsbury with experience of Harvard Fellowships and several able graduates from Princeton came to Shiplake from 1990. American Studies gained immensely and rowing men proved their value. However, experience has shown that Australian exchanges, starting in January, bring us oarsmen for two terms and rugby coaches during their final term.

James Johnson, in charge of Art from 1981, provided a permanent Australian presence. Christopher Taylor, from Canberra Grammar School, demonstrated the potential of the Australian school leaver in 1988. His scholarship, confidence, tact, charm, delicate batsmanship and rugby coaching set standards that were hard to follow. A decade later, *The Court* magazine spoke of 'an Australian contingent', a combination of gap year school leavers and two year Sports Fellows, which has proved successful. There is little doubt that pupils between thirteen and eighteen respond well to overseas helpers who are not much older than them.

Unfortunately, economic circumstances forced Pickering College to change from a senior boys' boarding school to an all age co-educational enterprise where boarding was less important. The contribution our leavers could make there was much reduced. As a consequence, our junior masters had to be replaced by mature students who were trainee teachers. One hopes that Shiplake will never have to transmute to such an extent.

In 1989 our ceramics expert, Angela Drinkwater-Lunn, was promoted to take charge of Art at Queen Anne's, Caversham. Angela's move foreshadowed several departures of personalities, who had been pivotal during the eighties. Many liked the place; certainly they liked the boys, but felt the need to move on.

The choice was so often between the convenient and a challenge elsewhere. In due course, Angela's move was followed by Mark Hayter departing to Monmouth and Ian Lowry to a prep school Deputy Headship. He remained based in Caversham and became a Shiplake parent instead of common room all-rounder.

The last days of summer term 1989 belonged to the hot weather and to the Boat Club. The lawns at Shiplake were parched brown by hot days and absence of rain. Seven hundred Old Vikings and their families celebrated thirty years of College history in what was almost a drought and the conditions at Henley were exceptional. A German crew lowered the record time for the Grand Challenge Cup final to under six minutes.

Henley finals on the Sunday coincided with our Speech Day, so many families went directly from College into Henley. The Guest of Honour, Colin Moynihan, had given some advice to oarsmen before presenting the prizes. Generally, the Shiplake community was in the best of spirits, even after we lost to Hampton in the Princess Elizabeth Cup. From the Buckinghamshire bank two things stand out in memory: the tremendous roar of support as the two schoolboy crews reached the Stewards' Enclosure and the surge of supporters leaving their seats in the enclosure to applaud our young men as they came back to the landing stage. Shiplake crews – being so very local – have always attracted otherwise neutral spectators and the nine Hampton Schoolboys must have felt somewhat alone as scores of Shiplake mothers and fathers consoled our crew after their near success.

The final that day was emotionally draining for everyone involved with Shiplake College and even now the disappointment of coaches and crew can easily be understood – especially as the opportunity to get so close again would be denied to those coaches of the 1980s: Mark Hayter, John Scottorn, Ian Lowry, and Nick Dunlop.

The First XV dominated the autumn of 1989, winning fourteen out of sixteen fixtures and taking the Oxfordshire Cup. In a tense and scrappy final we defeated the local Sixth Form College – vastly larger in numbers. The Under Fifteens drew their County Final at home, so Radley took the Cup under the away rule.

The 1990s were blown in by another great storm – this one on January 25th was in daylight so the full fury of nature could be seen. The College and our neighbours at Shiplake House lost many more mature trees than in 1987 and the devastation on the higher ground around Crowsley Park knocked out electricity and telephone services in parts of Shiplake parish.

Some planned moves were in preparation. Peter Hose would hand over Orchard House to Richard Mannix, 'Dick' Whittington would relinquish the direction of Modern Languages and Viv Daly would replace Richard Lee when he retired as Head of Science. Among the notable arrivals would be Dr. 'Bob' Snellgrove who, in no time at all, found himself starting one of those invaluable and difficult jobs – running the Second XI for cricket and hockey for a decade.

Dan Richards played three times at prop for England Under Eighteens (in 1999, James Bailey was selected for the England Under Sixteen XV, appearing as a wing three-quarter) and missed a fourth cap through illness. He proved himself a popular and respected member of the team. A number of Old Boys who had played with him were in the match crowds. Ben Hunt-Davies continued to make exceptional rowing progress in the Boat Club, eventually making it to the Barcelona, Atlanta and Sydney Olympics memorably winning a gold medal in the British VIII. One has memories of him vaulting an eight-foot high fence to help cricketers look for a ball.

The last term of the 1980s saw the start of work on the Goodwin Building, ushering in five years of disruption as the £3 million plus schemes were completed between 1990 and 1995. Those in Everett and Orchard were left feeling there were only two seasons – vacation and construction.

Naturally, the early 1990s at Shiplake had affinities with the late eighties – especially in terms of expeditions, charity contributions and public relations. The Trekking Society had mounted a Thirtieth Anniversary Expedition that spent four weeks in the Annapurna region, but this was the last occasion when Nepal and the world's highest mountains beckoned. Large parties went to Kenya in 1990 and to Venezuela in 1991. Kenya was again the destination in 1992. Our summer holiday was not the best time for high altitude walking south of the Himalayan summits and the skills needed to complete plans and foster discipline, endurance, team work and patience could be deployed in less remote parts of the world with more variety of scenery and opportunities for wildlife study. Expeditions to Kenya, a country with problems of balancing the needs of population against the preservation of the animal kingdom, have led on to permanent commitments, so Shiplake does still hear Africa calling.

Red Nose Day in 1989 raised £1,001 on a day when the Governors met at the school. During this charitable day, much genuine fun was had, no one overstepped the mark and we seemed to have more skilled mimics of staff than at any time since the 1970s. Green issues were voiced in 1989 in *The Court* magazine and for some years Burr took the lead in our recycling policy. In the early 1990s we found more practical opportunities to help with handicapped young people than for some time past and there was an attempt to find new ways of raising money for good causes. Eight J16 oarsmen took it in turns to row a sponsored Four from Oxford to Putney and there were 'Dogathons' in 1990 and 1992. Here the idea was to involve parents in fund raising on a Sunday in March. Pupils could show off their pets who were the sponsored walkers. Each time some £3,000 was raised, in 1990 for our local Centre at Dyson's Wood, for salmon ladders at Shiplake Lock and at Sonning (now in place) and in 1992 for the Alzheimer's Disease Society and the Battersea Dogs' Home. The money raised from the J16 row went to the British Heart Foundation. The sponsored dog walks took the easy route – six miles along the Thames to Aston and then back upstream to the College. However, the police were worried by the notion of some two hundred walkers and eighty dogs crossing Henley Bridge, so most went under it aboard motor boats provided by Hobbs and Sons!

The idea of the 'Mass Sponsored Walk' was revived as part of the week of events marking the first forty years of Shiplake College – Kikunduku Primary School was chosen as part of our thanksgiving, a combination of our Chapel and Summer Expedition interests. The children of Kosovo were added to the walk objectives following Easter Holiday tragedies in the Balkans.

By 1991 those teaching at Shiplake had moved into a world, familiar to parents and many Old Boys, where individuals talked over a previous year's work with the person to whom they were responsible. Such reviews came into schools when the Secretary of State was in conflict with the teaching profession and as a result 'Staff Appraisal' was viewed as a threat. At Shiplake we opted for 'Staff Development' as the label for a simple system confined to one piece of paper a year in which we all asked ourselves the same questions as a basis for discussion. We sought a high degree of confidentiality and avoided an over-elaborate structure. 'Who appraised the Headmaster?' was a question sometimes raised to

The first 'Dogathon' sets out

suggest the unfairness of the system. Having seen every report to the Governing Body – three a year – one feels that little was left to chance, especially when the Board formed specialist sub-committees. Staff Development had a trial run under Peter Lapping and resumed after Nick Bevan had been a year at Shiplake. As we were a small school, he had been successful at reviewing methods and progress and no one in a key position had been overburdened. Regular development discussions provided a better chance for junior staff to advance their ideas and encouraged a two-way discussion of concerns.

The Children Act, as it applied to independent boarding schools, was a case of hearing the message even if we did not like the television messengers. After H.M. Inspectors were withdrawn from independent schools at the end of the 1970s, there was no monitoring of academic or welfare standards during a decade when child abuse became more of an issue. The Children Act used existing machinery – in our case Oxfordshire Social Services – as the way of ensuring the all-round welfare of boarders. The legislation was not helped by its pedigree – child-care scandals and a criminal conviction at a small school with which we had occasional fixtures. The case arose via reports in a serio/comic TV show which almost ran out of control. It was all rather sad, but the emotions released did launch Childline. As a new school, we always had a constructive attitude to change. For example, we had worked with the fire prevention authorities and taken heed of safety at work regulations and, unlike the smallest schools, we had the resources and means to adapt and the sense not to see fresh legislation as intrusive.

Shiplake was one of the Oxfordshire schools that helped social services work out questionnaires for pupils and explore boarding routines and much as usual, our pupils were open and friendly towards official visitors. As Designated Officer under the Children Act, it fell to me to put all aspects of our boarding routines and policies on paper. Much of our accumulated experience – why and when boarders did things and our agreed approaches to unhappiness and bullying – had never been analysed or turned into standard documents.

In the same way, prefects had never been given written briefings. Definite procedures about listening, caring and reporting problems reduced the initiative of colleagues. It required much of the Easter holiday in 1993 to have files prepared for use by the staff. The Housemasters received the stoutest folders and the standard Children Act folder, which summarised our routines and responsibilities, established lines of communication and summarised the responsibilities of everyone who was a House Tutor. Also included was a briefing to prefects. The updating of our methods and the whole issue of protection and awareness passed to the new Deputy Head, Barry Edwards, from January 1994. At the end of 1996 he wrote of 'the need to take into account the latest legal and social welfare advice offered to us'. He doubted 'if any independent school could be entirely confident about identifying signs of distress among pupils and making sure that "secrets" were handed on through a system that was concerned, consistent and professional'.

There was little doubt that remodelling Everett had done much to improve the privacy looked for in the Children Act and those at school long ago will remember the danger was that 'Just having a bit of fun, Sir' can turn into mental or physical bullying. In the same way, a school system geared to persuasion and guidance instead of punishment has to lay down that staff and prefects may not devise their own systems of punishment.

Our first draft of Children Act policy was completed in the light of a first Social Services' inspection in October 1992. Boarders were somewhat disappointed that inspectors did not come to very early morning events and had left Houses by 9.30 p.m. At the end of reporting the early benefits of documenting all aspects of boarding life, Nick Bevan concluded that the Children Act was good for Shiplake because it had made us review everything outside the classroom. He then moved on to mention 'a demand from local people for places for girls in our Sixth Form' – a reference made in the Spring of 1992, twelve months before we were fully up to date with Children Act issues.

The last decade of the twentieth century is covered by almost a thousand pages of annual magazines and the Headmaster's reports to Governors weighing more than the *Oxford English Dictionary*. Such a wealth of detail presents problems of selection. *The Court* grew in size partly because illustrations in colour and black and white were now inexpensive to print. Part of the growth of Headmaster's reports stems from detailed accounts from masters in charge of activities – major sports, tennis and squash (success based on improved facilities) music, art, CCF and Duke of Edinburgh Award. Instead of the previous summaries, the Deputy Head, Director of Studies, Careers and Tithe Barn Society saw their reports included in full.

The Court entered the 1990s produced through Media Studies – a Sixth Form growth industry. There was some failure to pursue late reports so gaps occur, and proofreading appears optimistic. However, there was a marked intent to communicate with readers, notably with parents and staff. Chris Foster's explanations of GCSE showed the clearest vision – few could be in doubt about fresh methods of study and preparation. In 1992 Graham Vick, then newly installed as Director of Studies, outlined the need to build up a sound base for study in the Sixth Form while we kept in step with many aspects of the National Curriculum. He predicted that 'A' Levels – 'Very much as thirty years ago' – would change considerably. GCSE and the old 'A/S' Levels were beneficial to Shiplake boys. Indeed his whole survey was better than any staff meeting. His predictions proved sound; three years later he reported on the effects of Modular Syllabuses in the Sixth which required external exams in January and June. Furthermore there was a distinct shift towards employment related 'A' Levels. In 1992 *The Court* also reported on our Children Act work in tandem with Social Services to make sure our support and welfare arrangements were fully understood. It was also important to explain that boarding schools occupied very few clauses in this Act. Many of its provisions covered homelessness, deprivation and the care of the handicapped – modernising the legal structure without increasing resources.

From 1993, *The Court* set about the coverage of opportunities available from the first term to Upper Sixth. This was a welcome return to detailed recording at the expense of journalism and innovation. Rising costs led to the inclusion of advertisements in 1995. In 1998 *The Court* slimmed down with more emphasis on photography and much less text. As a result, it took three months less to produce.

In the autumn of 1991, the education pages of *The Observer* described Shiplake as a 'Super confidence-building establishment'. Nick Bevan observed that it was not a description he had used to any journalist so it was a welcome judgement from outside. Our magazines during the late 1990s, suggest we were doing even more to justify such a description.

Confidence is probably caught; it can be encouraged but not taught. In 1992 more of our Upper Sixth voted at a General Election than ever before and in November, the Windsor Castle fire unleashed prolonged and bitter press attacks on Her Majesty the Queen. This was probably a situation where staff and pupils were equally bewildered.

Wisdom lies in handling the unforeseen and in a daily world of one confounded thing after another, we tended to be parochial. Boys worked their way through a week and then had to find a way between advice offered here (the standards at Shiplake are not always those of the outside world) and the plans of their friends for Saturday night and Sunday morning. At the same time, the staff were addressing themselves to a drift from boarding. We needed local people to keep talking about us, but it was hard to see the value of some of our efforts. Visiting speakers on Sundays liked the boys – liked them very much – but how many people did they tell the next week? The Head preached at prep schools and he and Mrs Bevan attended prep school speech days. We supported National Boarding Weeks and Ian Lowry headed our teams at ISIS exhibitions, between issuing many a press release. We even advertised on Classic FM – everyone appeared to have tuned in! No one seemed to grumble that he or she came to teach not to do PR work. A genuine conviction of the value of our product made us want to have a full school every September, with another entry similar to those we were already helping.

There was a significant number of our university applicants who decided that their undergraduate years should be spent in a city environment very different from Shiplake, where life had perhaps been too privileged. This kind of decision came from the students themselves as, by and large, teaching at Shiplake avoided political bias. However one could pose ruthless questions: 'In June 1953, on the Saturday after the Coronation, 736 coal pits worked an extra shift to cover missed production earlier that week' – *that* under a Conservative Government and forty years later another Conservative administration was nearly annihilating the industry as a preliminary to privatising the remnant, via the 1994 legislation. Perhaps the bias would have come in if one had stressed the ministerial role of our local MP and our own Tim Eggar.

Economically 1991 was a milestone for the College. Our budget passed the £3 million mark and the payroll reached one hundred and three staff. Salaries and wages exceeded £1.2 million and (as in 1985) it was clear that our contribution to the local economy was growing - even allowing for inflation. In 1961 our income from fees was barely £55,000.

The average expenditure on new building work in the 1980s had been £310,000 per annum. While Appeals, supported most cheerfully by parents and friends, had totalled £500,000, the level of fees reflected the need to service loans. Furthermore, strict budgeting – up to £50,000 a year saved on routine spending – made a contribution to building funds after 1987. Holiday lets, the activities of Shiplake Enterprises at half terms and at some weekends were all geared to making a surplus approaching six figures. Hiring out the buildings helped to pay for fresh construction, even if the summer holiday strain on caterers and full time residents was considerable.

Dr Margaret Wells-Furby died in May 1991 after a short illness. Ill health had led to her early retirement the previous September. As Nick Bevan reminded boys and many staff, she had been part of Shiplake College since its third year. As a full-time professional, her involvement with boarders was limited to evenings and weekends, but staff valued regular contact with a member of another profession who was able to give unofficial advice – salted with Yorkshire common sense. At a crowded funeral service, Peter Lapping paid tribute to her and the family subsequently gave a Lower Sixth prize for Progress and Effort in the Sciences. At Bracknell, East Berkshire Health Services held a memorial service. Following some reorganisation, a Children's Resource Centre was named after her.

The role of the Housemaster's wife at Shiplake has never been defined. The first Shiplake Housemasters were bachelors or married men with very young children. Centralised feeding of the boarders, along with house matrons responsible to the Bursar for use of labour and resources, meant that Housemasters' wives had no practical responsibilities, day to day, for any part of boarding routines. However, their scope for listening and encouraging was limitless. Furthermore, several had career experience of their own which could enrich their imput. In the post-1945 world, divorce was still 'terminal' to any career in a boarding school; by the 1980s divorced housemasters were not unusual.

It was clear from the very earliest days that the Thames side frontage of Shiplake Court would give a new school a special opportunity. A minimum distance from boarding houses to boat houses and rural surroundings upstream to Sonning were obvious advantages. Proximity to Henley had helped to recruit schoolmaster coaches and given opportunities to lady coaches as well. However little now endures – the recreational use of the Thames has made the river less advantageous to Oxfordshire schools and Oxford University. Shiplake oarsmen have twice had their Easter Training camp in the USA and the school year has shortened so much that the Henley Royal Regatta, which used to be three weeks before the end of our Summer term, first became an end of term, and now a holiday, event. Parents no longer have to negotiate with Housemasters about pupils' availability and boys can attend without limitations of school routine – and without the opportunities of paid work in the Stewards' Enclosure while still in residence at College. Things were somewhat different for the First VIII when they could expect the cheers of two hundred organised to give tongue at the milepost. No doubt Old Boys could add other points to the list of 'How things were different in my day'.

The Princess Elizabeth Cup in 1992 ought to have been the perfect climax to several years of rowing endeavour. Our first appearance in a Henley Regatta final was only three summers earlier and the cox, Guy Jackson, survived from that crew. Several of the VIII had been in a successful First XV during the previous autumn – eight were selected for Oxfordshire Schools – and they were physically powerful. The average weight of the crew was thirteen stone and seven pounds and Caspar Ouvaroff, at sixteen stone, nine pounds, was then the heaviest schoolboy to appear in the Princess Elizabeth Cup. With two successes at Marlow just before the end of term, the Shiplake party settled into accommodation at Fawley, provided by Mr and Mrs Smee, parents of Alistair, rowing at number four.

For the first time Henley Royal Regatta was a holiday event in the Shiplake calendar. The newspaper headline: 'Shiplake pin Eton to the Canvas' emphasised a great success in eliminating the current holders of the 'P.E. Cup'. Instead of holding our rivals over the first half of the course before our main challenge, we took an early lead and just kept it. We met Westminster in the semi-finals; they had eliminated Hampton – this time it was our opponents' early lead that just survived to the finish. Our Thameside rivals, Pangbourne, won the final.

Staff changes during the 1990s reflect both changes within the independent schools system and the certainty that retirement would remove some long-serving members of staff. Furthermore some challenging positions, Director of Studies, English and Maths Departments, the Chaplaincy, in particular, gained from change at five or seven year intervals.

It is doubtful if the very experienced Eric Pollard intended to spend a decade with us, but the CCF and shooting absorbed his interests. While he claimed to be allergic to Headmasters, his advice was always sought. Jim Kroth came to help with weaker Maths sets and proved invaluable as Examinations Secretary.

His year as United States resident physicist at the South Pole had made him quite unflappable. Problems were things to be sorted out calmly and with deliberation, rather than haste. Jim died at home, most suddenly, in July 1993 after a holiday morning's work tidying away loose ends in his exam office. He was his usual cheerful self as he left messages for colleagues and at the office before driving home. At very short notice George Cassells took over, showing similar tolerance and patience over problems emanating from the exam boards.

Tenure can be both official and merely understood. Andrew Smail completed his full fifteen years as Burr Housemaster and showed considerable stamina in doing so; few schools now make appointments of such a length and Chaplains now join schools on comparatively short contracts. Having returned from Israel, Michael West was happy to work at Shiplake for a limited period. As Church of England Chaplain in Tel Aviv, he had acquired a knowledge of Galilee and other holy places so that knowledge of the New Testament world illuminated his preaching. He proved himself an all-rounder with a good sense of humour. He was assisted, and then followed, by Philip Parker.

Dick Whittington was almost thirty years at Shiplake – most of the time as Careers Master and for a dozen years as Head of Modern Languages. While he did have secretarial help, he gave himself too much to do. One saw his thoroughness in the summers he devoted to Tithe Barn restoration. His retirement from Shiplake was phased. He handed over Modern Languages to Helen Stewart-Clark and university entrance to Dr Snellgrove. After retirement in 1993, Dick remained with the RAF section of the CCF.

Helen Stewart-Clark remained eight years, some of them resident. She revitalised Modern Languages, bridged the gap between GCSE and 'A' Levels, persuaded Shiplake boys into dominating inter-school debates and acted as a special tutor to foreign students. Having made this exceptional contribution, she moved on. It is a tribute to HKSC's talents that she was twice Inspections Co-ordinator, (ISJC and HMC) a task that Headmasters had previously kept to themselves.

Family circumstances permitted David Welsh to take a well-deserved sabbatical in the autumn of 1991. He used the time to travel in Italy and to revive his skill in oil painting – not a secret to those few of us who had known him in the early 1960s. David had handed over as Director of Studies to Graham Vick and was officially recognised as Senior Master – a position that experience and wisdom had given him unofficially. His brief was to extend the part he long fulfilled on the Arts Committee – to plan and make decisions about anything not academic or sporting. The result was the Tithe Barn Society. Between September and March each year a wide range of performers, experts and demonstrators appeared in the Barn. Outside visitors were sold tickets and every boy had to attend at least one 'show' per term. In eight seasons David found over one hundred specialist programmes within a limited budget. Soloists, unusual instruments, stage make-up, one-person shows, a flute cocktail, stage fighting and choreography suggest the variety of the fare. Meetings of HEDFAS (Henley Fine Arts and Design) also continue to be held at Shiplake and are open to staff and pupils.

Mrs Doris Hinton – Shiplake's long serving bookkeeper – was known to many, sitting in her section of the Bursar's office from the mid-1960s onwards. Boys appeared with envelopes from parents with late requests for travel money, messages from Housemasters or with cash to pay for some sixth form social event and were met with understanding and a not always deserved patience. Staff who were businesslike in money matters found her ultra-efficient and most knowledgeable. Those who were late with requests or with money due to the Bursar's department, faced gentle reproach and hints to improve. Mrs Hinton had hoped to retire, but remained some two years longer than planned while school accounts were put on computerised systems. She was a very private person, but Shiplake owed much to her strong sense of duty, as did the five Bursars she worked with. Furthermore, she missed the benefits of moving to the modern offices, opened in 1991.

As the second half of the twentieth century moved into its final decade, one of our wisest recent graduates observed of the numerous Shiplake retirements 'Even Gladstone had to stand down in the end'. Michael Charles enjoyed several years of active teaching after thirty years of housemastering – half of it at Milton Abbey. Michael understood better than anyone at Shiplake how the prep school product was changing and took the lead in making sure that every pupil coming to Shiplake acquired the basic skills.

James Johnson said farewell to the Art Department with great regret. He had achieved marvels from a base in the old stables and the space, light and exhibition area of the new Art School – available from 1990 – kept up the momentum of a busy department. The exhibitions, Paris art trips, scenery painting and support for the Ceramics Department were all extensions of James's personality. Sometime wool buyer and Australian bush pilot, James was a little confused by routine and employed a droll sense of humour when changes in schedule left him bereft of pupils. Eric Pollard used to admonish boys with 'You didn't listen, did you?' James used to reproach himself with 'Well, it's here somewhere...'

Brian Burgess stepped aside when Design and Technology at GCSE and 'A' Level changed radically. He always taught near James Johnson and both men had the knack of making sure that every visitor knew what was afoot in their classes. John Scottorn, who had taught woodwork in the former basements, found that his subject no longer existed in GCSE terms. His greatest enthusiasm at Shiplake had always been for the river and he is now a successful professional rowing coach.

Some changes had unexpected long-term consequences. David Bryant was Clerk of Works between Dick Gapper and the arrival of Simon Brown – known to an earlier generation as proprietor of 'Fox's Shop' in Lower Shiplake. Simon also became involved with the RN section and his daughter had a successful Sixth Form career here – part of the Governors' scheme for the education of staff children. Single-handedly she proved that girls would succeed in our Sixth and the present scheme developed from her pioneering two years.

When Ian Lowry arrived to take over English from Mike Gilliat, we had no idea how versatile he would prove. He moved from Army Section and TA to run the Naval Section of CCF and his last major responsibility was as Head of History. His time with the BBC made him useful in drama and his experience in hospital management led to a contribution at Shiplake in public relations and the management of limited resources – including time itself. He was an exuberant conversationalist and first rate in looking after visitors to the Common Room.

The wide range of responsibilities that David Scoins gradually accumulated were divided amongst several: no one person could replace him. His speed to a decision was sometimes perplexing: 'That's it then' produced many a move forward. His stamina was remarkable and, by example, he turned cross country into an important inter-school sport. Athletics was near moribund when he arrived, but soon recovered its place in a crowded summer term. David Scoins acted within character, having begun life north of the Tyne and having attended a 'northern' college at Oxford, he decided to settle west of the Tamar!

Mark Hayter was another 1993 departure. The majority never saw his most important contributions as he was often at regattas or upstream coaching. His ability was on show every September Friday when utter novices, just in their teens, learned to scull in front of the landing stage. Mark's care and precision came in the little things. At Monmouth School, he remained involved in the world of schools rowing.

An author can only describe his own departure from the stage by dealing in events rather than emotions. In the kindest ways possible, every part of the Shiplake community made an official farewell to me. The Governors hosted a staff lunch and presented me with a carriage clock. Presentations at the Old Vikings' Dinner included a portrait and a drawing of Pickering College. The Head gave a private dinner party and the Sixth Form held an end of term dinner. There, the College gift – a David Welsh oil painting of Tudor Cottage – was presented and the Staff, at their dinner, gave me a table-top photocopier.

A multitude of memories of colleagues and of helping to keep Shiplake going is best summed up by looking at just one aspect of routine – organising 'cover' for absent staff. Curiously, even the most searching of would-be parents never asks 'what do you do about staff absence?' Twenty years of finding replacements showed the usual pattern and changes. Predictable absences for official reasons, such as away fixtures, regattas, CCF meetings and GCSE training grew with the passing years, but could be planned for. 'Please, Headmaster, no leave for anyone on October 10th – the Maths Department is at a conference'. The Common Room understood that the absence of seven staff was the maximum we could manage. It was policy to avoid any expeditions for the first six weeks of an autumn term, to give the year an uncomplicated start. After Christmas there was little respite. Sudden staff illness could be known the evening before, but normally there was only ninety minutes between an early morning alert and the start of the school day. It was at this point that the professionalism of the staff took over. The posting of an 'Emergency Notice' produced wry humour, but early arrivals did check to see if there was such a notice. During an epidemic, some doubling up of sets was possible. The Second Master always had a large classroom and could take two sets at once. The video era meant that progress of a set could be maintained. A high degree of co-operation was normal. 'If you need me could you leave such and such free as I have arranged a special meeting ...' It was never a case of the Roman Centurion – 'I say unto this man go and he goeth ...' The strengthening resources of the College improved the situation in three ways: private medical insurance meant that routine surgery could be booked in vacations, we could afford to employ part-time replacements when term-time illness exceeded a few days and from 1987 the presence of resident Junior Masters provided flexibility, especially early in the day. The boys were very tolerant of disruption; perhaps a change of face was welcome and inquiries about the sick were kindly. The feedback from parents about temporary arrangements was constructive. Furthermore, Peter Lapping and Nick Bevan were quick to support anyone, especially families, when sudden ill-health became a problem.

Before Easter 1993, the College entertained former staff to a lunch party. It was a chance for the Bevans to meet many who had once worked for Shiplake and the Second Master joked that it was a cost-free chance for him to say goodbye to old friends. It was the extra work done by so many in support of colleagues that he really had in mind, and for which he was particularly grateful.

Early in 1993, the Governors invited Barry Edwards to become Deputy Headmaster from January 1994. At the time he was appointed, Barry was Head of English at Highgate School and he was chosen from over one hundred applicants, many of whom were Housemasters at other independent schools. Shiplake was following an established trend by moving away from a Second Master traditionally found among senior staff in a school.

The edition of *The Court* covering late 1992 and the whole of 1993 was almost a hundred pages long and included as many photographs. The new Senior Editor, Jon Carley, tried to keep subsequent annual magazines to sixty pages, but Michael Edwards' first edition in 1997 climbed to eighty pages. The Headmaster and the Governors were keen to see activities and achievements fully reported. The revitalised magazine had an undoubted marketing value,

Winners of the Viking Ship 1992: Dan Marrett, Shola Macarthy, Dan Jones, John Polansky and Edward Horner

but more importantly it could record individual achievement in drama, the fine arts, debate, music and creative writing and pay tribute to the steady, routine contribution of Chapel helpers and the CCF NCOs. The inclusion of House and Team group photographs meant that everyone somehow appeared in the magazine.

Old editions of school magazines are insufficiently read – they provide useful accounts of conditions likely to be encountered when trekking in Asia, Africa or South America. There is recondite information a-plenty. Somehow over three decades the Reading Working Men's Regatta on the Dreadnought Reach has become the Thames Valley Park Regatta and photographs record changes in team shirts, jerseys and rowing garb. Not to be wholly forgotten was the achievement of eleven 'rather foolhardy individuals' – two Staff, two Junior Masters and seven boys on April 17th 1993. The challenge was to set foot on the three highest peaks in England, Scotland and Wales within twenty-four hours. The team completed the task in nineteen hours, thanks to the driving of Matthew Gardner, whose endurance at the wheel will be remembered long after his French teaching has faded into memory.

Some schools are convinced that Bishops always preach the same sermon at every Confirmation Service, but rapidly changing circumstances prevent Heads from repeating themselves on Speech Day after Speech Day. Amongst the points that Nick Bevan stressed in 1993 was that coming to know Shiplake over five years had not enabled him to relax. He was grateful for parental attendance at Sunday chapel and shared their concern about outside pressures on the young at a time when the nation was shocked by the number of murders committed by children. He found his time more and more consumed by the need to make potential parents aware of the variety of opportunities at Shiplake. A year later he stressed that the recent Parents Charter was rather strong on parents' rights and thin on parents' duties. He, himself, was a schoolmaster because he enjoyed working with parents and children. He also emphasised that because pupils at Shiplake had such opportunities to travel and to mix with other colours and creeds, they were blind to hatred and dislike.

In the autumn of 1993 our former Chaplain, Basil Wilks, died after twelve years' retirement from Shiplake. Inability to travel much meant he was little known to staff and boys after 1984. He had taught for two decades before his ordination and used this experience to combine his pastoral work with being part of normal school life. He liked to think that in the 1960s he instilled the idea that junior cricket and rugby practices had to be more thorough and far longer than quite talented youngsters deemed essential. In the same way, confirmation was something to be worked at. To colleagues, his ability to draw large numbers to voluntary events and Lenten services was a special gift. There were many things Basil was not: scholarship and piety were not his instruments, but common sense, patience and sincerity were.

1994 began with the saddest of events – the death in a road accident of Matthew Bevin, a Fifth Former in Everett House. The worst aspect of Shiplake's location is direct access on to a dangerous main road. Two college employees had been killed within yards of our grounds and we were fortunate that thirty-five years passed before traffic conditions claimed one of our pupils.

Helen Stewart-Clark paid tribute in *The Court* to this promising fifteen year old and a prize was established in his memory.

In the early 1990s we found elements of imbalance built into the timetable schemes we had adopted to help with GCSE courses. The number of periods had been increased; they were slightly shorter to provide more double periods, but no one had taken seriously what the effect of this would be on remedial English teaching. Extra English had been taught in place of French, but when the number of periods allocated to English and French is increased for exam preparation, those gradually overcoming dyslexia problems were simply getting too many English periods – in the long term, this was counter-productive. There were other places where change was necessary by 1994 – advertisements appeared in *The Court* and it seemed that the formula for getting old boys back in large numbers – the Family Days of 1984 and 1989 – had not worked so well in 1994.

Provided that lives are not endangered, it is no bad thing if Nature herself throws down the gauntlet and challenges a community. The Great Storms of 1987 and 1990 were challenges to the College's ability to clear up and return to normal. The freak rainstorm of July 1975 occurred in the summer holiday, but the flood of June 1994 gave another school generation the chance to demonstrate their emergency skills in fighting the elements during a power failure. This was no mere disruption of a routine evening. Parents had arrived for a barbecue; an outdoor pageant was due to start at 9 p.m. and valuable costumes hired from RSC were stored in rapidly flooding basement changing rooms. In describing events, Barry Edwards saw it as an enriching experience – chain gangs with buckets bailing out the basement and carrying borrowed costumes to safety, aided by the neighbourly assistance of Brian Doble's petrol powered pump. And of course, the next day was so typically Shiplake, a normal assembly at 8.30 a.m., with Old Boys and their families welcome, eighteen hours after the deluge and later, with some technical problems, the outdoor drama resuming in damp costumes and cheerful spirits. A week later on Speech Day, the Head paid tribute to the boys 'astonishing reaction and energy followed by a day of good humour and fellowship'. It takes nothing from the volunteers of 1994 in saying all performed worthily in a tradition that they, as distinct from senior members of staff, knew nothing of.

Shiplake's thirty-fifth year in 1993-94 was more obviously one of transition than any since 1980. Only one major building scheme lay ahead – the Pavilion-Orchard continuation of the Goodwin project – and there is a general 'before and after' impression. Things were different rather than worse or better, more flexible rather than clear cut. The explanation lay in events and social trends. To summarise is, to some extent, to repeat what has already been said.

Shiplake entered the 1990s with four boarding houses and a day boy community. Weekly boarding did not officially exist. This was unsustainable as very few entrants at thirteen had spent three to five years as prep school boarders.

The aftermath of the Great Storm: the author in the tree!

. . . all hands to the pump drying out the Entrance Hall

Saturday morning school was an integral part of life and we had large pupil and parent congregations at Sunday Chapel. One pre-1939 boarding school tradition had been adopted by Shiplake in 1959 – sport after lunch in the winter, followed by early evening teaching. All these were about to be adapted to reflect the demands of reduced numbers, the pressures of new public examination methods and in response to parental pressure.

Enough has been said about staff changes and retirements, but by 1996 only Malcolm Woodcock remained from the Housemasters of 1990 and by 1998 only half a dozen of the staff in the Silver Jubilee photograph remained. Retirement was only part of the picture because falling numbers meant that our exceptionally generous staffing with small teaching sets had to be made more economically sound. Furthermore, new areas of responsibility had to be covered. Naturally, every member of staff has to decide if Shiplake is the place for him or her in the longer term. A combination of career prospects, proximity to a rowing centre at Henley and the growth of rugby football in Henley had brought Shiplake many able staff. Marriage and a family kept many of them here for a decade or more. Between 1993 and 1998 Nick Bevan brought many able young teachers to Shiplake only to find that a significant number did not see their future at Shiplake or, indeed, in teaching. One begins to wonder if independent schools will be double victims of a decline in marriage and in career continuity.

During the latter 1980s and into the 1990s, Shiplake's links with universities such as Durham, Edinburgh and Bristol improved considerably. These, together with the occasional Oxbridge entry, were enjoyed by a dedicated staff who took equal pleasure in the GCSE success of the more average pupils whose subsequent career success occasioned even more delight. After 1993, it was Graham Vick's job to remind the staff that our smaller intake was closer and closer to the national ability average and we had rather fewer who would take 'A' Levels in their stride. In spite of this change in our intake, GCSE and 'A' Level results continued to improve. Nick Bevan was convinced that our teaching was better than ever and frequently said so. His impression was independently confirmed, first by a visit from an HMI (under the new OFSTED system) and then by inspections in 1997 (ISJC) and the visit of an HMC team in 1998. In November 1995, *The Times* picked out Shiplake as one of the ten most improved independent schools as far as A–C grades at GCSE were concerned.

Enough has already been said about Shiplake College attaining sporting peaks that could not be sustained with falling rolls and a dearth of the tall and strong who had sustained progress for almost a decade after 1985. Already First XI cricket was weak in 1993 and apart from First and Second XVs, rugby was woeful – in spite of every effort by coaches. We moved rapidly from mounting 'a strong challenge' to being 'an easy fixture' for our traditional opponents. A very well equipped Boat Club maintained its reputation without any of the headline winning exploits of the seasons before 1993. That we could continue to build confidence and achieve success for individuals lay in other areas of proven success before and after 1993: music, drama and public speaking. The all-round opportunities offered by a small school particularly impressed the OFSTED inspector.

In 1993, the benefits of new buildings for Art, Design and Technology and Information Technology were becoming clear and the future of Economics and Classical History was to be reduced, as the demand for the newer and very popular subjects increased. Business Studies was joining Art, Design and Technology and Media Studies as sought after options at 'A' Level. In 1997, twenty-eight Business Studies' candidates outnumbered Maths and the three main sciences for total entries at 'A' Level. Geography had more candidates than Art or Media Studies, and Design and Technology entered the same number as English and History had averaged since the 1980s. Essentially the 'new' subjects were being taken by pupils who might not have sat 'A' Levels at all or who would have attempted Economics and Classical History. At GCSE, Art and Design/Technology even put a strain on the much-expanded facilities.

CHAPTER 32

Combined Cadet Force Milestones

IN 1995 'THE CORPS' completed thirty years as a CCF Unit, having changed from ACF in 1966. Thanks to the Thames and reasonable road access to Portsmouth, an RN Section had long flourished, but it was only in the 1980s that an RAF section took off. Lt. Colonel Richard Lee had been in command for over two decades when he retired in 1990. He was replaced by the even more experienced Commander Eric Pollard and then Major Peter Webb took command. After twenty years service, Peter is now also Lt Colonel.

With a background in Physical Education, Peter Webb was well able to lead by example. He had played rugby for the Territorial Army, and through management of all those raw-boned characters in the Second XV, combined with the annual ski trips, he was able to create a willing atmosphere in what was a compulsory activity for part of every Shiplake pupil's school career. At one stage almost one third of the College staff were either officers or helped with CCF training. As Staff with National Service in the 1950s became fewer and fewer, the officer net had to be cast widely and included Flying Officer Rosemary Jones from the College Office, previously in the RAF! In 1995 the bi-annual inspection was carried out by the Headmaster's brother, Brigadier Tim Bevan. Unfortunately torrential rain gave him a less than kindly welcome and the parade was held uniquely in the Sports Hall. He was followed in 1997 by Group Captain D.M. Jones, whose son Richard was both Senior Cadet in the RAF Section and the Parade Commander on Inspection Day.

As a national youth organisation, the CCF provides opportunities that sometimes appeal more to day pupils than to boarders – camps, overnight expeditions, long days away from home, flying, boat trips and subsidised sailing lessons. Even so, these are also a break from boarding routine. There are hundreds of Shiplake Old Boys who achieved the Duke of Edinburgh Gold Award through CCF, as the sponsoring and training authority.

Any cadet force has problems large and small, together with image and organisation to maintain. The legislative ending of shooting as a skilled British sport came after the Dunblane tragedy provoked criticism that schools were

The CCF

Naval manoeuvres on the river

Officers and Senior NCOs, 1991

Phil Parker, Caroline Cheadle and the Tree-Climbing Society

training pupils to enjoy the use of firearms. Indeed was it the job of any school to keep weapons on the premises? From this problem, to finding enough staff to help cadet NCOs, to revising two-year training programmes during defence cuts were the mid-1990s agenda items of Peter Webb and his team.

Some may feel that the CCF at Shiplake alters but never changes. Climbing and the summer expeditions are spin-offs from CCF training – no matter if the required skills are taught to fourth formers or in the lower sixth. Members of staff move – a shortage of officers threatens and then there is a sudden influx – such as the five arrivals in 1997. Interest in going to Sandhurst may have waned slightly, but there is always the slightly unexpected, such as when the Army section put forward our sole girl cadet of the year for entry to RNC Dartmouth.

CHAPTER 33

Maintaining Links with the Past

MR PETER CARTER-RUCK was guest of honour on Speech Day in 1997. This was more than bringing back a former Chairman of Governors who had presided at our first Speech Day in 1960; it was an acknowledgement of how important the early terms were. We took a lot of boys that no other school wanted and, with rapidly growing parental loyalty, did a great deal for many of our early entrants. Of course, there were mistakes. Alexander Everett was keen to stimulate young people and Mrs Everett knew something of parental concerns. There was some good teaching in spite of limited resources and it was a mistake to think, as we probably did by 1963, that everything in the first months should have been done differently. Furthermore, Shiplake had attracted the support of men as varied as Aubrey Goodwin – a long-term Governor – and David Welsh, a long serving member of staff. What we probably needed at the time was more assurance. It was only later that a grandfather said to me 'What you went through at Shiplake was probably like turning a socially minded bunch of TA weekenders into a fighting unit ... Some of those in charge at the start had to stand aside' – a fair comparison between 1939–40 and Shiplake in 1960–62.

Nick Bevan has rarely been able to take his mind off the job of being Headmaster at Shiplake, but he has retained his sense of humour and kept alive his liking for young people. He has encouraged originality and taken the trouble to find out about our early days. He does understand their enduring achievement – the continuing partnership of parents, governing body, pupils and staff.

Shiplake is a little removed from the real world and very much subject to it. We cling to some values, quaint or out of date according to individual views. Some are seen as increasingly unfashionable due to the belief that 'The Brits have lost interest in leadership' during the last four decades. We also face changes so rapid that electronic equipment is out of date by the time it is paid for. The Staff are consulted in detail about new projects and the Governors have yet to erect any building with 'White Elephant' potential. Boys still expect games to be fun and training to have a purpose. However, it is now business

Forty years of Heads of College

Learning Support and
Geography fieldwork in 2000

leaders, not generals, who pay tribute to their schooldays in terms of learning to apply themselves through pre-match training and learning to be good 'company men' on the rugby pitch – as if a corporate mentality was acquired in the scrum!

In 1959, Shiplake set out to give a varied choice to a varied entry of boys and the school was already 120 strong when the first 'A' Level courses began in September 1962. Our first proper Sixth Formers sat Advanced papers in 1964. By 1998, the Sixth Form at Shiplake was as big as the whole school had been thirty-six years earlier.

In 1962, academic qualifications for all at sixteen was a distant prospect. The educational debate was then about two provisions of the 1944 Education Act – moving the school leaving age to the end of the school year in which young people reached sixteen or starting compulsory day release for occupational training for all employees between fifteen and eighteen. The latter, almost a century old in Germany, was deemed at the time to be the mainspring of the then West Germany's technological success. Certainly at Shiplake we had instances of pupils only six terms past their Common Entrance leaving, aged fifteen, to work in a parent's business or on the family farm. At the same time, the early careers work done by John Foster showed that professions were already abandoning entry via articled-pupil status between sixteen and twenty-one. This change made staying in the Shiplake Sixth more relevant to career intentions and, by the time the school leaving age was raised to sixteen, pupils could see a Sixth Form that looked worth joining. There were enlightened parents who believed that a Sixth Form career was worthwhile merely for the experience and responsibility rather than just for exam grades. In the Lapping years, we had a handful of slow developers who acquired 'A' Levels after three years in the Sixth. Some parents endowed a son's rowing career via Sixth Form fees! In 1980, a Shiplake Housemaster could have looked at his dozen Sixth Form members and seen twelve different reasons for staying on. Many looked forward to career-related courses at the expanding polytechnics, so the Upper Sixth eventually divided into UCCA and PCAS men until the polytechnics became a new generation of universities.

In Shiplake's early days Stewart Cowley – a May 1959 entrant – sensed 'a rich and original atmosphere' and Nick Bevan is convinced that Shiplake still has this ... indeed he has done much to preserve it. As a result, the 1990s generation never has to say 'What did our predecessors miss out on?' Nor, indeed, should old boys be jealous. The chore of weekend letter writing has been replaced by the fax machine in the House office and the queue for the House telephone is now replaced by mobile phones. The 'then and now' argument has the added spice of an increasing number of sons of Old Vikings in the school.

As a school for teenagers, Shiplake has proved trustworthy. It has a good record for 'getting it right' carefully and reasonably quickly and it has remained loyal to some basics. The ratio of nine pupils to one member of staff is as it was in 1962 and 1984. Boat Club membership is as it always has been, open to all without extra charge. Help for dyslexics has become part of a Learning Support Department. We improved as resources became more readily available. At some inconvenience to the resident community, the Sports Hall Complex is part-funded by evening lettings. Former parents and Old Boys would not expect anything else – 'that's the Shiplake way of doing things'. Furthermore, John Eggar's maxim 'The minimum of fuss and the maximum of results' has not been forgotten.

Continuity and change are both obvious. Former members of the Boat Club have rowed at international level – forty of them between 1981 and 1995. Beagling, fencing, clay pigeon shooting, judo and abseiling, come and go in contrast to mainstream activities, such as ski trips, The Duke of Edinburgh Award, CCF camps and courses and the Summer Trek which have long been annual events. At least four departments organise holiday courses, so that an autumn half term or an Easter holiday becomes an extension to term. Contributions that owe almost everything to pupil input have gone from strength to strength in the 1990s. Youth Speaks teams have marched to annual successes; Young Enterprise companies and the recycling scheme launched by Burr and Andrew Smail have grown from small beginnings into major commitments. Staff, pupils and parents combine to ensure that Shiplake is rarely a dull place. Teams using Henley Church Tower as a substitute for the elevation of Mount Everest to abseil down for charity are in the same tradition as the sponsored dog walk of years past. The staff market local wine under a Shiplake College label and parents and outdoor drama directors combine to bring realism to summer theatre through loans and demonstrations. Horses, donkeys and sheep have appeared in productions and evenings have been enlivened by fire-eaters, veteran cars and a World War One biplane.

By tradition, academic changes had been considered by the seven Heads of Department making up the Curriculum Committee and fresh developments were represented under subject umbrellas – Maths representing Computing plus Information Technology and English looking after Media Studies. The Head of Art would have represented Technical Drawing and Woodwork and historians were the main proponents of study skills for newcomers and for all starting 'A' Levels. Business Studies led an orphan existence with Economics and Careers as guardians.

From small beginnings many innovations have gained importance and now stand alongside the main subjects in the timetable. Information Technology, Learning Support and Design and Technology are available for all pupils, with Media Studies and Business at a later stage. Out of class, Health and Safety, Marketing and Activities (a rationalisation of all clubs, societies and the games list) are all important. To a retired schoolmaster this may seem evidence of rapid change, but to the Old Boy businessman this is merely schools having to 'be like the real world'. Not surprisingly, new areas of responsibility are in the charge of staff who have arrived in the 1990s. However, they still represent our traditional approach. As soon as we see a pupil need, action is taken, perhaps on a small scale at first. After due consideration we may realise, as so often happened in the early days, that we have found an area where our young people can succeed. It will always be true that long-term policy stems from dealing with today's problems, but Shiplake's planning structures now are superior to the often successful improvisation of thirty years ago. Analysis has replaced the guesswork of earlier times!

Former pupil and 1959 entrant Stewart Cowley was remarkably perceptive in stressing the 'rich and original atmosphere' of the early days. While the feel of the place has intrigued potential parents, many fresh from other school tours, it would be wrong to emphasise that this is the only important thing about Shiplake College. Staff are perhaps more likely to be appointed because they relish the challenge of making the difficult seem possible to our varied entry and because they like young people. Liking the atmosphere may help in selection between schools, but during the 1990s the challenge to staff has been helping Fifth and Sixth Formers to outperform previous generations. From the outset, Nick Bevan believed this was possible and pupils and staff have responded successfully to his challenge.

CHAPTER 34

From Reformed Catering to a Co-ed Sixth Form

INSTITUTIONAL FOOD is rarely forgotten. Old men talk of 'National Service Grub' and their wives still shudder at the thought of the culinary frugality at women-only colleges. Schools are judged by match teas offered to visitors and a 'good' school meal is always meagre in amount. Cafeteria queues stretch to the crack of doom, with central feeding often involving six daily walks in the rain and the changes brought about by new catering managers never endure.

The cafeteria system at Shiplake arrived in the late 1960s. While several modernisations of the 'Servery' have reduced the time spent in the queue, no answers were found to three problems: absenteeism towards the weekend, lack of choice for the unfortunates in the second half of supper and, for most teams and crews, the disadvantages of the main meal of the day being before all-out activity in the afternoons. Furthermore, first and second sittings by Houses never really succeeded. The rearranged meals system now makes allowances for changing fashions as well as nutrition. A longer lunch period now offers soups, hot dishes, salads, rolls, cheese and fresh fruit. Supper is more formal than previously, serving main courses and puddings, with queues assembling by age group instead of houses. Structurally, catering had been in a rut. No doubt many of our old boys in the catering business could have warned that format is just as important as variety of menus in a twelve-week term.

Shiplake remained a boys' school almost to the end of the century. There had been some girls in the Sixth during the 1970s and, in theory, places in the 'A' Level sets had always been on offer to daughters of staff. In the early 1980s a study in depth showed that buying any large and expensive house property in the Shiplake area could only be financed by it becoming an all-girls house. In the 1980s girls meant expansion, whereas in the next decade it means keeping up numbers. On the other hand there were plenty of bursars warning that it took a long time to recover the cost of building alterations that preceded co-education at

Head Chef
Steve Nicholson
serving supper

The first six girls

any level. However, co-education has been helped by changes of emphasis. Form orders and the publication of examination results in order of merit are things of the past. In co-educational grammar schools, girls used to claim it was easy to be 'top the Form' when half the competition were 'mere boys'. Girls in a boys' school Sixth Form are looking for 'A' Level courses in a different community. They may take an interest in rugby and cricket, but there will be a change of emphasis. A school of eight hundred boys has a wide choice for first and second teams, but when co-education at all levels is complete, the Marlboroughs and Kingswoods of an earlier era lose their sporting primacy. Independent schools do not survive upon memory like football clubs. 'We reached the Cup Final in 1947'. It is not a question of what we have been as a boys' school but what fresh opportunities will present themselves with girls in parts of the school.

The present structure of girls' independent schools, where most pupils will have arrived at between eight and twelve years old, encourages a change of school at sixteen. While Shiplake staff may think of female input in terms of better Music and Drama, girls arriving at Shiplake may regard that as more of the same. When your airliner captain is a woman and engineering is full of female graduates, it may be that it will be the Duke of Edinburgh Award and rowing that engage the interest of Shiplake's new Sixth Form girls.

The arrival of girls in the Lower Sixth in September 1998 resulted from many inquiries over a two-year period and a careful study, helped by the previous experience of a newly arrived Head of English with transition to a mixed school. A Sixth Form girls' study area in the Lodge is a good use of that building and poses an interesting challenge to Welsh House.

Having gone up to Oxford in 1929, Mrs Edna de la Praudiere was the most senior of the guests at Shiplake's Fortieth Anniversary service in 1999. She had come to a school of ninety-five boys in May 1960 to teach French on a part-time basis. 'I remained far longer than I expected because the boys were so pleasant and helpful'. One expects in future that Staff will stay because the girls and the boys continue to be just as friendly as their predecessors.

CHAPTER 35

'The Old Order Changeth . . .'

IN SPITE OF DEMANDS on their time, Shiplake Housemasters helped with appeals, coached cricket, hockey and tennis and turned up for everything on the calendar. Expeditions, music and drama depended heavily on two Housemasters during the 1980s, but whole areas of planning and innovation, from computing to curriculum, had to be left to others on the staff. When one looks back on the 1980s from a greater distance, it may well seem that this was when Housemasters ceased to be all-round schoolmasters and became specialists in welfare and relations with parents.

By 1993 one partial answer to Housemasters' problems was in sight. Nick Bevan was confident that more had to be delegated to House tutors. They were to be more than academic supervisors – 'work tutors' in our jargon – and more bachelor accommodation in refurbished houses, some of the requirements of the Children Act, the influence of Barry Edwards and a shortage of young staff who had been boarders themselves, all contributed to making tutors more important than ever before. This was one of the great achievements of the mid-1990s, but somewhat galling in the sense that these staff newcomers to Shiplake tended to learn the ropes, get to understand the pupils and then take their recently gained expertise to another school!

Andrew Smail left Shiplake in 1997 to continue housemastering elsewhere. In this he was emulating Michael Charles in completing fifteen years as a Housemaster in one school and then starting again. Andrew also left behind the Remedial English Department where he so patiently worked. Brought up in Cambridge, Andrew had something of Oliver Cromwell's 'Ironsides' about him – he was steadfast when things went badly and firm in his beliefs. Like Cromwell, he could entreat boys and parents to 'consider you might be mistaken'. Andrew was at his best in looking after boarders with some handicap and was most supportive of any boy who had suffered a bereavement. As President of the licensed JCR, he had an instinctive touch. As a determined cricketer, Andrew Smail was at his best in the relaxed atmosphere after a game – especially after well-earned victory. In private, he was a considerable raconteur and his confidential accounts of some senior boys' misdemeanours were, at times, hilarious. At the same time, a certain reserve prevented many boys, and some parents, from appreciating his support for traditional values.

Shiplake has prided itself as the school for a fresh start at thirteen or for those entering the Sixth Form. It has also served the same function for some members of staff. In the mid-1980s, the Jacklin family decided that Southern Africa was no longer for them and after a few years at Shiplake, they were in the heart of things, taking charge of the rebuilt Everett. Ivan Jacklin offered five years of interim management, which ended as seven. He was replaced by Graham Wells returning to the United Kingdom after a short spell in Canada. Caroline Cheadle came to England and to Shiplake in 1993 and her husband, Andrew, followed her onto the staff a little later. Together they moved into Burr in 1997.

Director of Art, David Stoker, had a variety of experience even more colourful than his predecessor. Having previously been Head of Art at King Edward VI, Birmingham, he came to Shiplake after running his own art school in France. Julian Seaton had been head of Design and Technology at Reading School before a spell of pioneering work at a rural secondary school in Zimbabwe, making him the latest in a long line of men with experience of work in Africa. While jokes about Shiplake's 'Afrika Corps' are as old as the College itself, it is not wholly paradoxical that those with experience of younger societies – particularly outside Europe – have found our freshness of outlook something they were seeking.

Two contrasting departures from schoolmastering in 1997 and 1998 combine Shiplake history: David Welsh retired after thirty-eight years and Michael Llewellyn after a dozen. As drama producers, their out-of-class involvement overlapped, but in other respects, their contributions to confidence building contrasted in style and content. David Welsh provided Shiplake with logical analysis of problems; his teaching was academic, sometimes austere but he challenged and supported the less able. Mick Llewellyn ran the danger of offering an 'alternative Shiplake' to the needy and to some 'dodgy characters', but all this was done in the best interest of getting more out of those who gained from informality. Occasionally, individuals failed to remember that their first loyalty was to their house. David Welsh came to Shiplake in 1960 to take charge of Latin and help with Mathematics. Mick Llewellyn arrived to work with small groups in 'Extra English' and was soon involved with the transition to GCSE and coursework in History. Both men could not have foreseen how their paths would change direction. David Welsh devoted much of his spare time from the early 1980s to 'computerising the College' and MLL launched 'A' Level Media Studies and coached interview skills in his latter days.

By the time Shiplake said farewell to Michael Llewellyn, his all round contribution had developed into a gallimaufry of interests and concerns – oversight of *The Court* magazine, years with the Third XV, village cricket for enthusiasts,

CHAPTER 36

Tradition, Religion and Status

CHRISTIANITY IS still important at Shiplake and many believe that the school is not so very different now than in the years of daily prayers and a liturgical Sunday Service and that the friendly co-operation sensed by visitors, reflects Christian values in daily life. 'I like to think so' was the response of the poet and novelist Thomas Hardy, when responding to questions without saying 'yes'. In one way – extensive parental attendance – Sunday Services never more positive in the 1990s than in earlier decades. Weekday services are now fewer – one senior morning chapel per week, one for juniors and a Friday Communion. Fewer may mean better in the sense that the challenge is 'Come buy without money' whereas one remembers the eternal discussions about how to get the boys more involved.

In a nutshell, the problem is how many hours a week does a school give to inculcating the meaning and purpose of human life and how many to the 'careers', qualifications and training to make 'serious money'? Many would ask, even in the decade of the one-parent family, whether it is the job of any school to discourage smoking, drugs and teenage pregnancy, and give lessons in how to avoid AIDS? Clearly, those clauses of the 1944 Education Act requiring compulsory Religious Education in class and daily collective worship on the part of all pupils have failed in their intent to give meaning and purpose to life in England and Wales. The Anglican Church, particularly, left too much to the state after 1944. LEA-agreed Religious Studies Syllabuses came up against the problem of a shortage of people able to teach well-structured courses. While sixty-six percent of all children received Anglican Baptism in the 1960s, we now have many school Heads without any faith and a public ignorant of the real meaning of the Millennium.

What has this got to do with Shiplake? Many parents and staff are products of the years in which Religious Education in state schools broke down, so there is less consensus about our moral purpose. Let there be no doubt about the work of College Chaplains at Shiplake in their attempts to meet the vital challenges of these times. As a young schoolmaster, I spent three years teaching twenty different classes a week for Divinity. Physically demanding on voice, challenging, always open to question, not often disappointing, sometimes exhausting, but to be relinquished when still fresh, so I often thought of my chaplain colleagues doing this and much more as a life's work.

A School Chaplain faces a multitude of demands – new boys know little of the Old Testament and not much more of the New when Confirmation Classes begin. His planned course of lessons may be delayed by the need to deal with some recent internal problem – a theft or drugs-related suspension, newspaper headlines, bullying and 'why should we do this, that and the other'? A Chaplain has to move with the times. He grew up when it was possible to say 'This is the truth ... write it down' and he has now moved into a society where an individual may do virtually anything in private. He must tolerate what was recently illegal in a world where Oscar Wilde's 'Love that dared not speak its name' now speaks loudly on any television programme after the nine o'clock watershed!

In recent years Shiplake pupils have run true to form; they decline to be 'disaster saturated' and support a wide range of charities. Work for good causes is mixed with an ability to get on with all races and a willingness to explore every continent. They are open-minded and inconsistent, support for discussion groups ebbs and flows; good causes are embraced and forgotten, Communion is taken in term time and the personalities of outstanding preachers remembered when their message is forgotten. Pupils are punctual for services and note if their Housemaster has not come. They may heed his advice to 'Work with the Chaplain on this one', but they will not worry if a Housemaster is not a communicant.

When Sixth Formers leave, we may take an interest in university years and career choice, but we do not think about the parishes where they live. The independent school problem is the same as that of the comprehensive school. There may be competent pastoral work in schools of all types; carols and cantatas are performed and distinguished speakers are heard, but the further the pupil travels to school, the more remote the chance of any link between the operational unit of the Church – St. Everywhere's Parish – and the school community, joining one after leaving the other. Since 1960, Shiplake Heads have all been Oxford educated Anglicans, but none have been 'High Church'. While weekday services are fewer, first interviews with visiting parents went quickly to a fundamental 'What do you want Shiplake/us/me to do for your son(s)?' One does not want to press the analogy with almost the same question in Luke's Gospel to a blind man seeking to regain his sight. This awareness was never far from themes chosen for the Fortieth Anniversary Thanksgiving Service, in the Sports Hall presided over by the Bishop of Dorchester.

Seven years after arriving at Shiplake, Nick Bevan joined the committee of the Society of Heads of Independent Schools – generally known as SHMIS. He was the first Shiplake Head to venture beyond merely belonging to professional associations and into entertaining as well as hosting meetings of SHMIS, Secondary Heads and IAPS meetings at the College. By February 1996, Nick was Chairman Designate of SHMIS and found himself on the Advisory Committee of the Independent Schools Joint Council. His early steps were cautious – a balance had to be struck between gaining ideas for conference speakers against returning to a backlog of decisions; catching up and consulting colleagues. Providing the SHMIS Chairman gave Shiplake College a high profile, especially as 1997 was an election year. Training to deal with radio, television and newspapers was part of preparing to take over as Chairman. In some ways this was an extension of the skills already needed in the yearly struggle to keep up numbers in one's own school.

Never one to be caught unawares, Nick Bevan warned the Shiplake governors about how much he would be away in 1997. He had to organise his own annual conference and would represent SHMIS at four other conferences, as well as being a guest at HMC. Committee work and representing SHMIS on National Committees involved being away at least one day a week, but being able to do good uninterrupted work on trains was a help. During his year at the helm of SHMIS, Nick Bevan made contributions to what one hopes will be long-term improvements. He belonged to the steering committee of the Lansdowne Group – working to create new perceptions of boarding school life – and this is now the Boarding Education Alliance. In 1998 Nick was Vice-Chairman of SHMIS and belonged to a Unity Working Party to develop the ISC. He was also concerned to lighten the load on future leaders of SHMIS, so a committee of past chairmen began to study how to delegate some of the work of attending conferences nation-wide.

With a considerable sporting profile and an ambitious building programme, Shiplake had the day to day look of success and many expressed surprise that the Head was not a member of the Headmasters' (and Headmistresses') Conference. John Eggar was always content to say that 'We were members of the "Second XI Organisation"', SHMIS, and recently Nick Bevan felt that SHMIS answered well all his professional development needs. Those long involved with Shiplake believed that HMC was not a conscious objective. In the summer of 1964, the Staff responded to John Eggar's insistence that we should define our long-term objectives. After the first five years of growth, in what directions should we progress? The size of the school estate meant we could never be a large school and no one thought of the possibility of seventy day boys when there were still several Grammar Schools in the area. Could we, or indeed should we, compete with the nearby independents for a more academic entry? After all, we had already fashioned our own style in helping our not very academic part of the Common Entrance field. The rewards lay ahead – the many parents who could say 'no one wanted him at thirteen, but Shiplake made a success of him'.

The 1964 consensus was that HMC membership should not be part of our plan. Of the twenty staff at that discussion, fourteen had been at HMC schools, but prestige was far from the point. We did not want to restrict our wide entry. We hoped to be more selective in the long run and prep schools already understood that we did not take all-comers. Every entrant had to have something to offer. It was some years before we were qualified to join SHMIS, the organisation which represented the smaller boarding schools. In 1995, SHMIS had fifty members (only twenty with above three hundred and fifty pupils) plus a further twenty elected in fairly recent years to HMC. Curiously our fellow members had changed more than we had; the majority were now co-educational throughout at a time when we were still thinking about girls at sixth form level.

Early in the 1990s we had an informal visit from the Secretary of HMC rather on the basis that we had become the kind of school that might be elected. At that stage our 'A' Level results did not qualify us, so the matter was quietly left. We knew what our boys could do at thirteen and the ability to measure value added over five years was close at hand. At Shiplake there was no feeling of being left out. Very few post-1950 foundations have seen their Heads elected to HMC membership. It was a long time since inter-war foundations like Stowe, Canford and Bryanston had quickly attained HMC status. We did not think 'there was anything odd about Shiplake not being a member', but perhaps some parents and some schools did.

In 1998, N.V. Bevan was elected to the HMC and thus Shiplake College became a new member of an organisation of large independent schools. (Taking 1995 as a typical year, only thirty HMC schools had fewer than three hundred and fifty pupils; of the remaining two hundred schools, seventy-five had no boarders.) HMC Inspectors were impressed by the high quality of teaching at Shiplake – confirming Nick Bevan's belief that day-to-day teaching had never been better. Nick himself is unlikely to see this development as a well-deserved recognition of his work, but of course it is. He could have been content with the many good things he found on arrival. He chose to expand facilities and had the support of governors and parents – this at a time when other schools were retrenching. He battled to keep up numbers and if he responded to the pleas of the easy going with 'well, tough!' he was also tough on himself. Recognition of John Eggar's long stewardship was the affection and admiration of many. Peter Lapping's persuasive vigour was rewarded by promotion. HMC membership confirms the value of the Bevan years.

CHAPTER 37

The Way Forward: The Debate Continues

IN 1984 THERE WAS abundant evidence that independent schools had been flexible when facing changing circumstances and Shiplake's further progress required freshness of outlook and continued adaptability. What, in brief, has happened since then? Independent schools in the Southeast were full until 1990, then they began to encounter the 'keeping up numbers problems' that northern and southwestern schools had already come up against. Until 1992, changing circumstances were mainly philosophical. 'Staff appraisal' was thought to be not quite proper in some schools. The 'new' GCSE was considered insufficiently challenging, computers made things rather easy and discouraged traditional skills – they must be used with caution – and a few even could be insensitive and snobbish over the impending Children Act. In all these areas, one likes to believe that Shiplake's youth as a school made us constructive in our response to so many schemes. However, there were some signs of premature hardening of the arteries of communication when Shiplake set about exploiting the improvements amidst so much innovation. In the absence of any endowments, never mind the substantial endowments of some foundations, Shiplake was heavily dependent on maintaining the number of boarders. The key to our early success lay in being a school that fathers and experienced schoolmasters could understand. As we built up fixture lists, established a house system, started 'A' Level work, introduced a Cadet Force, became known for rowing, employed a Chaplain, found jobs for leavers and produced the first University entrants, we became, clearly, a safe haven for middle of the road boys who could be prefects and all-rounders in a small school.

The Goodwin Building of 1990, with the new Art School in its shadow, are important achievements of the Shiplake community. They met many parental expectations, answered many educational needs and are, for pupils, a gateway to many fields. Of course there had been some carpentry, computing, design, painting and pottery, but mind, eye and hand found fresh challenges under one roof and in the face of new examination structures.

In a decade when a boarding school education is less sought after than in

Shiplake's heady days of rapid expansion, it is not surprising that the case for boarding is being re-thought. There is also a strong case for re-examining childhood itself, in far wider terms than the Children Act. The principle of 'residence' is under pressure and 'living what you are doing' needs explanation. In an electronic era why bother to reside at University? Essays can be emailed to a tutor after a week's Internet research in a room at home. It is easy to ignore the obvious until one borrows an idea from one context and applies it elsewhere. Having recently heard the Abbot of Downside stress that residence was fundamental to the Benedictine Rule, one's life work suddenly becomes clear. By extension, the 'Stabilitas loci' needed for the spiritual life to grow and which encouraged scholarship and art in past centuries, is still a vital concept. In the long run, University is what you learned from the people you were with. The main benefit of Scouting or CCF is going off to camp and expeditions are vital to the Duke of Edinburgh Award. Conferences and courses are fundamental to expanding adult careers. It is not easy to pinpoint the essence of residence, especially for boarders aged thirteen to eighteen, but it has something that the modern world has nearly lost, that continuity and security formerly obtained by a lifetime spent in the same village or in the same town, street and surroundings – both the familiar and family related.

Historically, boarding schools were for boys who had been brought up by servants. When beyond the control of Nurse or Governess, off they went. As already stressed, Shiplake was started near the end of a process which saw major boarding schools founded at the rate of two per year during the second half of the nineteenth century. In the same timespan, 'childhood' was invented by administrators and legislators.

We lament the demise of an idealised childhood, without considering how modern it really is. Infancy at home was spent with a non-employed mother and siblings who await father's teatime return from regular employment. Full-time school followed with the non-school hours at home with mother in charge. Spare time was spent with father and leisure time was easily filled with hobbies, clubs, youth movements and sports. Less affluent children were supported by free school milk, meals and medicals until they were allowed to leave compulsory school at thirteen or eventually later. Those at school were protected by laws limiting the amount of paid work permitted by school children.

The idealised childhood of western society, now being defended against erosion, is a product of market forces, social ambition and the vision of classically educated government officials. Industrial societies needed literate and numerate workers; the middle classes needed to establish their children on administrative or commercial career ladders and skilled workers had ambitions for their own children. Hard work and prosperity meant moving up a class and the content of teaching revealed what civil servants understood to be essential to the training of citizens. The priorities of 1880 are not all that different at the start of the twenty-first century. Can the state afford not to invest more in up-to-date education? Can better off parents afford not to pay fees at independent schools? Success is to be proved by tests and exams in almost every year of secondary education, further pressurising the immature.

Childhood, as we remember it, was partly the result of the skilled worker and his matriarch copying middle class attitudes and applying the discipline of an industrial age to all family members, at least until they were twenty-one. The whole concept was put under pressure during two world wars but it survived the inter-war depression and was at its most prosperous in the era of full employment from 1950 to 1970.

In retrospect, children and young people were preached at, rather than involved in any discussion about real values. Rapid changes in the attitudes of young people were blamed on everything from 'Rock 'n Roll' music to what the Germans bluntly call 'the anti-baby pill'. Major changes have multiple explanations, but every half decade has trumpeted a single cause, unemployment. Fathers away on war service, the cinema, television, too much prosperity, increased divorce rates, working mothers (caused by any of higher living standards, inflation or paying school fees), the Vietnam War, the proliferation of drugs, video games and mobile phones have all been blamed in their time. An experienced Housemaster in any kind of secondary school would see these, not as eroding childhood, but rather as factors getting in the way of pupils' progress and development.

One of the few comparative certainties is that higher living standards – especially in health and nutrition – mean than many, but not all, pupils are physically mature at an earlier age. In social and educational terms, technological toys, video games and travel have advantages and drawbacks. Boarding school life deprives children not only of home life, but also of home gadgets. One is being sent away from what remains available to friends in suburbia. The problem is not the adult world saying 'No' but insisting on 'Wait'. Far fewer are natural conformists, compared with forty years ago. In spite of parental concern and defensive housemasters, never mind the law of the land, late night parties, smoking, alcohol and drugs are attractive. Young people have to be tougher to survive a changing world in residential education. It is not a matter of surviving the discomforts, the routines of yesteryear, the former lack of privacy and the heartiness despised and rejected by the many artists and writers who proclaimed how much they hated boarding school. The toughness lies in keeping a balance between the pressures of youth culture and the need to work and to act responsibly.

The 1990s at Shiplake have produced Fifth and Sixth forms that have worked harder than their predecessors and have a sense of duty to their own kind much to be admired. There is more awareness of need. The new boy under pressure is spotted and support provided. Persistent breaches of rules are noted and, in the best interests of all concerned, authority is quietly informed. Not everyone will find his Housemaster congenial, so the development of the tutor system means a choice of staff to consult.

Even at the time, the 1980s appeared more favourable to Shiplake College than many expected and some knew that simply being in the southeast was an asset. While the building programme of the 1990s also exceeded expectations, the background was a clear reduction in the number of boarders. A comparison with industry was obvious – investment in new plant was essential to remaining competitive.

As one challenge was rapidly followed by another, the Shiplake story changed. Until the 1980s the story was straightforward, having many of the elements of a rattling good yarn. Objectives were simple – academic improvement and financial stability. The best possible 'O' Level results for our varied entry, at the right pace, would build up a Sixth Form. Through sports, and within a traditional house system, boys would get much the same experience as brothers in a long-established school. The Governors had the responsibility of providing the buildings vital to these aims and the duty of prudently expanding within a balanced budget.

The image then shifts from a long, steady voyage to the plot, if any, of a novel by one of James Joyce's many semi-detached imitators. So much so, that Shiplake's last twelve years may be more true to life. Disconnected occurrences, unfinished conversations, haphazard thoughts, the imagined and the unrelated, all banter away at the structure of the term and the planned day. Over a year, individuals enter and leave the lives of student and parent, Head and colleague, almost at random. Administration is just keeping confusion at bay or so it seems. Unexpected questions provoke hasty responses. Does one say 'Thank you' or 'Oh damn' upon receiving a message? The marvel is that with all the strains of the 1990s the pupils at Shiplake have received consistent care and been challenged academically as never before.

In 1984 no objection was advanced to the thesis that a twenty-five year old Shiplake College was a continuation of a Victorian tradition of founding independent schools. It was Peter Lapping who dubbed Shiplake a 'nineteenth-century event in a post World War II setting'. It is now becoming clear that these mainly unendowed schools, which now provide the bulk of HMC and GSA, are keeping faith with their past to a greater extent than other institutions once motivated by duty, thrift, piety, prudence, idealism, local patriotism and self-help. In the decay of the Cooperative Wholesale Society, the Trades Unions and the not wholly altruistic conversion of building societies and mutual life assurance undertakings, we see the alternate dangers of poor image or pure profit. At the moment 'better to be with the Woodard corporation than with the Woolwich!' Most of those involved with Shiplake's early days had been educated in nineteenth century foundations or had worked in them and were fifty or sixty years closer to the pre-1914 public school than Shiplake is. A century ago Britain was a confident state, yet the nineteenth century began amid fears of social and political change. In working hard to keep up to date, Shiplake has embraced the cause of progress. Even so, it is part of a community of independent schools where attitudes have changed so much since 1959. Religious communities no longer wish to conduct boarding schools so a number have passed to lay management and unordained Heads. A number of major boys' schools were committed to very low fees for the sons of clergy. This emphasis of forty years ago has slipped away. Of the three dozen Girls' School Association members named after saints, only one dates from after World War II. Under modern conditions, a geographical location is a safer marketing image. So much then, for now, when independent schools may search their souls at the beginning of a new century.

There is no urgent need to peer into the future. After forty years, Shiplake can proudly judge its current place by holding up the present against the past and against the experiences of any schools like ourselves.

CHAPTER 38

Afterword

WHAT CAN BE SAID about the Shiplake College of the early 21st century that has not already been outlined in this fascinating coverage of the College's early history? This final chapter, written seven years after Hans Wells-Furby's departure from the institution that he had served so well in so many capacities, will attempt to offer a snapshot of the needs, concerns and achievements of Shiplake as it chugs along inexorably towards its half century.

Let us consider as a starting point a real snapshot, the Millennium school photograph taken in September 2000*. What, if anything, can we glean from it? Firstly, where is it set? The photographer has his back to the A4155 (now, mercifully, with a speed limit of 30 mph following the tragic death of Matthew Bevin in 1994), and is facing the new Pavilion complex at the New Field end of the Goodwin Building. It is a fine construction, designed to attune with the Victorian Gothic feel of the original Court – note the grey criss-cross patterns in the brickwork. Although only opened in 1997, it is no longer the jewel in the crown of the building programme. That honour goes to the Humanities Block, so adroitly sited and designed at the heart of the school. Old Vikings, familiar with the long, thin, cold classrooms, until so recently in use for Geography, History and Modern Language teaching in the Stableyard, would be enthralled with the large, airy, carpeted computer-linked classrooms opened in April 2000 by Kate Adie. Even as I write, plans are afoot for an Upper Sixth House quite separate from the existing 13–18 houses familiar to most readers. Of this, more anon.

Who are in the photo? Well, naturally, the 280 or so students of Shiplake College plus the teachers and a few non-teaching staff. How good to count nine female pupils, all Sixth Form day girls, dotted here and there on the higher levels. The reasons for the introduction of girls to Shiplake College have been covered elsewhere, but it is significant, even symbolic, I think, that, in this photograph, they do not stand in a cluster but are fully amalgamated into the previously all-male institution that they have bravely and cheerfully opted to join. How many girls will there be in ten years' time? This is an intriguing

* See book jacket

question for the pundits. On the one hand, it may be possible to move towards a fully co-educational school, with girls, boarding and day, at all levels. This has certainly been achieved at many boys' independent schools in recent years. But perhaps, for that very reason, Shiplake should be different and offer, for that large number of parents who still want it, single sex education below the Sixth Form. Shiplake boys, for all their many talents and attributes, are often not brimming over with self-confidence, especially when they first arrive, and, so the argument goes, they would be further intimidated by the presence of voluble and maybe more physically and intellectually mature girls.

There are some parents who fear that their sons are entering some kind of monastic isolation as they drive towards Shiplake for the first time. Doesn't that breed, at best, social gaucheness, they ask, and, at worst, confused sexuality (though this latter concern is often implied rather than stated)? No and no are the answers to those. One has only to glance at the beautiful young ladies many of our leavers bring as partners to the Summer Ball. In the year 2000, we received no fewer than 23 invitations from girls' schools to parties, discos and other socials. I should know, because I seem to have taken on the duties of social secretary to the boys – my predecessor was spared that, I believe. It is certainly gratifying to hear, as we often do, that Shiplake boys, 13-year-olds as well as 18-year-olds, are regarded as amongst the most polite, well-mannered and modest young men that these girls' schools ever see – hence our popularity. Although not all invitations could be taken up, we still sent boys to seven different girls' schools for a total of sixteen functions, all under the watchful eye of willing members of staff. By way of reciprocation, our two Sixth Form dances, one for the Upper Sixth and one for the Lower, are amongst the most lavish on the circuit, while other smaller events, often on a house basis, are listed in the termly calendar or, more often, the updated weekly green calendar.

With the arrival of the girls has come a much more prominent female presence in the school as a whole. In the 1970 school photograph, I counted three ladies: thirty years later, twenty-one are included, not all teachers by any means, but all helping to soften the potentially rough ethos that can develop in a men only environment. Old Vikings and friends of the school may recognise Judy Smail and Marjorie White seated in the photo and, of course, Annabel Bevan sits on the Headmaster's right, but many of the standing female teachers are of more recent vintage. Their presence in the school is almost unreservedly beneficial, but two small difficulties have emerged here as elsewhere. With the best will in the world, ladies cannot coach rugby teams, of which we have a dozen in the school, and few feel drawn to the water to coach rowing, though there are exceptions to this, not least Suzie Ellis, a former Great Britain cox. They have to find other ways in which to contribute to the school: these contributions, often very considerable, are less ostensible and public. Teachers and pupils alike have to appreciate that, just because a female teacher is not dressed in a tracksuit, with a whistle in her mouth at every opportunity, it does not mean that she is giving nothing to the community. To take but two examples, Val Smallman, who joined the staff from a Bracknell comprehensive in 1999, has built upon the sterling work of Andrew Smail in the Learning Support Department and spends many afternoons drafting ITPs (individual teaching plans) for the benefit of all, whilst Lorraine Eccleston, who joined the History department from a Scottish prep school also in 1999, oversees the important house tennis leagues which keep so many boys busy long into the summer afternoons.

Another remarkable and distinctive feature of the College teaching staff at the beginning of the 21st century is the large proportion, over 15 per cent, who have taught or learned at southern hemisphere schools. Australia, New Zealand, South Africa and Zimbabwe are all well represented, not just from gap year students. Ivan Jacklin, an ex-housemaster, and Andrew Cheadle, a current one, have been mentioned in these pages, but Shane O'Brien, the head of PE, and Alex Hunt, in the CDT department, are also among those antipodeans who work hard and play hard and, by their mere presence here, highlight the internationality of our community.

In actual fact, Shiplake tends to have fewer overseas pupils than many of its competitors. In 1995, for example, there were about 25 boys who did not have at least one parent who was a British national: that number, in 2000, has decreased by half, not in any way as part of an agreed policy, but almost entirely because of the vagaries of the market. Shiplake always welcomes pupils from other parts of the world, whether natives of those parts or British ex-pats, but, as it happens, in the last year, EFL (English as a foreign language) has been deemed to be no longer required, and Michael Edwards has been less enthusiastic than some marketing directors to take our exhibition stand to all corners of the world, though recent marketing trips to Dubai and India have occurred. But Shiplake's cosmopolitanism is perhaps best demonstrated in the sustained and meaningful relationship that has built up between ourselves and Kikunduku Primary School in Kenya. The 27-mile sponsored walk from Shillingford along the Thames to Shiplake in 1999, followed by the Headmaster's moving and exhilarating trip to the school, stressed Shiplake's commitment to the cause. Several boys have been to Kikunduku, and Julian Seaton's six-week sojourn there recently, during which he used his woodwork and engineering skills to good effect, was a remarkable one. The humility and enormous gratitude demonstrated in the many letters from Kenya have taught us all quite a bit, too. This contact with Kikunduku is not merely an opportunity to ease our social consciences by slipping a fiver into a collecting tin every now and then. It is an ongoing and two-way relationship. Throughout the history of the College, as we read of it in this book, we can see that those in authority have decided that if a thing is worth doing, it is worth doing well. The rapid growth of the school, against all the odds, in the 1960s; a building programme that has eschewed, wherever possible, the merely functional and aesthetically unpleasing option; an extra-curricular structure that has allowed Shiplake, a really very small place, to play many sports at all levels against bigger and more established schools. These are all examples of the spirit that has carried Shiplake through to a new century in such fine fettle.

I doubt if there is any school in the country that has changed more than Shiplake in the last 25 years. Those last physical links with the early days, David Welsh and Monica Tomalin, have gone from Shiplake though, thankfully, not from the area. But, despite all the changes, there is still much that is preserved and cherished from the old days. Look again at the photograph. On the Headmaster's left is Harry Colvin, the Head Boy in 2000-2001, and, between myself and Richard Mannix, the outgoing Orchard housemaster, is the Deputy Head of College, John Robinson, whose brother Oliver also had a distinguished College career in the 1980s. The engraved names of the Heads of College on the Great Hall Honours Board go back to the very first year of our existence, when P.H. Morkel filled the role. In June 1999, all forty of these gentlemen, or their representatives, were invited to a very special dinner in the Hall. Well over half turned up, and were addressed by the then Head of College, Rory Smith, who reflected both on the changes that his predecessors would have spotted and on some of the similarities. 'Sometimes we even dress for Sunday Chapel in jeans and shirts rather than a more traditional suit,' he quipped, but added, 'What matters most is that Shiplake really does remain the friendly and supportive community that it always was. I would not want to be anywhere else.'

The other younger people seated in the photo are the heads of houses, houses that remain as fiercely individualistic and competitive as they could ever have been. Increasingly, Burr House has become the house for full boarders, many of whom spend large numbers of weekends in College: at the other end of the spectrum, Welsh House almost entirely empties at the end of the week, though its members have the option of staying in. Everett and Skipwith offer a middle course, with the latter edging more towards weekly boarding each year. Before traditionalists throw up their hands in horror, let it be stated that the 'weekend' does not start on Friday afternoon, but at the end of games, compulsory for all pupils, on Saturday, and that, for most boarders, the leave ends on Sunday evening.

Nonetheless, there are now as few as sixty pupils at the Sunday service, and the campus after that can seem almost spookily quiet, especially during the popular 'Tesco runs' in the minibus before lunch. Detention moved from its Sunday mid-morning slot to Friday afternoons in 1996. Those teaching staff who try to set up activities on Sunday afternoons meet generally with a polite lack of interest, perhaps not surprising in a place that is so busy for up to six days a week. On summer Sundays, the 'sunbathing lawn' near the recently enlarged swimming pool, fills up with those who (shall we be optimistic?) find that a congenial spot in which to revise for exams.

Most of this move away from full boarding is part of a national trend, one that Shiplake has neither the ability nor the desire to buck. Hans Wells-Furby, in earlier chapters, made much of the national and global issues which have provided the backcloth for the burgeoning of the College. It is indeed difficult to escape such parallels and links. At the most basic level, the televised England football matches on the evenings of two of the last four End of Year Suppers have resulted in timings and arrangements being overturned! More subtly, the collapse of the Far Eastern stock markets between 1996 and 1998 directly accounted for the decline in pupils from that part of the world. By contrast, the opening up of eastern Europe, the disturbances in the Balkans, the move towards a united Europe; all these resulted in new students from unexpected quarters. In 1997, the Labour Party returned to power after a gap of some eighteen years, but gone was the fiery rhetoric of the 1970s and earlier, gone the public dismissal of independent education as 'an anachronistic carbuncle' to be swept away at the first opportunity. The Direct Grant schools may have disappeared, or changed, and the Assisted Places Scheme scrapped, but, mercifully, the charitable status of schools like ours remains intact, and the emphasis nowadays is upon partnership with the state system. Certainly the College has enjoyed a fruitful two-way relationship with the local Primary School in recent years. Children and staff have used our computer room to good effect, for example, while some of our gap students, who hope one day to teach in the Primary sector, have been up the road, either to take games or to participate in classroom activities. Although it is fair to describe the Labour Government's attitude towards the independent sector as ambivalent, it nevertheless poses in 2001 no immediate threat to the existence of Shiplake College.

Let us return briefly to the Millennium photograph and take another look. It can hardly be disputed that the assembled young people look smart, perhaps surprisingly so to those of us used to the dishevelled look of the 1970s, the Lennon hair and glasses, huge tie knots and bell-bottomed trousers. There may even be disappointment amongst some aficionados of the school that these boys and girls seem so ready to conform. Where are the sports jackets, the checked and striped shirts, the weirdly designed pullovers that stretch the rules on such matters to the limit? These are surely a Shiplake tradition, an acknowledgment of the individuality of our children. Well, never fear, you are looking at the Sunday best, but in working hours (and indeed through to 7.00 pm), the boys do indeed have much more freedom and, my goodness, they use it. Partly in response to the wishes of parents who simply panicked when faced with the requirement to buy a 'plain, dark blazer', the College, since January 2001, insists that juniors (Y9, 10 and 11) who want to buy a blazer must do so through the school shop, where Paul Emerson stocks an unobtrusive little number with Viking buttons! But the tradition of sartorial freedom, at least compared with many other schools, is alive and kicking.

However, one must agree that the radicalism of earlier school generations has dissolved somewhat, perhaps under the constant pressure and demands of the exam syllabuses, course work and the like. To be a rebel, you have to be able to give a lot of time to being so, and you have to know that, when your rebel days are over (those 'green and carefree days' as Dylan Thomas calls them, when you 'sang in your chains like the sea'), you will have a niche in that society that you may or may not have changed with your protests. Many students, here as elsewhere, appear apathetic compared with their predecessors, but that can be misleading, as it stems from a perfectly natural concern about their own futures, a concern not to waste their parents' money.

As the threat of open revolt has receded over the years, as the fundamental conservatism (with a small 'c', possibly with a capital as well!) of our young people has asserted itself, so the Headmaster has felt legitimately that the democratisation of the school can move forward. In setting up School Council, Sixth Form Council, Food Committee, Shop Committee (with the intriguing acronym of SWHOOPBES) in the 1990s, the College could be reasonably sure that discussions would focus on whether prep should end at 20.50 or 21.00, whether croissants should be available on three or four mornings a week for breakfast, whether there can be an extra rubbish bin outside the shop. This is not to belittle such discussions: such things are important to those who live and work here 24 hours a day for 36 weeks a year. However, it is fair to say that, if and when resolutions are submitted, recommending the abolition of the prefect system, questioning the compulsory nature of lessons, demanding that a Sixth Form Council decision be honoured automatically by the Senior Management Team, well, that will be the time for the democratic process to come to a halt, albeit temporarily.

Of course, young people are still young people, adolescents struggling to come to terms with the changes in their own bodies and with the world in which they will shortly be taking their place. Seldom does such a turbulent period as the teens pass by without some hitch, and it would be wrong, in this sketch of Shiplake College at the start of a new millennium, to disguise the fact that there have been a very small number of pupils expelled for drug offences and that the most common cause of suspension is the persistent breaking of school rules on drinking and smoking.

Every school does its best to educate its young people in the dangers of alcohol, tobacco, cannabis and the harder drugs, and I think the Shiplake policy is well understood and fair. But it is a notoriously difficult area to legislate for and then to police, and it is even more difficult when so many boarders go home on Saturday evenings and are inevitably drawn to parties in London and elsewhere. Will cannabis be legalised? Is it more dangerous than, say, cigarettes? Is it all right to drink if you are not driving? These are the questions we want pupils to ask themselves and to ask their teachers.

All we can actually do is draw up a series of rules, complying roughly, but not exactly, with the laws of the land. We can discourage smoking by quoting the Children Act that the school, in loco parentis, has a 'duty of care' to its pupils, which means we cannot let them harm themselves with nicotine any more than we can harm them by, for example, leaving dangerous chemicals out. We can encourage sensible, moderate drinking by opening the JCR (Junior Common Room) four evenings a week for 17-year-olds and over. We can and must condemn all illegal drugs; in so doing, the school reserves the right to take urine samples and it will immediately expel any pupil who is supplying drugs to others, whether or not for payment.

Is this the right action? It approximates to most other schools' policies and probably has changed only in emphasis not, forgive the pun, in substance, here over the last thirty years or so. Nothing will totally deter the average adolescent from experimenting, but Shiplake's line, that fine balance between carrot and stick, is probably more successful than most, built, as it is, upon a consideration of values in general.

You will find nothing of what I have just written in any of the PR material produced by the College, and you would not expect to. In 2001, more than ever before, Shiplake is a commercial concern, marketing itself furiously, navel gazing on a grand scale with its SWOT analyses and the like. The discovery that the average number of schools visited by prospective parents and their children is now more than five was a sobering one, and the Headmaster's recurring lament about his job is that so much of it is geared to filling the school. Visiting parents are still shown round by College pupils. These tours, lasting up to an hour, are endearingly idiosyncratic, though they are supposed to conform to a pattern laid down by the Marketing Director. They are refreshingly different from what some parents experience at other schools, where no one lower than a prefect would be let loose on such valuable potential clients. What else does Shiplake try to do that is different? Reference has been made to the Facts Booklet, the last two editions of which I have had the honour to edit. In 1996, a pupil's prospectus was introduced to complement the standard glossy one. It is sent under separate cover to the child, and covers such matters as skateboard ramps and ice skating trips rather than GCSE option columns! Under the inspirational influence of Charly Lowndes, who arrived in 1997 to take over our ICT department, Shiplake has developed both an Intranet and an Internet site (www.shiplake.org.uk), the latter containing a vast array of information about the school and an opportunity for Old Vikings to stay in touch. I commend it to you. Who would have believed even five years ago that requests for prospectuses would now be e-mailed through on-line and that a 'virtual' tour of the College would be available to anyone in the world?

All recent marketing research has suggested that Shiplake should be looking increasingly to South and West London for more pupils. Demand for senior independent school places in London outstrips supply, and Shiplake, a mere 50 minutes or so via the M4 or M40, has much to offer, as we all know, the all-round child with plenty of potential who may not be an academic high flyer. There is no immediate likelihood of the College opening its doors to 11-year-olds, nor is it likely to acquire its own prep school, so the search goes on far and wide for the right pupils from a large batch of feeder schools, some of which, sadly, are finding it difficult to hold on to their senior (Y7 and 8) boys under pressure from 11 to 18 schools of one kind or another. One of the loveliest social occasions of the year is the prep school heads' cruise in June, when the paddle steamer, 'The New Orleans', sails down the Thames, packed with prep school senior managers who watch with awe as the First VIII row past, and listen attentively to the dulcet strains of the Big Band. This is an unashamedly PR occasion, but much appreciated by those very people on whom the future of Shiplake College depends.

One last look at the photograph, if you can face it. I have tried to consider some of the things that it tells us about the current strength of the school. But what happened five minutes after this special picture was taken? To what were these young men and ladies, not to mention the not-so-young teaching staff, returning after this brief and probably welcome break in their routines? Put crudely, they returned that Friday in September 2000 to their classrooms or, more precisely, their teachers' classrooms since, for the first time in 2000, every full-time teacher enjoyed the pleasure of being based in his or her own room. To learn what? 'O' Levels disappeared in 1987 to be replaced by GCSEs, and most pupils today tackle a total of seven or eight such courses. A declining number keep going with Learning Support right through until the end of Y11 (the old Fifth Form), though that is still a perfectly feasible and very 'Shiplake' option. The subjects are not very different from any other school's. Perhaps a higher proportion of pupils take subjects like Art, Ceramics, Design Technology, Sports Studies and the like, these being more practical while preserving a considerable academic component, too. There are no GNVQs, the vocational courses offered at some institutions considered to be our competitors. The theory is that boys are admitted to Shiplake on the assumption that they can at least tackle seven GCSEs: with small classes (the maximum is still only 18) and the very distinctive support on offer, most pupils will stand a very reasonable chance of passing. The Value Added statistics that place the school in the top five per cent nationally certainly justify the policy of letting all pupils sit GCSEs and the recent pass rate of about 70 per cent confirms that view.

Beyond GCSEs, most students embark on four AS courses. This is not the time or place to launch into a detailed explanation of this new tier of examinations studied in the Lower Sixth. Introduced only in September 2000, they allow students to accumulate 'units' or modules, rather than wait two whole years before sitting the life or death 'A' Level exams. It is hard to evaluate the impact of this radical initiative, either on individuals or on the school as a whole, but early signs are encouraging, not least in keeping certain young people, who might have found the old 'A' Levels beyond them, working away in an academic environment.

Time will tell. We cannot read the future; as 'time's subjects', we can merely do our best to ensure that this wonderful success story that is Shiplake College has the chance to go on, as Nick Bevan has stated as his avowed aim, to be 'amongst the very best small schools in England'. Perhaps it already is: the Head's inclusion in the ranks of the prestigious Headmasters' Conference would point that way. But this is no time to sit back. The College must continue to adapt to survive. The boarding houses, architecturally delightful though they are, are not really large enough to comply with Social Services' regulations, as our boarding numbers remain so buoyant. The solution, a bold one, is to cream off the top year of each house into a separate Upper Sixth Form house with its own ethos, rules and housemaster. Links will be retained with the houses from which the students originally came, but this new house, as yet unnamed, will give them the chance to prepare, academically, emotionally and socially, for University.

And beyond that? More computers to add to the 70 that the College already owns? Or none – everyone brings their own. Distance learning? An Arts Centre? The acquisition of new land, making the current hiring of river pitches, New Field and Sonning Astroturf unnecessary?

Mr Wells-Furby's book, quite rightly and unashamedly, has looked backwards. The recent visit (May 2000) of Alexander Everett, the school's Founder, highlighted how short this history has been. Mr Everett not only spoke cogently about those early days, but also passed around his business card because, amazingly, he is still operating a company in the United States! He remembers the arrival of that very first Viking in 1959, and he announced proudly to his audience in the Great Hall that he has every intention of living until he is at least 110. If the energy and spirit displayed by the school's Founder, and reflected in its current Headmaster, can be matched by the pride and confidence that the young people in the 2000 photograph seem to exude, then the future is indeed bright.

Appendix 1

Alexander Everett's Recollections of The Founding of Shiplake College

I WAS EDUCATED at Dorset House, a traditional private prep school in Sussex and at Aldenham, a small public school in Hertfordshire. My school days were not the proverbial 'happiest days of my life'. I was not that well co-ordinated and did not perform well on the playing fields. In the classroom my spelling was atrocious, foreign languages were just that, 'foreign' to me. Mathematics I did well at, but in general I was a poor student. I never was popular since I neither excelled at sports or academically. I even remember deliberately talking in prep time one evening in order to gain attention and receive three strokes with the cane in order hopefully to become accepted by other pupils.

So it was that at an early age I decided to start a school where all the boys would be happy, regardless of their abilities, and encouragement would be given to slow learners. At this time, in my mind, Shiplake College was already at the drawing board stage.

At the end of the Second World War I took the humblest of jobs in a prep school. The Headmaster noted my organisational abilities and in a short time I became the Second or Senior Master. By the time I was 28 years old, I started my own prep school at Bexhill-on-Sea, named Pendragon after Uther Pendragon, the father of King Arthur. Here I made a startling discovery, that it is easy to teach the gifted child. Michael Yarwood was aged twelve; I taught him everything I knew. He won a top scholarship to Kings Canterbury. What really happened is that I gave him the necessary textbooks from which he taught himself. However, it was the boys who found learning difficult that really needed the help. From that moment on I devoted my time to the slow learners.

It was at Pendragon that I met my wife to be, Eunice. She had lost her first husband in 1954 and her son Richard was shy and nervous and needed all the help he could get. By chance, I was asked to sell Pendragon, which I did and moved to Ashfold Prep School in Buckinghamshire. I was given all the backward boys who were formed into a class called 'Shell' and I built a reputation for helping the less likely to succeed. Some followed me to Shiplake. Richard, after Pendragon, became a pupil at Ashfold. His mother Eunice came and lived near Ashfold. During my stay at Ashfold, Eunice and I became closer and eventually were married in the little Dorton Church in the school grounds. Some boys sang in the choir and the wedding reception was held at the school.

There is a great similarity between Ashfold and Shiplake since the Parish Church was in both cases adjacent to the school buildings. Peter Carter-Ruck was best man and it was now that plans were laid in earnest to start a school for older boys.

Eunice and I went to Scotland to visit Kurt Halin at Gordonstoun where I learnt the concept that boys should compete[1] with themselves to achieve better results, rather than compete against each other. A master who was retiring promised to help me start my own school on the lines of Gordonstoun, when I found the right set of buildings, but unfortunately he died rather suddenly just before Shiplake Court was bought.

It was through Knight Frank and Rutley that I discovered Shiplake Court which was purchased for £17,500. My wife had private means and together with what I sold Pendragon for we were jointly able to scrape together the necessary amount of cash[2] to buy the buildings and equip them with sufficient furnishings as well as have enough money for operational costs. We moved to Shiplake Court late in 1958. I well remember the first Christmas – three of us – Eunice, Richard and myself, living in a forty-room mansion, huddled round a blazing log fire in the Great Hall.

Word was out that a school was being formed. Our first pupil, Alistair Barron, arrived from Reading in January 1959. Since I lacked the necessary academic qualifications, I employed George Spencer Brown as Senior Tutor. We were now in business in earnest. Plans were made, beds and furniture were ordered. A prospectus was printed and a company was formed; Eunice and I became directors along with my friend Peter Carter-Ruck, who was the first Chairman of the Board, and Eunice's solicitor Aubrey Goodwin. The Red House came on the market. I was criticised for not purchasing this building, but we plainly didn't have the cash to buy it. The front drive was tarred; the cricket field was ploughed, levelled and seeded. Staff – teaching and domestic – were hired. Somehow or other everything was ready for the start of Shiplake on May 1st 1959. We signed up 30 boys and turned away several pupils since I had ordered only 30 beds! I planned to take 120 students in all, since I measured the Great Hall to seat 120 boys for meals and the Church would hold 120 for Sunday service. Anyhow, I wanted to keep the school small so individual attention could be given to help every student's personal needs. In order to pay for this, I intended charging higher fees. I figured that there would always be 120 sets of parents who would pay to obtain the best education possible.

The first term was well on its way and problems appeared. The Senior Tutor did not work out with both boys and staff and was asked to leave. My wife and I were having personal problems. Richard, her son to whom I became stepfather,

[1] The concept behind John Foster's Tri-weekly order cards.

[2] It is hard to remember how difficult it was to borrow capital sums in the 1950s and 60s.

demanded much attention and I was never able to give him enough of my time. I personally always wanted to have a son of my own and, unknown to me, the day after we married I found out that Eunice had arranged to go to the London Clinic for a hysterectomy which didn't exactly cement our marriage. Also I had hoped Eunice would play her part as Headmaster's wife and handle the catering and kitchen staff which she never did. However, she was 'great at entertaining' the parents and always enjoyed mixing with other people. She and I both drank socially, but unfortunately she went beyond that. What with one thing and another it became apparent to all that something had to change. We struggled on for the remainder of the first two terms to the end of 1959.

Then, in order to save the Shiplake that I was proud to have founded and wanted to see continue, which I am happy to say has become the great school that it is 40 years later, I decided to leave and hand over the reins to David Skipwith. My wife Eunice opted to stay in residence after I left. Eventually I gave up my shares and in due course resigned from the Board of Governors. I knew that with Peter Carter-Ruck still involved the school would go on from strength to strength. Shiplake gradually turned in the direction of a more traditional public school. I am content in knowing that happiness reigns and the under achiever is being helped to become a successful citizen in life.

As the person who had the vision in the first place, I am extremely grateful to all those people who have brought the dream of Shiplake College into reality. I especially thank the author of this book, Hans Wells-Furby, who has devoted the major part of his life to helping make Shiplake College what it is today. I also wish to thank Nicholas Bevan, who is Headmaster at the time of revising this book for his part in arranging for vast quantities of bricks and mortar to be added to the physical structure of Shiplake College, as well as directing the academic aspect and general running of the school. For these two people, Hans and Nicholas, I will personally be eternally grateful.

Appendix 2

Founders, Chairmen of Governors, Headmasters and Senior Staff since the Foundation of Shiplake College

FOUNDERS

Mr Alexander de Morley Everett   Mrs Eunice Richardson

CHAIRMEN OF GOVERNORS

1959 – 65 P. F. Carter-Ruck
1966 – 71 R. Goodenough
1971 – 78 A.H. Southorn
1978 – 89 A.P. Goodwin
1989 – B.N. Gilson

HEADMASTERS

May/Dec 1959 A. de M. Everett
Jan/Dec 1960–62 D.J. Skipwith
Sept/Aug 1963–79 J.D. Eggar
Sept 1979–88 P.H. Lapping
Sept 1988– N.V. Bevan

SECOND MASTERS

Feb/Dec 1962–65 J.F. Foster (Acting Head Jan–Aug 1963)
Jan/Aug 1966 H.E. Wells-Furby
Sept/Aug 1966–80 M.M. Gilliat
Sept 1980–93 H.E. Wells-Furby

DEPUTY HEADMASTERS

Jan 1994– B.P. Edwards

BURSARS

1960 E.M. Burr
1960 H.W. Newell
1964 R.F. Jenks
1968 R.A. Alexander
1972 J.A. Corbett
1976 M.C. Whicker
1986– T.J. Mansergh

HOUSEMASTERS

EVERETT

1959 A. de M. Everett
1960 J.F. Foster
1966 M.W. Mash
1970 H.E. Wells-Furby
1982 D.S. Partridge
1991 I.S. Jacklin
1999– G.P. Wells

ORCHARD

1974 R.A. Esau
1978 D.S. Partridge
1982 P.G. Hose
1990 R.T. Mannix
2001– C.E. Allcock

WELSH

1965 D.F.K. Welsh
1978 R.A. Esau
1992– P.C.T. Gould

BURR

1959 E.M. Burr
1960 W. R. Hartley
1964 M.M. Gilliat
1980 P.J. Caston
1982 M.A. Smail
1997– A.R. Cheadle

SKIPWITH

1959 D.J. Skipwith
1961 H.E. Wells-Furby
1966 D.H. Drury
1972 M.J.H. Charles
1985 M.L. Woodcock
2001– N.J. Brown

Appendix 3
List of College Heads

No School Prefects before Spring 1961

Sept 1961–Jul 1962	P.H. Morkel Jan–Jul	(S)
1962	N.J. Findlay Sept – Dec	(B)
1963	A.H. Slatter Jan – Jul	(S)
1963	R.M. Shingler Sept – Jul	(B)
1964	J.P. Turner	(B)
1965	A.H. Patmore	(E)
1966	J.C.B. Clayton	(W)
1967	J.C. Pype	(B)
1968	N.J.C. Godwin	(W)
1969	I.K.F. Robertson	(E)
1970	A.G. Ridell	(B)
1971	J.W. Lundie	(B)
1972	A.D. Gordon	(E)
1973	J.M.P. Clayton	(E)
1974	F.G.A. Lambert	(E)
1975	S.S. Barnes	(W)
1976	J.R. Hardy	(B)
1977	I.C. Munday	(W)
1978	R.M.M. Davies	(W)
1979	R. Mackay	(B)
1980	R.A.S. Pim	(B)
1981	A.C. Kayll	(E)
1982	A.G. Baird	(E)
1983	A.H. Marsden	(O)
1984	R.S. Beccle	(W)
1985	C.J.W. Howie	(O)
1986	J.R. Bartlett	(S)
1987	J.C.A. Buck	(B)
1988	L.A.S. McCall	(S)
1989	N.R. Copcutt	(O)
1990	M.J. Tilney	(O)
1991	J.W.P. Ostroumoff	(S)
1992	E.J. Horner	(B)

1993	O.S. Macarthy	(S)
1994	D.J. Dickinson	(E)
1995	A.C. Hambrook	(E)
1996	J.G. Hitchen	(B)
1997	T.S. Page	(W)
1998	R.O.R. Smith	(W)
1999	T.P. Scoffham	(E)
2000	H.A. Colvin	(B)

B: Burr; E: Everett; O: Orchard; S: Skipwith; W: Welsh.